DATE DUE

DEMCO

WATER AND THE FUTURE
OF THE SOUTHWEST

Water and the Future of the Southwest

Zachary A. Smith, Editor

University of New Mexico
Public Policy Series
Fred Harris, Series Editor

UNIVERSITY OF NEW MEXICO PRESS

Albuquerque

Library of Congress Cataloging-in-Publication Data

Water and the future of the Southwest / Zachary A.
Smith, editor.
    p.   cm. — (University of New Mexico public
policy series)
  Includes index.
  ISBN 0–8263–1156–3
  1. Water—Law and legislation—Southwest, New.
2. Water-rights—Southwest, New.   3. Water resources
development—Government policy—Southwest, New.
4. Water resources development—Economic aspects—
Southwest, New.   I. Smith, Zachary A. (Zachary Alden),
1953–   .   II. Series.
KF5569.W37   1989
346.7304'691—dc20
[347.3064691]   89–33728
                                                      CIP

Contents

Tables

Foreword

I am pleased to introduce *Water and the Future of the Southwest* as the third volume in the University of New Mexico Public Policy Series. A primary goal of the series is to make available to a wide audience of scholars, students, policy makers, and the general public recent research and scholarly perspectives on contemporary policy issues of importance to the nation and the southwest region. A secondary goal of the series is to stimulate participation of scholars from different academic disciplines in the analysis of public policy issues. By their very nature, public policies intersect with a variety of academic disciplines and research traditions, beginning with political science but also including, among others, economics, sociology, public administration, law, and history. In addition, no analysis or attempt to understand the development and impact of public policies can be complete without some account of the viewpoints and experience of policy makers and public administrators whose acquaintance with the subject is firsthand.

Water and the Future of the Southwest is a future-oriented and interdisciplinary analysis and discussion of the significance and role of the Southwest's most critical natural resource, water. It is a comprehensive collection of essays that deal with water law, with the social and political contexts of water policy, with environmental concerns, with the role of the various levels of government involved, and with the central question for the future of the region: who gets water and why?

The Public Policy Series is sponsored by the University of New Mexico's Institute for Public Policy as part of its mission to promote public policy research and analysis, seminars and symposia, and policy-related publications. The Institute gratefully acknowledges the support of the College of Arts and Sciences in helping to establish the series.

Fred R. Harris
Series Editor

Introduction

Zachary A. Smith

In the history of the Southwest few issues have stirred the passions and emotions of people more than the allocation and distribution of water. Many think of water wars as a thing of the past, but the high-stake battles over water rights and uses in the Southwest may be just beginning. Rapid population growth and a boom in agricultural development after World War II resulted in a steadily increasing demand for water. Although most of the Southwest is an arid environment, there are numerous examples of poor water management. As the region has grown, greater attention has been focused on the use and development of water along with a realization of the importance of water management for the future prosperity of the Southwest.

This book makes a unique contribution to our understanding of water problems by drawing together scholars from a number of academic disciplines to address a central concern: What is the role and significance of water in the future of the Southwest?

The book is divided into three parts comprising fifteen chapters. In the first part the nature of the policymaking environment is discussed, including an examination of the legal doctrines that govern water use and distribution, along with the social and political context in which water decisions are made in the Southwest. The second part examines the roles of major governmental entities, particularly the federal government, in water policy formulation in the region.

The third part deals primarily with water allocation and other related management issues by examining broadly who gets water and why.

Chapter 1 summarizes the policymaking environment, discussing the historical development of water resources in the Southwest; the major participants in water policymaking; the importance of policymaking institutions, and the orientation of the policy formation process in the Southwest.

In Chapter 2 Richard A. Wehmhoefer sets the stage for much of the later discussion in the book by summarizing the law of water as it has been applied in the Southwest. Describing the physical properties of water as they relate to the law; trends and problems in groundwater law and surface water law, providing a state-by-state breakdown of legal trends; and concluding with a discussion of water law issues to be anticipated in the future.

In Chapter 3 Tim Miller examines the water "crisis" and discovers some interesting perceptual differences about the pending Southwest water "crisis."

It would be impossible to discuss the future of southwestern water without examining U.S.–Mexican relations in connection with water and pollution control. Albert E. Utton, in Chapter 4, provides us with a detailed account of these relations by summarizing pertinent treaties, agreements, and disputes along with making suggestions for avoiding disputes in the future.

The next two chapters examine the seemingly ever-increasing and controversial role of the federal government in the management of water in the Southwest. In Chapter 5 Ryan J. Barilleaux and C. Richard Bath argue, using conflict over water in the El Paso region as a case study, that struggles over water may lead to the nationalization of southwestern water in the future. In Chapter 6 R. McGreggor Cawley and Charles E. Davis discuss the shift in governmental responsibility over water resource management and development, finding increasing state involvement. Also they examine, through the experience of Wyoming, the conditions and prospects for a larger state role in the development, financing, and management of water resources.

The next three chapters deal with various aspects of the management of federal and Indian lands and the implications of that management for future development. In Chapter 7 Daniel McCool addresses policy and issues of water management on lands controlled by the U.S. Forest Service, National Park Service, Bureau of Land

Management, and the Fish and Wildlife Service and discusses how the water future of the Southwest may be affected by these federal land holdings. Lauren Holland examines the relationship between federal control over water resources and the deployment of weapons systems and other military activity in the Southwest in Chapter 8, paying particular attention to the role of state governments in water and weapons decisions in the future.

In Chapter 9, Lloyd Burton explores American Indian water rights, their origins, dispute-settling methods, and the possible impact of Indian claims on the future availability of water in the Southwest.

Three chapters deal with distributional questions or the values contained therein. Kent W. Olson, in Chapter 10, examines interbasin water transfers within the context of three projects designed to provide water to farmers on the Southern High Plains and finds among other things that the cost of some transfer proposals far exceeds their benefits. John Merrifield, in Chapter 11, provides an analysis of the costs of legal and institutional barriers to interstate water transfers and concludes that a system of water allocation responsive to market forces would lead to more efficient allocation of those resources. In Chapter 12, Timothy De Young and Hank Jenkins–Smith argue that market-oriented approaches to water allocation may have their advantages, but that there are numerous obstacles to a free market in water, and in any event such markets will be heavily regulated if and when they are created.

In Chapter 13 A. Didrick Castberg examines the crucial role of water for energy development in the Southwest and finds a need to take a number of steps immediately to ensure a future for southwestern energy supply and development.

Chapter 14 provides a worst-case scenario of groundwater management: *i.e.*, the management of resources to eventual depletion. Otis W. Templer provides a case study of Texas groundwater management and the adjustment to groundwater depletion. With unmanaged overdrafting taking place in a number of places in the Southwest, the Texas experience may well provide valuable lessons.

Finally in Chapter 15 I summarize the major trends and issues dealt with in the book.

The chapters are designed to be read either together or alone, depending on the reader's interests. Read together they share an orientation toward the future and the importance of water in Southwest development. Beyond this future orientation the authors are sometimes at odds with one another. We wouldn't have it otherwise. There is, for example, no *correct* level of federal activity in water management or *best* means of allocating water resources. These are among the value judgments about which experts as well as lay persons may disagree.

Not all the issues that have an impact on the future of water in the Southwest have been addressed in this book. For example, the protection and enhancement of environmental values, the role of federal water pricing (as opposed to the federal involvement) of water used, and the role of local water districts and other local units in water management are not dealt with in detail. We have, however, covered the topics that in our opinion will have the greatest impact on the use, management, and role of water in the Southwest in the future.

Although some writers, including several in this book, refer to a water "crisis" it is probably more useful and realistic to think of the Southwest's water future in terms of problems and issues that may or may not result in a crisis situation. Problems of pollution, for example, are of crisis proportions in some areas, but, in aggregate, water pollution should not reach a "crisis" level in the Southwest in the foreseeable future. Also, problems of supply and demand for water should be understood in terms of total water availability within a region. It is often the case that there is no shortage of water but only a shortage of water at a desirable price and for a particular use.

To further understand any pending crisis in water in the future of the Southwest one needs to appreciate the issues that confront water policymakers and users. An important change in the water policy environment in the last several decades has been the lack of federal dollars to mitigate perceived water shortages. It is anticipated that federal dollars will not be available in the future to develop additional major sources of water supply in the Southwest. Another important area that will have a direct impact on any future crisis concerns the mechanisms used for marketing or otherwise allocating water resources and the impacts that such devices have on third parties and interests that are not directly involved in the market mechanisms (for example, environmental concerns such as maintaining instream flow levels and possible damages to third parties). As a related factor the other mechanisms used for the transfer of water and the severability of water rights from land ownership promise to be a concern in many southwestern states. Other management issues that will have an impact on the future of water in the Southwest include the extent of the use of conjunctive management (the integration of surface and groundwater management); the impact of future energy development on water; the incentives and mechanisms that are used to increase agricultural and municipal water conservation; the role of agriculture (given that farmers use most of the water) in the future of the Southwest, and competition between agriculture and municipalities for water resources; the adaptation of waters of varying quality to suitable uses (or matching quality to use); and the form and intensity of competition for water resources between regions and, in the case of shared groundwater resources, within groundwater basins.

Although every effort has been made to prevent duplication in the presentation of material, there are some areas where it is necessary for a subject to be dealt with more than once. So, for example, the "Winters doctrine" (governing federal and Indian water rights) is discussed in several chapters where it is important, as is the Colorado River Compact.

As these and other issues are discussed throughout the book, it is important to remember that a water crisis in the future would be because of a failure to address these problems during the present. Through this collection of essays it is hoped that readers will emerge with a greater understanding of the importance and role of water in the future of the Southwest and also with a knowledge of what choices we should make now to facilitate the most desirable future.

I The Policy Environment

1   The Policy Environment

Zachary A. Smith

As we shall see in this and subsequent chapters, optimism about the Southwest water future will not always be easy to maintain. This chapter provides an introduction to the water policymaking process in the Southwest, with particular attention to the institutional and cultural environments that influence water policymakers, and a view of future developments that will have an impact on water policy in the Southwest in the decades to come.

STATE LEVEL

To put the water policymaking process of the states into proper perspective it may be useful to summarize some of the major water issues facing policymakers in the Southwest. Most of the political conflicts over water resources in the Southwest are due to scarcity and the related questions of allocation. Many of the allocation conflicts arise from the economic and social changes that have taken place during the decades immediately preceding and following World War II. For example, changes in demand related to agriculture are the result of steadily increasing prices from the 1930s to the 1950s (aided by government subsidies) for a variety of agricultural commodities. The price of cotton rose consistently from the mid-1920s to the mid-1950s, reaching an all-time high of 43.17 cents a pound. During this period agricultural production expanded rapidly in many parts of the Southwest as farmers and investors put more land into production to take advantage of the favorable market conditions. In Arizona, for example, land devoted to cotton production alone increased from 282,000 acres in 1948 to 678,000 acres in 1952.[1] For the most part the water necessary to support this increased production came from the ground. Developments in pump design that led to increased capacity and reduced costs, aided by high crop prices, resulted in the rapid development of groundwater resources. Though the prices for various agricultural commodities dropped and then flattened out in the mid- to late-1950s, farmers, needing to protect their investments, did not stop pumping.[2]

The early and rapid growth of agriculture in the Southwest had resulted in the vesting of water rights to farmers and thus laid the grounds for future conflict as other users began to compete with agriculture for the rights to water. Demands of others for a share of available water were, in metropolitan areas, quick to present themselves.

Throughout the period from World War II to the present, southwestern states have been among the leaders in the nation in terms of their percentage of population growth rates and manufacturing employment.[3] In the 1980s, Arizona, New Mexico, Oklahoma, and Texas have been among the ten fastest growing states in the country in terms of population.[4] In addition to the pressure an increasing population put on water, the growth of industrial, manufacturing, mining, and energy development increased the demand for water resources as well.

Today, most surface water has been entirely appropriated and groundwater has been appropriated in all but the most inaccessible locations. In addition, for a variety of reasons to be discussed below and in subsequent chapters, it is unlikely that major surface water projects will be built in the Southwest at any time in the near future. Thus the politics of water in the Southwest in the future will likely be even more confrontational than in the past.

THE PARTICIPANTS

The major claimants for water in the Southwest are the Indian tribes, the federal government, and the established water users such as farmers, mining companies, and municipal and manufacturing interests.[5]

On the state level the most influential participants in Southwest water-policy formulation are farmers, the extractive industries (for example, mining, oil, and gas), municipal and manufacturing interests, the federal government, and, to varying degrees, environmental organizations.

Farmers hold the bulk of water rights in the Southwest. In some of the states agriculture controls in excess of 90 percent of the available water. On the state level farmers are organized in a variety of ways. For example, in Arizona the local farmers' associations are represented by the Arizona Agri-business Council, and in California medium-size farmers are represented on the state level by the California Farm Bureau, whereas larger firms are represented by the California Chamber of Commerce. The influence of farmers on state water policymaking in the Southwest naturally varies from state to state. For example, agricultural interests are strong and well organized in Arizona, and in California agricultural interests have been successful in preventing the passage of water legislation they oppose.[6] In contrast, surveys of legislative leaders in Texas failed to identify agricultural interests as among the most influential lobbying organizations in the state capitol.[7] Not surprisingly, agricultural organizations are frequent contributors to political campaigns in southwestern states where they have been influential in water policymaking.[8]

The influence of agriculture in state politics in the Southwest is enhanced by the trend towards larger farms since the Great Depression. Thus most agriculture in the Southwest today is characterized by the large farm organization and is truly agri-business.[9]

The influence of extractive industries also varies from state to state. For example, oil and gas interests are influential in Texas,[10] Oklahoma, and New Mexico,[11] and mining interests have been influential in Arizona and New Mexico.[12] These extractive industries in the Southwest have traditionally been influential in the state policymaking process.[13] They frequently make campaign contributions at the state level, and the state legislatures in the Southwest have long had a reputation for being sympathetic to these industries.[14] As with farming, the trend since the Depression has been toward consolidation of holdings in extractive industries into larger and larger units.[15] This consolidation of course enhances their political influence.

Another major group involved in water policymaking at the state level in the Southwest are municipal interests and manufacturers.

11

Municipal interests and manufacturing are grouped together here primarily because manufacturers often receive their water from municipalities even though their interests at times conflict.

The interests of municipalities are represented in a variety of ways at the state level. In many states there are statewide organizations representing water purveyors, irrigation districts, or cities and towns. For example, in California, the California Association of Water Agencies represents most public water retailers and wholesalers. In other states, municipal interests are represented by blanket organizations such as the League of Arizona Cities and Towns and the Texas Municipal League. Municipal water interests also are often represented by large water purveyors. For example, the primary water wholesaler in Southern California is the Metropolitan Water District (MWD) of Southern California, and when matters of concern to the MWD are before the California legislature the legislature is lobbied directly. The same is true of the Salt River Project in Arizona and the New Mexico Public Service Company.

The influence of municipalities and the access of municipalities to legislators is generally strong. For example, if municipal interests feel threatened, they can pressure legislators through city mayors, legislators representing municipalities, and indirectly through city newspapers. Municipal interests are further favored in southwestern water policy formulation by the fact that western water law and public opinion generally favor municipal use over competing uses. In addition, municipalities have the power of eminent domain and can take water or water rights with the payment of fair compensation.[16]

Growth projections indicate that many municipalities will be increasing their demands for water in the future. With farmers and agricultural interests holding the bulk of water rights in the Southwest, the potential for conflict is evident. Such conflict has already taken place in some localities.

It is important to remember, however, that not all municipalities in the Southwest will want more water. Some communities, such as Santa Barbara, California, may work to prevent the development of future water supplies as a means of limiting growth and urban development.

Environmental organizations have, in varying degrees, been active participants in water policymaking in the Southwest. They were, for example, successful in defeating the dam construction that would have impacted Dinosaur National Monument and Grand

Canyon National Park. With the possible exception of California, however, they are not particularly influential in southwestern state legislatures.[17] For example, when an official in the Arizona Department of Water Resources was recently asked what influence Arizona environmental organizations had on the department's decisionmaking, the reply was, "There are no environmentalists in Arizona."[18] Although this statement was made in jest it illustrates the current weakness of environmental organizations in most state capitals in the Southwest. Political campaign contributions are one means of developing political influence. In a comparison of campaign contributions made by various groups concerned with water policy in Arizona, California, and New Mexico it was found that environmentalists rarely, if ever, made such contributions. Quite a contrast to agricultural, mining, and manufacturing interests, which were frequent contributors to political campaigns.[19] As the population in the region increasingly becomes urbanized (as has been the trend), the influence of environmental organizations will no doubt increase, as their greatest strength is in urban areas.[20]

POLITICAL CULTURE AND ORIENTATION

Daniel J. Elazar, in a study of politics in the American states, identified three primary political cultures: individualistic, moralistic, and traditionalistic. Elazar found individualistic and traditionalistic culture to be predominant throughout the Southwest. He defines traditionalistic culture as follows:

> Political culture rooted in an ambivalent attitude toward the marketplace coupled with a paternalistic and elitist conception of the commonwealth. It reflects an older, pre-commercial attitude that accepts a substantially hierarchal society as part of the ordered nature of things, authorizing and expecting those at the top of the social structure to take a special and dominant role in government.[21]

The individualistic culture views government as a marketplace, created to satisfy public demands placed upon it. The individualistic political culture avoids government intervention in the private sector and generally views politics as a dirty undertaking. The moralistic political culture views government as a means to achieve good through positive action. Social and economic regulations are considered legitimate, and participation in politics is viewed positively. Although it would be an oversimplification to define the politics of a state, much less a region, strictly in terms of these three cultures, the political orientation of the Southwest seems to fit Elazar's descriptions.

A variety of authors writing on the politics of the Southwest have found that much of the public as well as the policymakers hold a general orientation against governmental intrusion into the private sector.[22] Related to this dislike of government intervention, there is a widely accepted view of the desirability of a *laissez-faire* economy; *i.e.*, economic individualism. This orientation toward individualism was in large part responsible for keeping the city of Phoenix out of comprehensive land use planning and zoning until the 1960s,[23] and keeping the city of Houston out of land use planning in the 1980s.[24] It should be noted, however, that federal government involvement in local issues is often tolerated, at least when accompanied by federal dollars.

Another characteristic of politics in many southwestern states is for interest groups to be strong (*i.e.*, influential)[25] and political parties to be weak.[26] Related to the fact that political parties are often weak and interest groups often strong is the fact that bargaining over major legislation in the Southwest often takes place outside the legislature between the major interests that are affected. For example, in the 1950s it was not unusual for the New Mexico Cattle Growers Association to determine what their legislative needs were and to submit them to the New Mexico legislature for enactment.[27] Recently in Arizona, in response to federal pressure to enact a groundwater management code, representatives from the mines, major cities, and agriculture met behind closed doors for nine months to produce a groundwater bill. After these interests had agreed on the groundwater legislation it was submitted to the governor and subsequently to the legislature. The Arizona legislature then passed the 1980 Arizona Groundwater Management Act, considered to be one of the most comprehensive of its kind in the nation, in less than eight hours with over two thirds of the members voting their approval.[28]

There is a deeply rooted tradition in the Southwest that water should be treated differently from other commodities, and that its allocation "should not be governed by purely economic motives."[29] Fundamental to this idea is the feeling that water is essential to life and that no one should be cut off from a water supply regardless of inability to pay. These attitudes, to the extent that they hold in the future, will undoubtedly affect water policy in the Southwest.

POLICYMAKING INSTITUTIONS

To understand the water policymaking process in the Southwest it is necessary to understand the institutional environment in which the major actors participate. Specifically, one needs to examine the institutional arrangements or policymaking arenas where water decisions are made. These arrangements vary from state to state. In most states water allocation and distribution decisions are made by a centralized bureaucracy, usually the state engineer's office. In other states, notably California and Texas, water allocation decisions are decentralized and often made at the local level or in the courts. The significance for water policymaking is that certain groups may be benefited when water allocation and distribution decisions are made in certain policy arenas, whereas other groups are at a disadvantage when water decisions are made in the same arena. This is because groups have varying resources that are useful for influencing the policymaking process or more specifically for influencing decision making in different institutional environments. When policy is formulated in a political environment that can be influenced by the resources that a group possesses, that group is benefited when decisions are made in that policy environment. For example, if allocation decisions are made in legislatures and if one accepts the argument, as a number of political scientists have,[30] that legislators are primarily motivated by a desire for reelection, then we would expect groups that can provide electoral support to be influential in the legislative policymaking arena. In contrast, if water allocation and distribution decisions are made in the courts we would expect groups that have resources useful in litigation to be more successful. Resources beneficial in court systems include time (water cases are notorious for the amount of time they can take from initiation to resolution) and access to legal talent. If these decisions are made in a state bureaucracy by a state engineer, department of water resources, or water rights board or commission, then groups with resources useful for dealing with bureaucracies may benefit. These include expertise (or at least the ability to use the same jargon); time (implementation can take place over a long period of time); and the support of legislative leaders (particularly those in the legislature in a position to influence funding decisions of the agencies the group is dealing with).[31] The most influential participants in Southwest water policy formulation (*i.e.*, farmers, extractive industries, and municipal and manufacturing interests) are likely to have the resources necessary to participate effectively in the legislative, administrative, or judicial policymaking arenas.

Those without the resources necessary to be influential in the policymaking process are obviously disadvantaged. These groups, for the most part, include environmental organizations and other "public interest" organizations, and in many cases include Indian tribes.[32]

California's experience with water policymaking illustrates the importance of group resources and the impact this can have on the ability of a group to influence state water policy. California courts have developed the *correlative rights doctrine* in California groundwater law. Under this doctrine each owner is entitled to a reasonable share if the groundwater supply is inadequate to satisfy the whole needs of the overlying land owners. The courts in California determine the reasonableness of extractions in such cases and restrict overlying land owners to their reasonable share. Absent the adjudication of groundwater rights in a groundwater basin in California, extractors are free to continue pumping regardless of the effects the water withdrawals have on adjacent land owners. Consequently, pumpers with the resources necessary to fight costly and long-drawn-out legal battles are at an advantage with regard to those interests lacking such resources. In contrast, if decisions were made quickly by a state engineer, those pumpers would be less likely to continue their extractions.

The influence of any group in a state will depend on the utility of the group's resources for influencing the policymaking process in that state. Although generalizations are difficult to make, it is clear the major water users in the Southwest today have the resources necessary to influence water policymaking in the future regardless of the institutional and policymaking environment in the state.

Separate from state governments yet intimately involved in their water policymaking are the various officials in the federal government. These participants include members of Congress and the relevant congressional committees that deal with water-related issues and the federal administrative agencies involved in water use or allocation. Additionally, although they cannot be classified as falling into an identifiable group, are the "water professionals"—those water lawyers, scientists, engineers, administrators, and others who are involved in water management on an ongoing basis. They play an important and influential role in the water policy formation process in the Southwest.

NOTES

1. Robert G. Dunbar, "The Arizona Groundwater Controversy at Mid-Century," *Arizona and the West,* 19, No. 1 (1977), pp. 14, 19.

2. Zachary A. Smith, *Interest Group Interaction and Groundwater Policy Formation in the Southwest* (Maryland: University Press of America, 1985), p. 133. [Hereinafter cited as *Interest Group Interaction.*]

3. *Ibid.,* pp. 132 and 199. See also Jerome Olson, "Trends in Texas Manufacturing," and Niles Hansen, "Employment Patterns in the Southwest Borderlands," in Joseph E. Pluta (ed.) *Economic and Business Issues of the 1980s* (Austin: University of Texas, 1980).

4. U.S. Census Bureau as reported in the Hawaii *Tribune–Herald,* 14 January 1985. The ten fastest growing states from 1980 to 1984 were as follows: Alaska, 24.4 percent; Nevada, 13.8 percent; Utah, 13 percent; Florida, 12.6 percent; Texas, 12.4 percent; Arizona, 12.3 percent; Colorado, 10 percent; New Mexico, 9.3 percent; Oklahoma, 9 percent; and Wyoming, 8.9 percent.

5. Allen V. Kneese and F. Lee Brown, *The Southwest under Stress* (Baltimore: Johns Hopkins University Press, 1981), p. 71.

6. Zachary A. Smith, "Rewriting California Groundwater Law: Past Attempts and Prerequisites to Reform," *California Western Law Review,* 20, No. 2 (1984), p. 251.

7. Eugene W. Jones, *et al., Practicing Texas Politics,* 5th ed. (Boston: Houghton Mifflin, 1983), p. 170.

8. Smith, *Interest Group Interaction,* pp. 44–57.

9. Mario Barrera, *Race and Class in the Southwest* (Notre Dame: University of Notre Dame Press, 1979), p. 104.

10. Jones *et al.,* p. 171.

11. Smith, *Interest Group Interaction,* p. 61.

12. *Ibid.,* pp. 46, 61.

13. Helen M. Ingram, Nancy K. Laney, and John R. McCain, *A Policy Approach to Political Representation* (Baltimore: Johns Hopkins University Press, 1980), p. 5. See also, Ross R. Rice, "Amazing Arizona: Politics in Transition," in Frank H. Jonas (ed.) *Western Politics* (Salt Lake City: University of Utah Press, 1961), p. 58.

14. *Ibid.*

15. Barrera, p. 404.

16. Jones *et al.*, p. 26, and Smith, *Interest Group Interaction*, chaps. 7–9.

17. Smith, *Interest Group Interaction*, Chap. 4.

18. Interview conducted by the author on a not-for-attribution basis, 15 December 1981.

19. Smith, *Interest Group Interaction*, Chap. 4.

20. *Ibid.*, p. 56.

21. Daniel J. Elazar, *American Federalism: A View from the States*, 3rd ed. (New York: Harper & Row, 1984), p. 118.

22. Dean E. Mann, *The Politics of Water in Arizona* (Tucson: University of Arizona, 1963) and Smith, *Interest Group Interaction*.

23. Smith, *Interest Group Interaction*, p. 128.

24. Jones *et al.*, p. 4.

25. Harmon Zeigler, "Interest Groups in the States," in Virginia Gray, Herbert Jacob, and Kenneth N. Vines (eds.), *Politics in the American States*, 4th ed. (Boston: Little Brown, 1983), p. 100. See also Jones *et al.*, p. 173.

26. John F. Bibby *et al.*, "Parties in State Politics," in Gray, Jacob, and Vines, p. 82.

27. Frederick C. Irion, "New Mexico: The Political State," in Jonas, p. 238.

28. Smith, *Interest Group Interaction*, p. 147.

29. Kneese and Brown, p. 97.

30. Smith, *Interest Group Interaction*, p. 21.

31. *Ibid.*, pp. 21–23.

32. *Ibid.*, Chap. 4.

2 Water Law in the Southwest

Richard A. Wehmhoefer

As water becomes scarcer in the Southwest[1] and the quality of water declines, legislatures and courts will be called upon with increasing regularity to intervene in determining who gets what water; when they will receive it; how much water will go to each user; and where the water will be delivered.[2]

This chapter examines the law of water, both surface and groundwater, in southwestern states. It also presents an overview of some of the pressing conflicts that have found their way into the legislatures and courts and that suggest future alternative public policy and legal outcomes.[3]

SETTING THE STAGE

Litigation surrounding water rights has been most prevalent in the southwestern states. This is so because conflicts generally arise when there are shortages. Historically, the name of the lands lying west of the one hundredth meridian was the "Great American Desert."[4] This region often receives less than twenty inches of average annual precipitation,[5] which makes farming virtually impossible without irrigation.[6] In fact, more than eighty percent of the irrigation in the United States takes place in the western states, and ninety percent of the available water resources in the western states goes to agricultural purposes.[7] Thus, with the rapid population growth in these states, conflicts between urban and rural areas over water allocation have become inevitable.

Waters in nature (and often for legal purposes) take two major forms: water *on* the ground and water *in* the ground. Each of these may be further divided, so that water *on the ground* takes two patterns: diffused surface waters, and streams, or watercourses. The term *diffused surface waters* refers to waters moving over the surface of the earth but not a part of any defined stream channels. Examples of this are precipitation runoff, flood waters extending well beyond the banks of streams, and water standing in swamps and marshes. Streams, or watercourses, are familiar to all. However, the courts have held that for a body of water to qualify as a watercourse the following requirement must be met: It must be a body of water that flows, usually in a definite channel having a bed and sides or banks. This flow may be constant or intermittent.

Waters *in the ground* are also divided (according to the laws of some states) into two categories: subterranean streams and percolating waters. Subterranean streams, in order to qualify as such, must meet the same requirements as surface streams described above. Percolating waters are those that pass through the ground beneath the surface of the earth without traveling through definite channels.

SURFACE WATER LAW—RIPARIAN RIGHTS

Around each class of water has grown a body of law, usually supported by both statutory and case law. The law of surface water is generally divided into two categories—riparian and appropriation. In the eastern states, where water has historically been quite plentiful, and to some extent in the West, a body of law developed called the *riparian doctrine.*

The construction of the riparian doctrine has been best summarized as " . . . one who owned lands touching upon a stream was entitled to have the full flow of the stream come by his place undiminished in quantity and unimpaired in quality, except that each landowner was entitled to make reasonable use of the water upon his own lands, provided: (1) that he returned the stream to its natural channel before it left his lands, so as not to deprive succeeding lower riparian owners of their rights, and (2) that use on his own land was reasonable in respect to the corresponding rights of other riparian owners lying below him (*rule of reasonable use*)."[8]

This principle of law was the rule of decision used by most of the states before 1850; it still is the law, exclusively, in all of the states east of the Mississippi River and in the tier of states just to the west. It permitted use of water in quantities sufficient to satisfy most domestic needs.

Under the riparian doctrine, the right to use water is considered real property, but the water itself is not property of the landowner.[9] The right is a natural right that is an appurtenance of the property. It is a property that enters materially into the value of an estate; it may not be separately transferred, sold, or granted to another person.

While it is generally held that such rights are natural rights, they are subject to state regulation. Rights of individual owners are subordinate to the public interest. Thus the states, exercising their police power, may subject water rights to reasonable regulation.[10]

Reasonable use refers to the uses that are necessary to the sustenance of life and enjoyment of property. A hierarchy of uses has been recognized by the courts. First priority is given to water used for drinking, cooking, and stock watering; second priority is to industrial and irrigation; and third priority is to water transported away from the land contiguous to the stream.

In situations where there is a conflict among owners over the amounts of withdrawal for reasonable uses, it has been determined that when the conflict is over domestic uses in times of short supply all owners must bear the burden of the shortage equally.[11] When there has been a conflict between an upper owner for domestic uses and a lower owner for a secondary purpose, *e.g.*, industrial, the lower owner has had to forgo his right. And when the conflict is between lower and upper owners for the same secondary use, then the upper owner has a claim senior to that of the lower owner.[12]

Owners of riparian rights also have certain responsibilities. These responsibilities are logical results of the law of riparian rights. If every owner is entitled to the full flow of the stream diminished only by the necessary withdrawals of upper owners for reasonable purposes and to the water in its natural state of purity,[13] it logically follows that a riparian owner may not obstruct or pollute a stream.[14]

The riparian law, as a rule of decision, is not even fully effective in the achievement of its own ends. A judicial decision on a water right holds only so long as another judge does not interpret the law or the facts differently. Thus the landowner is never certain of his or her rights until a judicial determination has been made. Under this system, a landowner's investment is not always secure.

In the light of modern knowledge and modern economic conditions, there is a more serious defect in this kind of law. The riparian doctrine presents no basis or framework for efficient water management. As court-made and self-enforced law, it can not provide such. The *full flow* requirement of the doctrine tends to encourage waste or nonuse. In short, a state water management program cannot be expected to evolve from a common law system.

SURFACE WATER LAW—
THE APPROPRIATION DOCTRINE

In the Western and Southwestern states, the needs and the laws have been different. Most importantly, this area has been consistently dry so that the water supply remains relatively short. This part of the country has a tradition somewhat different from other areas, in that it has been under a succession of Indian, Spanish, and Mexican regimes. These peoples had different customs with respect to natural resources. The early unwritten law with respect to gold and silver "finds" closely parallels the present water laws of the West. With respect to gold, the procedure, had it been formalized into law, would have read something like this: "He who first discovers gold, if he develops his claim within a reasonable period of time, and continues his development diligently, may have the benefits of his labor. If he fails to develop and work them diligently his rights are forfeited."[15]

When questions of water rights arose, the same rule prevailed. This procedure and its rule acquired the name *appropriation doctrine.* As the territories became states, some of them adopted the law of riparian rights, but some of them rejected it even to the point of repudiating it in their constitutions. Some of the western states used their constitutions as a means of declaring state water policy, and some even employed the constitution to establish the machinery for state administration of appropriation law.

Appropriation statutes generally follow the mining-camp principle for gold prospecting illustrated above. Perhaps the best definition of appropriation law is this description from the Report of the President's Water Resources Policy Commission:

The appropriation doctrine ... rests on the proposition that beneficial use of water is the basis, measure and limit of the appropriative right. The first in time is prior in right. Perfected only by use, the ... right is lost by abandonment.... An appropriative water right is not identified by ownership of riparian lands.... Its existence and relationship to other rights on the same stream are identified in terms of time of initiation of the right by start of the work to divert water coupled with an intent to make beneficial use of it and the diligence with which the appropriator prosecutes to completion his diversion works and actually applies the water to beneficial use.[16]

Although details vary greatly, this statement is the essence of water law in the appropriation states. Throughout appropriation law, the elements of beneficial use and water conservation play important roles, because in these states water has been relatively scarce.

STATUTORY WATER LAW IN THE WEST

Generally, the states of poorest water supply manage their water most closely. Some southwestern states have never recognized riparian law. Other southwestern states adopted the riparian doctrine as a rule of decision, but also passed appropriation statutes. As water problems became more acute and conflict between the two systems developed, the riparian doctrine usually yielded to the statutory law.

These state systems merit an examination to show the philosophy of government involved in the appropriation system, to illustrate the administrative procedure involved, and to show the contrast between the two systems.

Seven of the southwestern states have statutory water law. In Arizona, Colorado, Nevada, and New Mexico *appropriation law is exclusive.* In three other states—California, Oklahoma, and Texas—the *appropriation doctrine and riparian doctrine coexist.* Each of the states differs from the others in mechanics of administration, so that a consideration of each is in order.

States Where Appropriation Law is Exclusive

In *Arizona,* the constitution provides that the common law doctrines of riparian rights shall not obtain or be of any force or effect in the state.[17] It states further that all existing rights to the use of any water in the state for all useful or beneficial purposes are recognized and confirmed. To implement this policy, the state of Arizona has adopted a comprehensive water code. In addition to reiterating the state's policy regarding water, the code declares that all water of the state from all sources of supply is subject to appropriation. Preferred uses of water are (1) domestic use, (2) municipal use, and (3) irrigation.

To implement administration of the water policy, jurisdiction originally was given to the Office of the State's Land Commissioner, and, more recently, to the Department of Water Resources. Applications for a permit to appropriate water are made to the director of the Department of Water Resources. The application is approved if it (a) does not conflict with vested rights, (b) is not a menace to public safety, or (c) is not against the interests and welfare of the public. While an application may be approved for less water than applied for, no application can be approved for more water than may be put to a beneficial use. Where conflicting applications for the use of water from a given supply arise, preference is given to the relative values to the public of the proposed uses. These values are: domestic and municipal uses; irrigation and stock watering; power and mining; and recreation and wildlife, including fish. If the director determines that a person entitled to the use of water has not beneficially used it for a period of five or more years, the water right reverts back to the state. An exception to this reversion procedure is an appropriation for a hydroelectric power development of 25,000 horsepower or more. In this instance, an act of the legislature is required; the right is then leased to the appropriator for a period of not more than forty years with a renewal option provided.[18]

This may seem to be a rigid program. But Arizona has an average annual precipitation of less than fifteen inches, so it is clear that this strict management may well be a necessity.

Colorado, another of the exclusive appropriation states, follows much the same pattern as Arizona. The state constitution declares all water of natural streams to be public property and subject to appropriation. It states further the principle of the superiority of prior appropriative rights and the preferred uses of water: (1) domestic, (2) agricultural, and (3) manufacturing.[19]

Responsibility for administering the law of water is vested in the state engineer. He or she can make and enforce rules, but adjudications are handled solely by special courts, referred to as "water courts." There are seven water courts in the state; each court is responsible for separate drainage basins in the state.

Applications to appropriate are made to the water court for the stream basin in which the diversion is requested. Following a time period for other users on the stream to object, the court may hold informal or formal hearings, after which a decree will be entered.[20]

Nevada does not present any great departure from the principles followed in most other appropriation states. Appropriations are made through the state engineer, who administers the law. The state engineer also makes determinations which must be entered in the courts; these have the effect of complaints in a civil action. All waters are subject to appropriation with the exception of wells for domestic use which have a draw of less than 1,800 gallons per day. Rights are lost by five consecutive years of nonuse.[21]

In New Mexico the situation is exactly the same as in Nevada with two exceptions. There is a statutory four-year nonuse forfeiture, and adjudications are made in the courts, with any state action being initiated through the Office of the Attorney General.[22]

States Where Appropriation Law and Riparian Rights Coexist

In the other Southwestern states surveyed here—California, Oklahoma, and Texas—the appropriation doctrine and riparian doctrine coexist with varying degrees of compatibility. The question of how the doctrines coexist deserves special examination.

In California a system of limitations is imposed on each type of law. A grant of water rights does not convey ownership of the water; a grantee receives only the right to use the water for useful and beneficial purposes.[23] In addition, only certain water is subject to appropriation: water on public lands and the surplus for private lands. The riparian owner must adhere to a strict interpretation of reasonable use, and the use must be both reasonable and beneficial.

There was much litigation over the relative rights of riparian and appropriative users. This led to a constitutional amendment in 1928 that restricted riparian rights to reasonable use and reasonable methods of diversion. Beyond that, riparian rights are not recognized. The riparian owner's rights to this extent are protected by law. These rights can be lost through prescription (*i.e.,* the acquisition of a personal right to use water by reasons of continuous past usage, much like adverse possession) and judgment, but the owner must be compensated. All surplus above the riparian owner's rights is declared part of state property and is subject to appropriation.[24]

In Oklahoma, at least until very recent times, the situation has been unclear. Both systems operate, but they have operated in rather exclusive spheres. No decisions testing the strength of each in opposition to the other have been rendered.

In Texas, riparian rights seem to prevail over appropriation rights. The language of the appropriation statutes always has protected vested riparian interests. When the two have come into conflict, the riparian doctrine has been the basis for adjudication. In effect, the riparians have a vested right over the amount of water beneficially used and are not entitled to water in excess of that quantity.[25] The riparian doctrine was affirmed by the courts as early as 1863 and as late as 1982.[26]

COMPARISON OF THE TWO SYSTEMS

Comparison of the major features of appropriation law with those of riparian law shows that under the statutory system a framework is provided to correct the deficiencies of the common law system.

In the determination of rights, the issue is settled by a state agency, and the appropriate right is a permanent, exclusive right guaranteeing security of investment.

Appropriation statutes are the implementation of a beneficial use policy. Waste, nonuse, and nonbeneficial uses can be discouraged. While the appropriative right in some instances is monopolistic, it is so only in terms of beneficial use.

Water agencies in the appropriation states are empowered to make and enforce rules. An administrative agency with such authority can frame its regulations in terms of need, and these rules can be based on scientific principles. With scientists and water resource experts participating in making a policy, there is greater likelihood that the law will keep up with the knowledge of hydrology.

It appears that comprehensive and effective management of watercourses probably could occur only when a state adopts the major principles of the appropriation system. Therefore, when both systems are compared and analyzed, the appropriation system usually gets higher marks.

Beneficial Use of Water

Uneconomical, wasteful, or inefficient uses of appropriated water are rejected by the beneficial use concept.[27] Colorado is typical of other southwestern states in its interpretation and development of the beneficial use concept. This element has been a condition of the appropriation doctrine since the 1882 case of *Coffin v. Left Hand Ditch Co.*[28] The Colorado Constitution has also incorporated the beneficial use requirement.[29] The Colorado Constitution recognizes several uses as being beneficial, including domestic, agricultural, and manufacturing.[30] Court decisions later added uses such as watering trees and grass,[31] and statutory enactments have added recreational purposes.[32] Other than these vague categories, there is no specific list including all those applications considered beneficial.[33]

There are, however, certain characteristics of beneficial use that Colorado courts have recognized. The most basic is that a failure to continue beneficial application of appropriated water will cause a loss of the appropriation rights.[34] A corollary is that there is no right to appropriate more water than can be beneficially applied; only the amount of water reasonably necessary for the intended beneficial use is allowed.[35]

The necessity of efficient and economic use of appropriated water has not been limited to methods employed on land to which the water is applied.[36] Colorado courts have expanded this requirement to include the manner utilized for conveyance of the water from the point of diversion to the point of application. For example, in *Town of Sterling v. Pawnee Ditch Extension Co.*,[37] the court stated that water was too valuable to be wasted by an inefficient method of conveyance when this loss could be averted by reasonable diligence.[38]

An extension of the requirement that the means used to convey water be reasonable and also efficient occurred in *City of Colorado Springs v. Bender*.[39] The court held that no senior appropriator had a right to employ inefficient methods of diversion, such as shallow wells.[40]

An earlier Colorado case, *Empire Water and Power Co. v. Cascade Town Co.*,[41] recognized the right of an appropriator to take advantage of the natural flow of a stream as a beneficial use, but it limited this right to an efficient application.

Colorado statutes also recognize the need for efficient diversions, by requiring appropriators using ditches to keep them in a state of repair that will prevent unnecessary loss through overflow or seepage.[42]

Maximum Utilization

The doctrine of maximum utilization is a natural outgrowth of beneficial use.[43] Again, Colorado typifies other states with respect to this concept. The Colorado Constitution implicitly recognizes the need for water to be applied so that it will produce the best and highest benefits for the greatest number of people through the recognition that all water not appropriated is the people's and for their benefit,[44] and the establishment of the preference system,[45] Article XVI, Section 6, provides that when a conflict of use occurs, domestic application of water will be preferred over agricultural use, and agricultural will be preferred to manufacturing activities.[46] This preference system reflected a realization by the lawmakers that some water uses are more beneficial for more people than are others.[47] Court decisions concerning beneficial use and limiting wasteful or inefficient application were a recognition that the water in Colorado should be developed in the best interests of all the people in the state.[48]

An extensive discussion of the concept of maximum utilization for several states in the Southwest comes from several law review articles written in the mid-1960s by Professor Frank J. Trelease.[49] In his articles, Trelease stated that western water should be shifted to more efficient uses in order to accommodate the rapidly increasing population of the western states.[50] Trelease's suggested method of shifting the water uses to more efficient and productive uses is to encourage free marketability of water rights; the most economically desirable uses of water will cause private interests to buy out less beneficial applications. Government regulation would be used only where private interests were not promoting public welfare, and only on the condition that the less desirable use be condemned and the prior appropriator compensated.[51] The purpose is to shift to more beneficial uses without injuring prior appropriators.

In Colorado,[52] the Supreme Court warned water users that the time had come to recognize maximum utilization as a necessary policy to be integrated with the doctrine of prior appropriation.[53] Subsequent decisions applied the doctrine of maximum utilization and upheld the state engineer's right to issue regulations and limitations on use of underground water.[54]

The Colorado legislature officially adopted the concept of maximum utilization in its Water Act,[55] stating that the policy of water use in Colorado was maximum utilization of all water available, including an integration of ground and surface waters.

THE LAW OF GROUNDWATER

The ultimate source of water in the ground, or groundwater, is precipitation. Hydrologically, water falling or melting on soil will percolate through a zone of aeration (unsaturated zone) until it reaches the saturated zone (aquifer), where it can be mined by wells and pumps.

Aquifers are of two types: artesian aquifers and water table aquifers. Artesian aquifers are those in which the groundwater is under pressure, usually because an impervious layer of clay or rock restricts upward movement of groundwater in a portion of the aquifer. As water percolates into the aquifer, pressure increases. Because of changing pressures after this type of aquifer is tapped, water level fluctuations may be dramatic.

Water table aquifers are not under pressure and, therefore, changes in water levels are much less dramatic.

Just as with surface water, irrigation is the major use of groundwater in the southwestern states. Approximately 90 percent of groundwater consumption goes to irrigation.[56]

Groundwater Allocation Doctrines

Groundwater allocation doctrines are typically common law or statutory. Common law doctrines include the overlying rights doctrines of absolute ownership, reasonable use, and correlative rights. Arizona, California and Texas follow common law allocation principles to a significant degree.[57] Oklahoma, originally a reasonable use jurisdiction, now follows a statutory adoption of the correlative rights doctrine. Colorado, Nevada and New Mexico have adopted a statutory prior appropriation and permit system form of administration by an office of the State Engineer.

Historically, the common law theory of absolute ownership gave the landowners absolute "ownership" of all groundwater underlying their land. This meant they could withdraw water without legal liability to neighboring overlying owners.[58]

The *absolute ownership* doctrine originally was followed in most southwestern states, including California, Nevada, New Mexico,

Oklahoma (by statute), and Texas.[59] Texas still abides by this doctrine, except that today landowners in Texas can be liable for land subsidence resulting from "negligent" groundwater withdrawals.[60]

A second common law doctrine—that of *reasonable use*—holds that groundwater may be used without waste on overlying land. Such a use is unreasonable if it is wasteful or if it occurs on nonoverlying lands. Arizona uses the reasonable use doctrine, which is also called the *American Rule*. In Arizona, the State Supreme Court interpreted "overlying land" as the tract of land from which the water was pumped, not all land overlying a common groundwater supply.[61] (The Arizona Groundwater Management Act is discussed below.)

The California rule of *correlative rights* is an extension of the reasonable use doctrine to allow nonoverlying groundwater use by nonoverlying users (referred to as "appropriators"). The correlative rights theory includes pro rata sharing during times of shortage and also allows rights to be established for water stored underground. This concept of underground storage is referred to as "recharged groundwater."

For many years Oklahoma followed the concept of reasonable use. Today, groundwater rights are allocated by statute. Allocations are given by the state to each overlying owner based on the owner's proportionate share of the supply, based on a minimum aquifer life of twenty years, a statutory adaptation of the sharing principle of the correlative rights doctrine.[62]

The remaining southwestern states examined here—Colorado, Nevada, and New Mexico—have adopted prior appropriation statutes. Under these statutes, a permit must be given by the state engineer before a well can be drilled or put into use. A groundwater appropriator must meet the same requirements as for a surface water appropriator: due diligence, perfection of the water right, actual use, and beneficial use. Junior groundwater appropriators may be subject to a variety of conditions, thereby protecting the rights of senior groundwater appropriators, including restricted withdrawal rates and maintenance of reasonable depths.

SURFACE WATER AND GROUNDWATER: CURRENT AND FUTURE LEGAL ISSUES

Historically, several forces have shaped surface water and groundwater law. These forces include themes of prior appropriation under state law, stable priority for historic uses, concern for private rights over public rights, preference for consumptive (usually commercial) uses, and the provision of subsidized water for irrigation.[63] While such historic forces are relevant today to some degree, many other issues have come to the forefront and must now also be addressed by current water policy.[64]

First, the era of cheap or federally subsidized water has passed. Subsidies are giving way to a user fee approach in which the eventual users pay directly for water and water storage projects. For example, in the Denver, Colo., metropolitan area, more than forty municipalities have banded together to pay the costs of planning and completing a 1,000,000-acre-foot reservoir on the South Platte River near Denver (so-called Two Forks Dam). While still in the planning phase, the municipalities have recognized that there may be little federal money to build such a project. Planning costs alone already exceed $50,000,000, with project completion costs expected to exceed $350,000,000. Similar projects may be in the future for the Southwest, and to the extent they conflict with existing water rights these systems may generate legal problems.

Second, as population has increased in the Southwest much attention is being paid to conservation techniques, particularly by agricultural users because these are the greatest consumers of water. However, there is disagreement as to the potential for real water savings depending on assumptions concerning factors such as evaporative losses, reuse of runoff, percolation to reusable groundwater, and contribution of runoff to other beneficial uses. With severe economic uncertainty facing American farmers, there are clearly arguments that various conservation techniques must be low in cost and tax deductible in order to be acceptable. Some examples of conservation techniques include: improved on-farm management like irrigation scheduling (low cost); crop mix changes or rotation (moderate cost); land fallowing and retirement (moderate cost); improvements in distribution systems, such as lining canals (high cost); and changes in irrigation application methods, such as changing from flood irrigation to drip or trickle irrigation (high cost).

Third, we have learned that often groundwater and surface water are intertwined. As a result, the traditional system of managing surface and groundwater separately fails to reflect hydrologic reality. In effect, conjunctive management of both systems is required.[65]

Fourth, water quality has become a concern recently. Moves to abate water pollution are an issue that has been given little or no attention in prior appropriation law.[66]

In early 1986, residents in Adams County, Colo. (a suburban area directly north of Denver), began buying bottled water and home-filtration systems after the Colorado Department of Health warned them in February of 1986 not to drink their groundwater supply until it had been boiled for five minutes. The reason: traces of trichloroethylene (TCE), a cleaning solvent, were found in the wells supplying the forty-five thousand residents of the area. In an unusual gesture, the U.S. Army, conceding that some of the contaminants had seeped from its Rocky Mountain Arsenal, agreed to fund a $1,000,000 purification system.

Agricultural users, although sometimes water polluters themselves (e.g. runoff from feedlots, polluted tail water), have also become very concerned about pollution, particularly when forced to use water that has been used by upstream municipal and manufacturing users. Such uses often leave high levels of nitrates and heavy metals that have disastrous effects on land, crops, and cattle.

Fifth, due largely to increased demand for water in arid areas, uses of water have become increasingly comprehensive and complex since the late 1800s and early 1900s. No longer is water simply a commodity taken from the river for farm or city use. As a result of growing public awareness of the need to protect our physical environment—including wilderness, recreation, and wildlife—southwestern states have begun to recognize and adopt aspects of riparianism: i.e., sufficient water must be left upstream for protection of public lands, recreational uses, ecological needs, and pure aesthetics.[67]

Sixth, policymakers and the courts have recognized that prior appropriation law must account for the rights of the federal government and the Indians. While the federal government has generally delegated water issues to the states,[68] a body of law based upon a U.S. Supreme Court decision, Winters v. United States,[69] holds that Indians have rights to western waters. (For a detailed examination of Indian water rights and the Winters case, see Chapter 9.)

The Western States Water Council recently prepared a report for the Western Governors' Association concluding that Indian water rights across the West may total over forty-five million acre feet per year, an amount equal to more than three times the annual flow of the Colorado River.[70] That figure was only an estimate, no more than a conscientious attempt to approximate the magnitude of the issue. But it stands in stark testament to the fact that Indian water rights are of front-line significance in modern western water policy.[71]

Seventh, the geography of the Southwest means that the states and even Mexico must compete for this scarce resource. Several rivers in these states are multistate or international, including the Platte, the Arkansas, the Rio Grande, and the Colorado. As a result, it has become illogical for water policy to be left to the sole discretion of any single local jurisdiction. (These issues are discussed in detail in Chapter 4 of this volume.)

The states continue to play a paramount role in western water law and policy, especially in determining rights to the use of water.[72] This dominance of state law, however, has seen a series of inroads since World War II. The Secretary of the Interior has effectively decreed water rights on the lower Colorado River among the lower basin states by entering into water delivery contracts, and the Supreme Court has upheld the administrative action.[73] The Supreme Court enforces the demands of federalism by refereeing disputes among states in interstate watersheds.[74] The federal pollution laws have taken effect.[75] The Endangered Species Act requires sufficient flows to protect covered species.[76] Various laws regulating salmon and steelhead harvesting have affected water allocations.[77] The 1982 decision in *Sporhase v. Nebraska*[78] made it clear that the demands of interstate commerce can override the desire of any single state to ban exports of water. The court found that states regulate water, but do not own it, calling the notion of state ownership of water "a legal fiction."[79] A new era in management of the federal public lands, which comprise 48 percent of all land in the eleven western states, has imprinted water policy by promoting erosion-preventing practices on federal timber and range lands, by protecting key high elevation watershed lands, by establishing wild and scenic rivers, and by setting reserved rights in many federal landholdings, including national parks, wildlife refuges, and wilderness areas.[80] And of course the balance point has shifted—although we are years from knowing how far—by the determination of Indian tribes to assert their *Winters* rights to help fulfill the essential treaty promise that their reservations be homelands.

State domination of water policy, then, has been grudgingly eroded, in fits and starts, on a number of fronts. We have developed, and will hold to, a policy matrix that recognizes a set of legitimate state interests in the allocation of water, but that also accommodates larger national interests including the needs of downstream states and nations, water quality, recreation, the environment, and Indian tribes.

Eight, the most far-reaching statutory water conservation program ever adopted by any state is the 1980 Arizona Groundwater Management Act.[81] The Arizona experience[82] foreshadows the possibilities for effective combat against waste and overuse, particularly through the use of management plans for active management areas (AMA's).[83]

The central provisions of the Act and recent management plans are a blueprint for the serious conservation of western water.[84] Among other things, the Act provides for a strong state regulatory agency[85]; the imposition of mandatory water limits for individual farm units based upon specified conservation practices[86]; a prohibition against opening new irrigated acres within the AMA's[87]; a program for retiring land from irrigation[88]; compulsory conservation within metropolitan residential areas[89]; and the imposition of "groundwater withdrawal fees" (a politically necessary euphemism for pump taxes).[90] By any reasonable standard, it is a remarkable piece of legislation.

Ninth, in the wake of the U.S. Supreme Court decision in *Sporhase v. Nebraska ex. rel. Douglas,*[91] water is now subject to the construction of the Commerce Clause. This decision has had considerable impact on water resources allocation because many southwestern states traditionally had statutes controlling the export of water.[92] Such state statutes are now subject to "dominant Commerce Clause analysis."[93] In addition, the *Sporhase* decision may hinder the enforcement of interstate compacts and equitable apportionments concerning interstate waters given the actual or potential role of the federal government in such arrangements, which is now possible because of the decision. All these issues and accompanying legal and public policy changes will have a real impact upon the future.

What Does the Future Hold?

Americans once saw clean and inexpensive water as a kind of national entitlement, which was all but inexhaustible. Today, however, water has become relatively scarce, particularly in the Southwest, and conflicts among competing users are common.[94]

Clearly, several past and current actions jeopardize our future generations' access to fresh water that will meet both quantitatively—and qualitatively—derived standards. Such actions include surface water diversions on an excessive scale; consumption of groundwater supplies in excess of natural recharge rates; pollution and contamination of surface water and groundwater supplies through toxic and other discharges; and ongoing local, state, national, and international debates as to who gets what, when, where, and in what quantity and quality.

Edith Braun Weiss has argued that there are three principles that can ensure our children and grandchildren enough good water. These principles are: 1)the conservation of options; 2) conservation of quality; and 3) equitable access and use. *Conservation of options* means that we should retain as wide a variety of freshwater sources as possible along with available points for diversions. *Conservation of quality* means a ban on persistent toxic contamination of streams and lakes and of aquifers that are linked hydrologically to streams. Issues of *equitable access and use* arise both among generations and among members of the same generation. Conservation of options and of quality is intended to ensure that all generations will have an equal relationship to the resource.[95]

Managing for Future Generations

Preventing actions that deplete the water resources or degrade quality will be far more effective and less costly than will remedial efforts or attempts to impose liability for damages after the fact. This means giving priority to identifying dangers, assessing the likely effects of proposed actions, monitoring the consequences of actions already taken, and consulting among affected parties. It also means increasing the efficient use of water, including recycling it for different uses.

Whether all these priorities can be accomplished depends in large measure on the capability and capacity of legislatures, courts, and other policymakers to adapt to changing conditions and needs. It is interesting that there seems to be little agreement among water professionals on what precisely the water "crisis" is or will be. Certainly changes in policy will have to be made to address the issues that have been raised.

Historically, however, policymakers, legislatures, and the courts have generally risen to the occasion, *i.e.*, making changes when needs have arisen. If past history is to be our guide, it is likely that the laws of water appropriation in the Southwest will continue to be amended and changed to account for changing needs and public uses. Because water is vital to our survival, such flexibility has been, and will continue to be, a necessary part of water law.

NOTES

1. For purposes of this chapter, the southwestern states include Arizona, California, Colorado, Nevada, New Mexico, Oklahoma, and Texas.

2. Albert E. Utton, "Overview," 22 *Natural Res. J.*, 735 (Oct.1982).

3. Armstrong, "Anticipating Transborder Water Needs and Issues in the United States–Mexico Border Region," 22 *Natural Res. J.*, 877 (Oct. 1982) and Charbeneau, "Groundwater Resources of the Texas Rio Grande Basin," 22 *Natural Res. J.*, 957 (Oct. 1982).

4. *Sporhase v. Nebraska ex rel. Douglas*, 458 U.S. 941, 952–53, n. 13 (1982) [quoting *California v. United States*, 438 U.S. 645, 648 (1978)].

5. U.S. Department of Interior, Geological Survey, *The National Atlas*, 97 (1970).

6. Soil Conservation Service, U.S. Department of Agriculture, *America's Soil and Water: Conditions and Trends*, 25 (1980).

7. *Idem.* See also U.S. Department of Interior, *Westwide Study Report on Critical Water Problems Facing the Eleven Western States*, 46–47 (1975).

8. C. Busby, "Water Rights and Our Expanding Economy," *Jour. of Soil and Water Conservation*, 9, 68 (Mar. 1954).

9. H. Farnham, "The Law of Water and Water Rights," 1 *Lawyers' Cooperative Publishing Co.*, 280.

10. *Idem.* at 284.

11. *Canton v. Shock*, 66 Ohio St. 19, 63 NE 600 (1902).

12. *Idem.*

13. *Lambeck v. Nye*, 47 Ohio St. 336, 24 NE 686 (1890).

14. Annot., 70 ALR Fed. 221 (1931).

15. C. Busby, "Water Rights and Our Expanding Economy." *Jour. of Soil & Water Conservation* (Mar. 1954) at 9, 68.

16. *Report of the President's Water Resources Policy Comm.*, 156 (1950).

17. Ariz. Const., art. 17, ss1 & 2.

18. See Ariz. Rev. Stat. s45–101 *et seq.* (1984). Decisions of the director are subject to judicial review. When conflicts arise, petitions for the adjudication of rights may be brought and maintained in the superior court of the county in which the largest number of potential litigants reside. The court may appoint a master to report on all legal and factual issues. The adjudication is governed in all respects by the Arizona rules of evidence and civil

procedures, and any decision is subject to review by the Arizona Supreme Court.

19. Colo. Const., art. 15, s5 & 6.

20. See Colo. Rev. Stat. s37–92–100 *et seq.* (1984).

21. See Nev. Rev. Stat. s48–532.010 *et seq.* (1983).

22. See N.M. Stat. Ann. s72–1–1 *et seq.* (1978).

23. *Eddy v. Simpson*, 3 Cal. 249, 252–53 (1853).

24. See *Lux v. Haggin*, 69 Cal. 255, 4 P 919 (1884); *Herminghaus v. Southern Cal. Edison Co.*, 200 Cal. 81, 252 P 607 (1926); and *Peabody v. Vallejo*, 2 Cal. 2d 351, 40 P2d 486 (1935).

25. Alexander Hamilton, "The Plight of the Riparian under Texas Water Law," 21 *Harv. L.R.*, 577, 582 (1984).

26. *Rhodes v. Whitehead*, 27 Tex. 304 (1863); *Chicago R.I. & Gulf Ry. v. Tarrant County, W.C. & I. Dist. No. 1*, 123 Tex. 432, 73 SW2d 55 (1934). See also Tex. Water Code Ann. s1.001 *et seq.* (Vernon 1985); III *Report of the President's Water Policy Commn.* app. B (1950). See also *In re the Adjudication of the Upper Guadalupe Segment of the Guadalupe River Basin*, 642 SW2d 438 (Tex. 1982). See also the Water Rights Adjudication Act, Chap. 45, ss1–12, 1967 Texas Gen. Laws 86, Texas Water Code Ann. zz11.301–341 (Vernon Supp. 1985).

27. *Gossner v. Utah Power & Light*, 612 P2d 337, 341 (Utah 1980); *John Meier & Sons v. Horse Creek Conservation Dist*, 603 P2d 1283, 1288 (Wyo. 1979); *People v. Hinderlider*, 57 P2d 894 (Colo. 1936). See note, "A Survey of Colorado Law," 47 *Den. L.J.*, 226 (1970).

28. 6 Colo. 443 (1882).

29. "The right to divert the unappropriated waters of any natural stream to beneficial uses shall never be denied." Colo. Const. art. XVI, s6. See Colo. Rev. Stat. s 37–92–103(3) (1973), which states: " 'Appropriation' means the application of a certain portion of the waters of the state to a beneficial use."

30. Colo. Const. art. XVI, s6.

31. *City & County of Denver v. Sheriff*, 105 Colo. 193, 209, 96 P2d 836, 844 (1939).

32. Colo. Rev. Stat. s37–92–103(4), which states, " 'Beneficial use' . . . includes the impoundment of water for recreational purposes. . . . "

33. The problems created by the lack of specific beneficial use standards is discussed in Carlson, "Report to Governor John A. Love on Certain Colorado Water Law Problems," 50 *Den. L.J.*, 293 (1973). "The existing water law of Colorado does not recognize the possibility that appropriators may seek to develop water rights which, although beneficial uses under existing law, are nonetheless socially undesirable for the public at large." *Idem* at 324.

34. Colo. Rev. Stat. s37–92–402(2) (j) (1973). See *Farmers Reservoir & Irrigation Co. v. Fulton Irrigating Ditch Co.*, 108 Colo. 482, 120 P2d 196 (1941).

35. *Enlarged Southside Irrigation Ditch Co. v. John's Flood Ditch Co.*, 120 Colo. 423, 210 P2d 982 (1949). "The time during which water may be diverted thereunder is measured by the reasonable needs of the land, and when the water is not so needed, it may no longer rightfully be diverted from the stream, but must be left therein for use of subsequent appropriators." *Idem* at 428–29, 210 P2d at 984–85. Accord, *Snow v. Abalos*, 18 N.M. 681, 140 P1044 (1914).

36. *Colo. Rev. Stat.* s37–92–103(4) (1973).

37. Colo. 421, 94 P 339 (1908).

38. "It is a matter of common knowledge that in . . . [conveying the water in the manner proposed by the city] necessarily a very great proportion of such volume would be lost by seepage and evaporation before it was conveyed any considerable distance. The law contemplates an economical use of water. . . . Water is too valuable to be wasted, either through an extravagant application for the purpose appropriated or by waste resulting from the means employed to carry it to the place of use, which can be avoided by the exercise of a reasonable degree of care to prevent unnecessary loss, or loss of a volume which is greatly disproportionate to that actually consumed." *Idem* at 429–30, 94 P at 341. Accord, *Glen Dale Ranches Inc. v. Shaub*, 94 Idaho 585, 494 P2d 1029 (1972).

39. 148 Colo. 458, 366 P2d 552 (1961).

40. "[E]ach diverter must establish reasonable means of effectuating his diversion. He is not entitled to command the whole or a substantial flow of the stream merely to facilitate his taking the fraction of the whole flow to which he is entitled. . . . [P]riority of appropriation does not give a right to an inefficient means of diversion. . . . " *Idem* at 462, 366 P2d at 555.

41. 205 F 123 (8th Cir. 1913).

42. Colo. Rev. Stat. ss37–84–107–119 (1973).

43. This discussion appears at Comment: Maximum Utilization Collides with Prior Appropriation in *A–B Cattle Co. v. United States*, 57 *Den. L.J.*, 103 (1979).

44. Colo. Const. art. XVI, s5.

45. *Idem*, s6.

46. *Idem*. For an interesting and revealing history of the conflicts concerning which uses were to have priority during the constitutional convention of 1876, see "Colorado Water Study, Directions for the Future," *The Current Legal System*, II=9 to II=14 (Colo. Dept. of Nat. Res., 1980). See also Trelease, "Preferences to the Use of Water," 27 *Rocky Mtn. L. Rev.*, 133 (1955).

47. *Black v. Taylor*, 128 Colo. 449, 264 P2d 502 (1953); *Town of Sterling v. Pawnee Ditch Extension Co.*, 42 Colo. 421, 94 P 339 (1908); *Montrose Canal Co. v. Loutsenhizer Ditch Co.*, 23 Colo. 233, 48 P 532 (1896). See Thomas,

"Appropriations of Water for a Preferred Purpose," 22 *Rocky Mtn. L. Rev.*, 422 (1950).

48. *Suffolk Gold Mining & Milling Co. v. San Miguel Consol. Mining & Milling Co.*, 9 Cal. App. 407, 48 P 828 (1897). "[T]he title to the waters of the state always remains, in a measurable sense, in the people. . . . The appropriator may acquire title, but that title is necessarily subject to many conditions." *Idem* at 9 Cal. App. 407, 412, 48 P at 830. See generally, G. Radosevich, K. Nobe, D. Allardice & Co. Kirkwood, *Evolution and Administration of Colorado Water Law, 1876–1976* (1976).

49. Trelease and Lee, "Priority and Progress—Case Studies in the Transfer of Water Rights," 1 *Land and Water Rev.*, 1 (1966). See also Danielsen, "Water Administration in Colorado—Higher -iority or Priority," 30 *Rocky Mtn. L. Rev.*, 293 (1958); Milliman, "Water Law and Private Decision-Making: A Critique," 2 *J. of L. & Econ.*, 41 (1959).

50. See Fox, "Water: Supply, Demand and the Law," 32 *Rocky Mtn. L. Rev.*, 452 (1960).

51. Contra. Carlson, *supra*, note 33 at 341: "One approach . . . would be to treat existing uses in the way that nonconforming uses are treated in zoning law. In this way, undesirable existing uses might be phased out over a period of time without the necessity of payment of compensation arising."

52. For a Colorado case, for example see *Fellhauer v. People*, 167 Colo. 320, 447 P2d 986 (1968).

53. *Idem* at 336, 447 P2d at 994 (1968): "It is implicit in these constitutional provisions [protecting the rights of appropriators], that, along with vested rights, there shall be maximum utilization of the water of this state. As administration of water approaches its second century the curtain is opening upon the new drama of maximum utilization and how constitutionally that doctrine can be integrated into the law of vested rights." *Idem* at 336, 447 P2d at 994 (1968).

54. *Hall v. Kuiper*, 181 Colo. 130, 510 P2d 329 (1973); *Kuiper v. Well Owners Conservation Assn.*, 176 Colo. 119, 490 P2d 268 (1971).

55. "It is hereby declared to be the policy of the State of Colorado that all waters originating in or flowing into this state, whether found on the surface or under—have always been, and are hereby declared to be the property of the public, dedicated to the use of the people of the state, subject to appropriation and use in accordance with law." Colo. Rev. Stat. s37–92–102(1) (1973).

56. See J. David Aiken, "Western Groundwater Law: Overview and Recent Developments," *Western Water Law in Transition*. Proceedings from a short course presented by the Natural Resources Law Center, University of Colorado School of Law, June 3–5, 1985, at pp. 1–2.

57. Zachary A. Smith, "Centralized Decision Making in the Administration of Groundwater Rights: The Experience of Arizona, California and New

Mexico, and Suggestions for the Future," 24 *Natural Resources J.*, 641–644 (July, 1984).

58. This theory is based on the 1843 English decision of *Acton v. Blundell*, 152 Eng. Rep. 1223 (1843). The first American case adopting this rule was *Wheatley v. Baugh*, 25 Pa. St. Rep. 528 (1855).

59. See Aiken, "Nebraska Ground Water Law and Administration," 59 *Neb. Law. Rev.*, 317, 324 n 19.

60. See *Houston & Tex. Cert. R.R. v. East*, 98 Tex. 146, 81 SW 279 (1904) and *Friendswood Dev. Co. v. Smiths–Southwest Industries*, 576 SW2nd 21 (Tex. 1978).

61. See *Farmers Investment Co. v. Betty*, 113 Ariz. 520, 558 P2nd 14 (1976).

62. See Jensen, "Allocation of Percolating Water under the Oklahoma Ground Water Law of 1972," 14 *Tulsa L. Rev.*, 437 (1979).

63. Charles F. Wilkinson, "Western Water Law in Transition," 56 *Colorado L. R.*, 317, 321 (1985).

64. *Idem*. The following summary can be seen in greater detail at pp. 321–45.

65. On groundwater, see R. Freeze and J. Cherry, *Groundwater* (1979). On conjunctive use, see F. Trelease, "Conjunctive Use of Groundwater and Surface Water," 27B *Rocky Mtn. Min. L. Inst.*, 1853 (1982).

66. W. Rodgers, *Environmental Law*, 354–550 (1977) and 187–205 Supp. (1984).

67. These conclusions are reflected in a number of modern movements, including the setting aside of large areas of land as wilderness, *e.g.*, R. Nash, *Wilderness and the American Mind* (1983 rev. ed.); the increased concern for the rights of animals, *e.g.*, M. Bean, *The Evolution of National Wildlife Law* (1983); the increased demand for recreational uses of water, *e.g.*, *Wilderness Public Rights Fund v. Kleppe*, 608 F2d 1250 (9th Cir. 1979); the provision in most western states for the establishment of instream, nonconsumptive water flows, *e.g.*, Tarlock, "Appropriation for Instream Flow Maintenance: A Progress Report on 'New' Public Water Rights," 1978 *Utah L. Rev.*, 211; and the attention given to water issues in essays and works of fiction by modern western writers, *e.g.* E. Abbey, *Beyond the Wall* (1984); J. Nichols, *The Milagro Beanfield War* (1974); W. Stegner, *The Sound of Mountain Water* (1969).

68. The leading statement by the U.S. Supreme Court on congressional deference to state water law is *California v. United States*, 438 U.S. 645 (1978).

69. 207 U.S. 564 (1908).

70. See *Western Governors' Association, Indian Water Rights in the West* (1984).

71. For example, Indian water rights are discussed in great detail in National Water Commission, *Water Policies for the Future*, 474–75 (1973).

72. For a comprehensive review of *California v. United States*, 438 U.S. 645 (1978); the Reclamation Act of 1902, and congressional deference to state water law, see Kelley, "Staging a Comeback—Section 8 of the Reclamation Act," 18 *UCD L. Rev.*, 97 (1984).

73. *Arizona v. California*, 373 U.S. 546 (1963).

74. See *e.g. Colorado v. New Mexico*, 104 S Ct 2433 (1984); *Texas v. New Mexico*, 103 S Ct 2558 (1983).

75. See *e.g.*, the Clean Air Act, 42 USC ss7401–7642 (1982); Resource Conservation and Recovery Act, 42 USC ss6901–6987 (1982); Toxic Substances Control Act, 15 USC ss2601–2629 (1982); Federal Water Pollution Act (Clean Water Act), 33 USC ss1251–1376 (1982).

76. 16 USC ss1531–1543 (1982). See *e.g. Carson–Truckee Water Conservancy Dist v. Clark*, 741 F2d 257 (9th Cir. 1984), *cert. pending, Riverside Irrigation Dist v. Andrews*, 758 F2d 508 (10th Cir. 1985).

77. *Idem.*

78. 458 U.S. 941 (1982). See Tarlock, "So It's Not 'Ours'—Why Can't We Still Keep It? A First Look at *Sporhase v. Nebraska*," 18 *Land & Water L. Rev.*, 137 (1983). The most recent decision on the issue is *City of El Paso v. Reynolds*, 597 F. Supp. 694 (DNM 1984) upholding constitutionality of most aspects of New Mexico's statute regulating groundwater transports, N.M. Stat. Ann. s72–12B-1.

79. 458 U.S. at 951. This has not stopped state courts from continuing to rely on the fiction of state ownership of water. See *e.g. Montana Coalition for Stream Access v. Curran*, 682 P2d 163, 166 (Mont. 1984). State authority over water is ample, but it is based on reserved power under the 10th Amendment, not on ownership. The famous statement in *California Oregon Power Co. v. Beaver Portland Cement Co.*, 295 U.S. 142, 163–64 (1935) ("What we hold is that following the [Desert Land Act] of 1877, if not before, all non-navigable waters then a part of the public domain became *publici juris*, subject to the plenary control of the designated states . . . ") is itself a legal fiction based on concepts of ownership. There was no need to "sever" water from the public domain (*idem* at 158) to establish state regulatory authority—such power always existed by the Tenth Amendment unless preempted by federal authority. Thus state courts were correct in applying state water law on the public lands from the beginning. See *e.g. Irwin v. Phillips*, 9 Cal. 140 (1855). *Cf., California v. United States*, 438 U.S. 645 (1978) (state law applies to federal reclamation projects unless overridden by specific congressional provision); *United States v. New Mexico*, 438 U.S. 696 (1978) (Congress has authority to establish federal reserved rights, but state water law applies unless federal power actually exercised); *Andrus v. Charleston*

Stone Products, Inc., 436 U.S. 604, 614 (1978) (congressional water policy in the mining laws has been "passive" and has "affirmed the view that private water rights on Federal lands were to be governed by local law and custom"). See generally, Trelease, "Uneasy Federalism—State Water Laws and National Water Uses," 55 *Wash L. Rev.,* 751, 758–68 (1980); Wilkinson, "The Field of Public Land Law: Some Connecting Threads and Future Directions," 1 *Pub. Land L. Rev.,* 1, 19–23 (1980).

80. See *Cappaert v. United States,* 426 U.S. 128 (1976) (national monument); *Sierra Club v. Block,* 14 ELR 20626 (D. Colo. 1984) (wilderness areas); *United States v. Denver,* 656 P2d 1 (Colo. 1982) (national park and monument); "Federal Water Rights of the National Park Service, Fish & Wildlife Service, Bureau of Reclamation and Bureau of Land Management," 88 *Interior Decisions,* 553 (1979) (Interior Department agencies, National Wilderness Preservation System, and National Wild and Scenic River System). Reserved rights in national forests were construed strictly in *United States v. New Mexico,* 438 U.S. 696 (1978).

81. Ariz. Rev. Stat. Ann. ss 45–401 to 45–637 (Supp. 1984–85). See also Zachary A. Smith, "Centralized Decision Making in the Administration of Groundwater Rights: The Experience of Arizona, California and Suggestions for the Future," 24 *Natural Res. J.,* 541 (1984).

82. The history of the 1980 Act is told well in Connall, "A History of the Arizona Groundwater Management Act," 1982 *Ariz. St. L.J.,* 313. The state established a Groundwater Study Commission in 1977 to address the increasingly serious overdraft situation, *idem* at 323, but the long-simmering tensions among the various interest groups made progress difficult. For example, Jim Bush, the colorful Phoenix attorney representing mining interests, laid the blame for the overdraft condition at the irrigators' feet and fought against potential profits to the farmers if agricultural land were to be retired: "We're not going to buy farms so that farmers can move to La Jolla and raise martinis." *Idem* at 325. Connall extols Governor Babbitt's abilities to grasp the difficult factual and legal issues and to move the negotiators toward consensus. *Idem* at 331–32. A key impetus was Interior Secretary Cecil Andrus's personal visit to Phoenix and his insistence that his department would allocate no Central Arizona Project (CAP) water unless the state enacted an effective groundwater code. *Idem* at 329–30. Andrus was satisfied with the 1980 Act and CAP water was not delayed. *Idem* at 344.

83. See *e.g.* Arizona Dept. of Water Resources, *Management Plan. First Management period: 1980–1990* (1984) [hereinafter cited as Phoenix AMA (Active Management Area) Management Plan]. Management plans were also issued in December 1984 for the Prescott and Tucson Active Management Areas. The 1980 Act established four initial AMA's (Ariz. Rev. Stat. Ann. s45–411, Supp. 1984–85), which included about 80% of Arizona's population, 70% of the state's groundwater overdraft, and 60% of the groundwater

pumping. K. Ferris, "The Development of the New Arizona Groundwater Code" [Oct. 30, 1984], published in 1985 in the proceedings of a groundwater symposium entitled "Groundwater, Crisis or Opportunity," sponsored by the Univ. of Texas at Austin and Texas A. & M. Univ., October 29–31, 1984, and also excerpted from *Groundwater Management: A Key Issue for the 80's* (T. James & S. Ballard, eds.), soon to be published [hereinafter cited as Ferris]. The director of water resources must develop a series of five successive management plans for each AMA through the year 2025, when groundwater withdrawals may not exceed discharge; the conservation requirements will become more rigorous in each successive plan. Ariz. Rev. Sta. Ann. ss 45–561 to –566 (Supp. 1984–85). The initial plans, cited above, cover the management period ending in 1990.

84. The Act was challenged on constitutional grounds on the theory that existing Arizona law provided for ownership of groundwater by overlying landowners and that the restrictive provisions of the code constituted a taking. State and federal courts, however, have both upheld the Act. See *Town of Chino Valley v. City of Prescott,* 131 Ariz. 78, 638 P2d 1324 (1981), *appeal dismissed,* 457 U.S. 1101 (1982); *Cherry v. Steiner,* 543 F. Supp 1270 (D Ariz 1982), *aff'd* 716 F2d 687 (9th Cir 1983), *cert. denied,* 104 S Ct 1719 (1984). The Arizona Supreme Court dismissed language in earlier opinions ("dictum thrice repeated is still dictum," 638 P2d at 1327) and held that "there is no right of ownership of groundwater in Arizona prior to its capture and withdrawal from the common supply." *Idem* at 1328.

85. The negotiators in conservative Arizona finally settled on the creation of a new agency—the Department of Water Resources—with broad-based powers to implement the Act. See *e.g.,* Ariz. Rev. Stat. Ann. s 45–102 (Supp. 1984–85). Ferris, *supra,* note 83, has explained some of the reasons:

"The concept of concentrating decision-making authority at the state level was not accepted without controversy. In its 1979 Draft Report, the Groundwater Management Study Commission recommended that management of groundwater should be carried out primarily by local management entities according to statewide guidelines with the state exercising oversight and enforcement powers.

"The negotiators, however, ultimately recommended that the Commission reject giving local management entities decision-making authority. Agricultural representatives had begun to fear that municipalities would control any election for members of a local management entity and that management by local entities would therefore mean management by the cities. Other representatives, most notably, mining, had always worried that members of the local management entities would be unable to withstand political pressure from their neighbors and that management by a local entity would therefore mean no management. Finally, several negotiators became increasingly concerned that each local management entity might interpret a complex law differently resulting in strikingly divergent management plans for each AMA and numerous legal challenges. Gradually the consensus shifted toward centralized state management with AMAs as the focal point of management activity." (Ferris, *supra*, note 83 at 10–11.)

86. In each management plan a water duty is calculated for each farm unit (one farm or contiguous farms with similar soils and cropping patterns). For the first management plans, the calculations assume the use of conservation practices such as lined canals and land leveling. See *e.g.*, Phoenix AMA Management Plan, *supra*, note 83 at 39–60, 130–35. Later plans will be based on more advanced practices such as drip irrigation. After a phase-in period (January 1, 1987, for the initial plans), an irrigator may not apply water in excess of the prescribed duty. See Ariz. Rev. Stat. Ann. ss 45–561 to –566 (Supp. 1984–85), and Ferris, *supra*, note 83, at 15–16.

87. No water, including CAP water, may be used to irrigate land that had not been in production as of January 1, 1980. Ariz. Rev. Stat. Ann. s 45–452 (Supp. 1984–85). Existing irrigation rights are grandfathered and can be transferred. *Idem* s 45–472 to –474.

88. Ariz. Rev. Stat. Ann. s 45–566 (Supp. 1984–85). Once retired, land cannot be returned to irrigation. *Idem* s 45–473. '

89. Residential users are subjected to per capita reductions. *Idem* s 45–564(A) (2). The initial management plans, (*supra*, note 83) are based on reasonable use of 140 gallons per day per capita. Tucson has come close to that figure through its highly successful "Beat the Peak" program, but use in Phoenix still exceeds 250 gallons per day. (Ferris, *supra*, note 83, at 16–17.) Existing supplies of municipal water are not required to meet the 140 gallon per day limit, but must reduce per capita deliveries by 6 to 11% within two years. New municipal providers must meet the 140 gallon per day standard. (See Phoenix AMA Management Plan, *supra*, note 83, at 61–81. See also Rocky Mountain Mineral Law Foundation, *Water Law Newsletter* No. 3 at 1–2, [1984].)

90. Ariz. Rev. Stat. Ann. s 45–611 (Supp. 1984–85). The Director set a fee of $0.75 per acre foot for calendar year 1985, which will be applied toward the annual administrative costs of approximately $1.5 million. Ferris, *supra*, note 83, at 10. No more than $1 per acre foot may be used to defray administrative costs, but during the second ten-year plan an additional $2 fee can be levied to create a fund for augmenting the water supply. Ariz. Rev. Stat. Ann. s 45–611(2) (Supp. 1984–85). During the third planning period another $2 fee can be imposed and applied toward the retirement of agricultural land. *Idem* s 45–611(3).

91. 458 U.S. 941 (1982).

92. Ariz. Rev. Stat. Ann., s 45–153B (Supp. 1981); Colo. Rev. Stat., s 37–90–136 (1973) (Supp. 1983); New Rev. Stat., s 553.520 (1979); N.M. Stat. Ann., s 72–12–19 (1978); Okla. Stat. Ann., title 82, s 1085.22 (West. Supp.

1983); see also Colo. Rev. Stat., s 37–90–136 (1973) (repealed 1983). A similar Texas statute was struck down by the district court in *City of Altus* 255 F. Supp. 840, and subsequently was repealed. Act of Aug. 30, 1965, ch. 568, 1965 Tex. Gen. Laws 1245, repealed by Act of Apr. 12, 1971, Tex. Gen. Laws 658.

93. This expression refers to restrictions the judiciary has held to be placed on state regulation by the Commerce Clause even though Congress has not exercised its regulatory authority. Alternate expressions of the same doctrine are "silent Commerce Clause" and "the negative implications of the Commerce Clause."

94. Kent A. Price, "A Water Crisis?" 83 *Resources*, 1 (Spring, 1986).

95. Edith Brown Weiss, "In Fairness of Future Generations," 83 *Resources*, 4 (Spring 1986).

3   The Pending Water Crisis

Tim R. Miller

Of the many themes and concerns appearing in the writings on water policy in recent decades, perhaps none is as routinely cited as the alarm concerning the pending great American water crisis. Indeed, fears of an allegedly pending water crisis have dominated much of the literature since at least the mid-1960s and have, if anything, grown more numerous and ominous each year since.[1] "Drought, waste and pollution," we are told, "threaten a water shortage whose impact may rival the energy crisis."[2] And, the doomsayers caution, we are grossly unprepared to deal with its possible life-threatening and economically devastating consequences.

The water crisis issue is of particular concern to the future of the American Southwest, so it is not surprising that many of the contributors to *Water and the Future of the Southwest* write, in the following chapters, about water's scarcity and its availability. Taxed by an era of rapid population growth and correspondingly great economic development, and having a generally arid climate, the region stretching from Texas through southern California is uniquely vulnerable to the dangers of a potential water crisis. In fact, for these reasons it could be quite sensibly argued that of all the nation's regions, the water crisis issue is most relevant to the American Southwest.[3] But what, exactly, is a "water crisis" and how is such a crisis perceived by water professionals? In an effort to answer these questions we will attempt to clarify two key aspects of this potential southwestern crisis. First, do knowledgeable water professionals in the region agree that a water crisis is likely in the foreseeable future (defined as within the next fifteen years); and if so, what specifically is seen as the nature of that potential crisis? In other words, is there a consensus across state boundaries on (a) the likelihood and (b) the specific type or form of the allegedly pending water crisis? Second, how well-prepared is the Southwest to deal with the crisis, should it in fact occur?

Answers to these questions will provide insights into (a) the meaning of "water crisis" in the context of the Southwest, (b) the extent to which the crisis is seen as a realistic feature of the region's future, and (c) the state of readiness for a response to the future crisis.

The discussion that follows is based largely on relevant themes found in the literature on water policymaking, and on extensive telephone interviews with the directors of the Water Resources Research Bureaus (WRRBs) in the eight southwestern states conducted during the early summer months of 1986.[4] The basis of the selection of these authorities for analysis is the assumption that their career positions provide them with unique perceptual insights into the relevant issues. Each is a water professional who deals with water issues on an everyday basis and is by definition among the foremost student-scholars of water policymaking in each of the respective states. The directors have for the most part devoted their career energies to the study and/or management of this precious resource. Accordingly, this study's application of the perceptual approach, as used throughout the social sciences, "is based on the premise that perceptions of complex social phenomena are no less valid than other measures of reality."[5]

With one exception, a series of open-end questions were asked regarding the likelihood and nature of the hypothesized water crisis. The rationale behind the questions gauging the adequacy of state crisis preparation traces to Harvey Doerksen. According to Doerksen:

> Overshadowing the normal intra-organizational problems are the technical, legal-political, and philosophical (value) problems associated with water. Water resources management must be understood as policymaking where agencies, laws, and political entities converge.[6]

Following Doerksen's lead, directors were asked to "grade [their] state" on a series of items (legal, political, etc.) regarding their state's present capacity to respond "to a possible water crisis within the foreseeable future, say the next 15 years." Letter grades of A through F (using pluses and minuses) were assigned, with "A as an excellent or extremely high score, B as a good or high score, C as an average or adequate score, D as a poor or low score, and F as a failing or extremely low score." The author acknowledges, of course, that the legal, political, agency-technical, and social-values categories are not entirely distinctive nor mutually unrelated issue areas. Still, questions oriented around these themes provide an excellent broad-based starting point for examining these four major aspects of water and policy.

The discussion below will necessarily make regular reference to the individual states studied. When feasible, however, points are dealt with in the aggregate. This approach not only protects the identity of respondents whose candor might be troublesome for them in light of their in-state political situation but also responds to Keith Baker's charge that "most of the participants in the struggle for water in the West became so preoccupied with questions of state sovereignty (water imperialism) as to lose sight of the common good."[7] Thus, approaching the issues in the regional context will help focus attention on the more comprehensive regional issues of the Southwest.

Finally, for the purpose of this paper, *Southwest* is so defined as to include the states ranging from Texas and Oklahoma west through California. Eight states are included here: Texas, Oklahoma, California, New Mexico, Colorado, Arizona, Utah, and Nevada.

At the outset of the interviews, respondents were reminded of the many books, articles, and discussions predicting a pending water crisis in this country in general and the Southwest in particular. Table 3.1 shows their responses to the question of whether they "would say it is likely or unlikely that your state will face a major water crisis within the next 15 years." As shown, a clear consensus does not exist on the likelihood of the allegedly impending crisis. In fact, respondents from Arizona, New Mexico, and Texas thought it quite *unlikely* that there will be a serious water crisis by the year 2000.

These responses are somewhat surprising in light of the tone of most crisis writings, which tend to express an "air of emergency" if not outright prediction of "impending doom." Essentially, though, these last three officials take exception to the label "water crisis,"

Table 3.1 The Likelihood of a Major Water Crisis Before the
Year 2000: The Perspective of Water Resources
Bureau Directors from the American Southwest
(n=8)

Responses	State
Very or extremely likely	Colorado
	Oklahoma
	Utah
Quite likely	Nevada
Slightly likely	California
Quite unlikely	Arizona
	New Mexico
	Texas

more than they deny the reality of impending danger. Portraying the situation in crisis terms misses the mark in at least two ways, they contend. First, the term may have a counterproductive effect of generating a community-wide sense of hopelessness.[8] In recent years, for instance, Americans have survived a series of political crises (*e.g.* civil rights, Vietnam, Watergate, terrorism, Iran), the energy crisis, a crisis of confidence, institutional crises (*e.g.* schools, marriage), and a never-ending string of economic crises. The "crisis of the week" syndrome, it is argued, may actually lead to inaction if the public perceives that "wolf" is being cried once too often.

The term likewise has pejorative connotations for professional water managers and elected leaders. As Wayne Jordan, of the Texas Water Resources Institute, put it:

> Crisis is . . . not . . . the proper way to describe the water problems of the West. As you look historically at the actions taken, the people who manage water in the West are probably as progressive a bunch of people as you're likely to find anywhere because they've had more experience in marketing, regulation, policy development, conservation—the whole gamut. So I think that "crisis" implies a lack of foresight and a lack of future planning. I will say that we do have water problems, but I believe that we are probably going to be able to anticipate those problems and take care of them and others as they arise.[9]

So the point here is *not* that these eight southwestern water authorities are divided on the issue of whether the region is at risk. The dissenters to the term "water crisis" were equally direct in noting that serious water "problems" may indeed loom in the region's near future. The disagreement that these three authorities have with their colleagues from the other states in the region, then, is more semantic than substantive. In fact, Jordan went on to say that his opposition to the term is based on the fact that *crisis* is a rhetorical term that tends to incite rather than enlighten.[10] In that context, a clear consensus does exist among these water professionals that the immediate future of water in the Southwest is one of peril, whether or not it is termed a "crisis."

Respondents proceeded to identify three concerns as "at the heart of the potential water crisis or problem." These responses, shown in Table 3.2, provide some indication of the nature of the potential problem in each of the affected states. Seven of the eight directors cited water quality as central to the danger faced in their state. Clearly, in the Southwest as elsewhere, "the quality of the nation's ground waters has become a major problem."[11] Five directors defined the potential "crisis/problem" in terms of quantity shortages tracing to the region's arid climate, and four directors said the dangers are related to state and federal institutional and legal frameworks (particularly the legal standards that encourage water use rather than conservation or that tend to block water transfers).

These responses are in keeping with the themes sounded throughout the water "crisis" literature. The logical question to arise from this, then, is, "How well-prepared is the region to respond to the potential crisis/problem?"

As Table 3.2 indicates, the directors provided mixed assessments of how well prepared the Southwest is to respond to a water crisis or serious problem before the turn of the century. The respondents from California, New Mexico, and Texas were optimistic and felt that their states either are, or soon will be, well prepared for the anticipated problems. The California representative cited the high degree of environmental awareness, organized conservation groups and legislative activity, and the constitutionally anchored legal system for determining prior use and riparian rights as underlying his state's readiness. New Mexico's director pointed to his state's physical and institutional infrastructure for managing water, and took particular pride in the evolution of New Mexico's water law since statehood.

Table 3.2   WRRB Directors on the Nature of the Potential Water "Crisis" and the Adequacy of Response Preparation, By State

State	"Crisis" Defined in Terms Of:	Adequacy of Present Response Preparation Future Crisis/Problem
Arizona	Quality—Groundwater pollution	At risk, although Groundwater Management Act (1980) is a beginning
	Institutional Inadequacies—Legal standards which encourage use of water in order to stake claims to ownership	Early state of improvement
California	Quality—Groundwater pollution	High level of preparation
	Quantity—Secondary problem exaggerated by political rhetoric	High level of preparation
Colorado	Quantity—Defined in terms of location; 75 percent of water is in west	Not well prepared
	Institutional Inadequacies—"Prior use" private property ignores legitimate public interests	Not well prepared
Nevada	Quality—Groundwater pollution	Not well prepared
	Institutional Inadequacies—Legal obstacles to transfers from one purpose to another	Not well prepared
New Mexico	Quantity—In light of population growth	High level of preparation
	Legal Inadequacies—Legal obstacles to transfers between states and basins	High level of preparation
	Quality—Cleanliness	High level of preparation
Oklahoma	Quantity—Depletion of the Ogallala Aquifer	Somewhat—preliminary data-gathering is underway
	Quality—Groundwater pollution	Not well prepared
Texas	Quantity and Quality—Both tied to population growth; geological factor of water not being where population is; and the recent arrival of northerners with user, as opposed to conservation, value systems.	High level of preparation— state plan in place
Utah	Floods	Localities well prepared; Great Salt Lake solution yet to be achieved
	Salinity—Issue of upstream users damaging Colorado River quality for downstream users	Not well prepared
	Quality—Local drinking water	Reasonably well prepared

And Texas was depicted as having shown foresight with the passage of a state water plan, having good state and local managerial institutions and mutual interaction, along with ongoing educational and research efforts.[12]

Arizona and Utah were portrayed as having mixed response capabilities. Arizona's situation is seen as one of vulnerability of groundwater quality, although the 1980 reform legislation is seen as having enhanced the development of the administrative machinery for more effective groundwater management.[13] Likewise, the state's water consciousness—particularly among public policymakers—is seen as high. Local officials are credited with having taken steps to correct Utah's local flooding and drinking water quality problems, but the state is depicted as deficient with regard to pollution of the Colorado River.

Respondents from Colorado, Nevada, and Oklahoma were less optimistic regarding their state's capacity to deal with a future water crisis (or "problem") as they defined it. In Colorado, for instance, the legal system's emphasis upon water as an individual property right essentially deters any statewide planning efforts. Although the state influences events by granting or withholding low-cost loans, individual owners who can raise independent funding are unrestrained by government and are largely supported by a political climate that favors the status quo.[14] Although the Colorado director anticipates that his state will resolve the planning shortcoming at some point in the future, he envisions considerable confusion and litigation before his state's individually oriented water law is tempered to include provisions to protect the broader "public interest," however defined.[15] Nevada's spokesperson, like the directors from several other states, was disheartened by the extent to which planning to deal with the anticipated problems has been replaced by a patchwork process of litigation. Rational planning, he fears, is not a likely result. Consequently, Nevada's representative was the only participant to say that the crisis is actually upon us at the present time. This is interesting in light of the fact that in many of the states examined here litigation plays a major role in water management.

Oklahoma's director was only slightly more optimistic. His view is that Oklahoma is in the very early stage of addressing the quantity issue, by attempting to educate eastern Oklahoma residents (where annual rainfall is fifty inches per year) on the need to move some of their water to the more arid western part of the state. Of course, he continued, "Water becomes a very precious commodity when you talk about taking it away from people. They don't think much about it until you begin to indicate that you may want to transport it to somewhere else." This education process, he cautions, is quite informal and at a preliminary stage. The picture with regard to Oklahoma's future water quality is potentially more bleak, however. Because all seventy-seven counties there have oil wells, all of the state's reservoirs run the risk of being polluted by runoff or salt water plumes. On this issue, the state is largely in a preplanning phase.[16]

Up to this point the "readiness" issue has been examined on a state-by-state basis, and with "readiness" defined in general terms. The question can be explored more precisely, however, in light of the region's response to three specific forms of water crises (or problems) that are most feared—quality, quantity, and institutional/legal inadequacies. On only one of these three potential crises or severe problems is the region judged high in terms of the adequacy of preparation. Largely because of existing compacts and reservoirs, three of five directors give their state high scores for preparing to deal with water shortages (California, New Mexico, and Texas); only one director (Colorado) is critical of his state's efforts (the fifth director, from Oklahoma, judges his state's effort as modest, but not bad). Opinions are rather evenly divided on the quality dimension: three states (California, New Mexico, and Texas) are seen as exhibiting a high level of preparation; two are portrayed at the opposite end of the spectrum as not well prepared at all (Nevada and Oklahoma); and two (Arizona and Utah) are described as largely at risk, but with at least a few initial accomplishments in this regard. Among the directors who cited their state's legal/institutional format as the source of a potential crisis, one director thinks that his state is at a high level of preparedness (New Mexico), one director sees his state as at an "early state of improvement" (Arizona), and two directors view their states essentially as yet unable to correct their corresponding deficiencies (Colorado and Nevada).

The preceding discussion brings us to a preliminary conclusion regarding the readiness of the American Southwest to deal with a serious water problem or crisis within the foreseeable future. These interviews—although not intended as a statistically valid measure of exact percentages of risk—nevertheless strongly suggest that the region is only marginally prepared for a water debacle before the turn of the century. Their readiness, in other words, depends entirely on which specific problem or problems occur in fact and which geographical portion of the Southwest is being considered. This, in itself, suggests that the Southwest as a whole is at considerable risk.

But can we go further in assessing the readiness question? As noted earlier, the literature on water policy suggests that the readiness issue has four major components. Each, therefore, is a unique piece of the region's readiness puzzle. We will now explore these four major components one by one.

LEGAL INFRASTRUCTURE

As often as not, water disputes are legal disputes. This study probed two issues that have historically served as focal points of legal contention over water.[17] Respondents were asked (in terms of the grading system noted earlier) whether their state has: (a) an adequate legal basis (in terms of statutes and case-law precedents) by which to determine water ownership rights and to resolve ownership disputes, and (b) an adequate legal basis by which to determine priority usage during times of shortage.

In terms of the legal mechanisms employed, the eight states considered here fall into two categories in response to these questions. Arizona, Colorado, Nevada, New Mexico, and Utah follow the "prior appropriation" doctrine in surface water law. California, Oklahoma, and Texas adhere to the California doctrine's mixed riparian and prior appropriation rights.[18]

As Table 3 illustrates, most WRRB directors from southwestern states are satisfied with their states' mechanisms for determining legal ownership and priority uses during times of water shortages.[19] In fact, six of the eight authorities grade their state A or B on both counts. The regional average on both factors is likewise in the high B range (i.e. 3.125 on a 4.0 grading system). Nevertheless, the author's "reading" of these interviews is neither that these high scores reflect an absence of problem-oriented conflict in southwestern water law nor that the various legal mechanisms are seen as having completely made up for the planning and policy inadequacies noted earlier.[20]

This distinction was more explicitly made regarding Arizona and Colorado. Colorado was faulted as a result of the haphazard body of precedents that has arisen over the course of the state's history. "Colorado," Dr. Evans facetiously explained, "has 80 percent of the water attorneys in the seventeen western states. Their 'water policy'

Table 3.3 WRRB Directors' "Grading" of State Readiness to Respond to a Water "Crisis" in the Southwest

| | State | | | | | | | | Grade | Numerical |
Factor	AZ	CA	CO	NV	NM	OK	TX	UT	Average	Average
Legal										
Basis upon which to determine ownership rights	C	A	D	A	B+	B	A–	A	B	3.125
Basis upon which to determine priority rights during shortages	C	B	B–	B	A	B	B+	A	B	3.125
			Overall Average, All Legal Factors =						B	3.125
Political										
Water policy in relation to state's overall political agenda	A	A–	A	C	A	B	A	C	B+	3.337
Farsightedness of present legislature on water management issues	—	—	—	—	—	—	—	—	C+	2.4
Expertise of legislature's water committee leaders/chairs	—	—	—	—	—	—	—	—	B–	2.662
Farsightedness of present governor on water management issues	—	—	—	—	—	—	—	—	B	2.971

										Average
Comprehensive water policy already in place	C	B−	F	D	A	A−	B	B−	C+		2.387
Overall Average, All Political Factors =									B−		2.751

Agency-Technical

											Average
Incentives to conserve	B	C+	D	F	B−	C	C−	C	C		1.837
Funding levels of management and planning agencies	C	B+	C	D	A	C	C−	A	B−		2.5
Manpower/staff levels of management agencies	C	A−	C	C	A	C	B	A	B−		2.837
Expertise and skill of management agency leaders	—	—	—	—	—	—	—	—	B−		2.685
Overall Average, All Agency-Technical Factors =									C+		2.464

Social Values

											Average
Level of public concern with water issues	B	B	A	B−	A	B	B	B	B		3.125
Level of consensus regarding appropriate water policy needs, direction	B	D	F	D	C	A−	B	B	C		2.087
Overall Average, All Social-Values Factors =									B−		2.606

Averaging Format: Averages were figured by converting letter grades to numbers based on A=4, A−=3.7, B+=3.3, B=3, B−=2.7, C+=2.3, C=2, C−=1.7, D+=1.3, D=1, D−=.7, F=0.

is litigation."[21] Arizona's director concurred (C grade) in depicting his state's ownership rights as "soft," making transfers especially difficult. Both respondents noted that although the doctrine of prior appropriations is supposed to determine priority assignments during times of shortages, the reality in these states is that the hierarchy of rights is often easy to get around for a variety of reasons (*i.e.* legal ambiguities, informal agreements by property-right holders, etc.). Consequently, C (Arizona) and B– (Colorado) grades were assigned.

Over all, then, the responses of these WRRB directors suggest that although the methods for determining ownership and priority uses during times of shortage in the Southwest are "satisfactory" to "good," the realities in at least a few states are that there is a patchwork quilt of litigation and corresponding uncertainty that is not conducive to the establishment of viable water policy. In other words, the high confidence levels in these legal mechanisms may actually have the counterproductive effect of increasing the volume of water litigation, thereby undermining legislative policy formulation. In such settings comprehensive policymaking takes a backseat to litigation.

POLITICAL SETTING

In their article on New Mexico's effort to protect its water from encroachment by the City of El Paso, Robert F. Durant and Michelle Deany Holmes note the distinction James Q. Wilson makes between "conditions" and "problems." Conditions, they explain, do not become problems unless or until public opinion perceives that action is necessary, often as a result of some "triggering" or "focusing" event.[22]

This distinction is especially useful in the context of the potential water "crisis." It suggests that effective public policy is not likely to be achieved until attention is focused on the magnitude of the potential crisis. In Wilson's terms, viable policy is more likely to result when water changes from being understood as a "situation," to being seen as a pending "crisis." Three issues are directly relevant here: 1) the extent to which water policy is an item of prominence on the region's political agenda, 2) the water-oriented capabilities and consciousness of political leaders, and 3) the degree to which the southwestern states already (or soon will) have a comprehensive water policy in place. Simply put, appropriate action is more likely to occur if water has assumed a position of prominence on the region's political agenda; a precrisis response requires political leaders who are capable and interested in addressing the issues of water policy and the potential crisis; and the future is more likely to be assured if comprehensive steps are already being taken.

According to pluralist theory, politics in democratic societies is largely a process of organized groups making competing demands in a pluralist context. Over the course of this competition, issues rise and fall in terms of public concern. Society's "political system is concerned with the manner, from symbolic representation to formal policy response, in which it deals with them."[23] Issues that are high on the political agenda are of greatest public concern and saliency. As Table 3.3 demonstrates, these water authorities are persuaded that water problems are currently a top priority throughout most of the Southwest (B+ grade over all).

In fact, in five states water is seen as one of the leading issues on the agenda: Arizona ("the Number One issue right now, both in the legislature and the over-all political agenda"), California ("very popular, important, gets lots of headlines"), Colorado ("right behind jails and maybe highways"), New Mexico ("third to the revenue crunch and education"), and Texas ("high because of the tensions between agriculture and the cities"). In only Utah and Nevada is water not judged a top priority. Utah's director acknowledged that while flooding is a top priority in the state (A grade), other water issues hardly appear on the agenda at all (quality = C grade; supply, etc. = D grade). Likewise, Nevada's participant in this study said that the state's spring 1986 flood had raised the issue to the C level, but that water would quickly be forgotten again. As an illustration of the issue's stature on the political agenda, he continued, water was not mentioned in the recent platform of the state Republican Party. Still, these perceptions of Utah and Nevada are clearly in the minority in the region.

The directors were also asked to grade their *present* state legislature and governor (as of mid-1986) regarding their "farsightedness on water management issues" as well as the expertise of the leaders of the water-oriented committees in their state legislatures. These scores are reported in aggregate form (critical comments expressed to the author are being withheld due to their sensitive nature) in Table 3.3. Two major points are evident from these responses. First, the marginal scores (legislatures = C+, expertise of committee leaders =

B–, governors = B) are considerably short of a solid vote of confidence in the abilities of elected officials in the Southwest to take the steps necessary to head off a future water "crisis." No A's were given on the farsightedness of the state legislatures (New Mexico's B+ was the highest score). And the expertise of the appropriate committee leaders with jurisdiction over water issues was graded only slightly higher, with Texas's A– the only A assigned. The brighter picture— and second conclusion to be drawn from the interviews— is the high level of confidence voiced in the region's governors. Three state governors received A or A– marks—Arizona, California, and Oklahoma (Utah's former governor was included here as well). The reassuring point is the fact that these states would generally have to rely on their chief executives for leadership in responding to the crisis, should it occur. The current crop of executives, in turn, are generally seen as up to the task, at least in a "guarded" sense (B is not A, after all).

The issues of the political agenda and leadership skills in the Southwest raise the logical question of whether or not the respective states in fact have comprehensive water policies in place. Today's policy, after all, is the primary bulwark against the anticipated water crisis or problems of tomorrow. Acknowledging that there is no universally agreed-upon definition of "comprehensive water policy," directors were encouraged to respond in their own terms, focusing on the extent to which their states have to date devised broadly based, integrative policies in anticipation of serious future water problems. Although this approach is admittedly general, it has the offsetting advantage of allowing the authorities to conceptualize around the aspects of policy that *they* see as most salient, on a state-by-state basis.

As seen in Table 3.3, the responses are not particularly encouraging across the region as a whole (over-all grade = C+), although five of the eight states were graded B– or higher. The perceived contrasts are sharpest between New Mexico (A grade) and Oklahoma (A–) on the one hand, and Colorado (F) and Nevada (D), on the other. New Mexico's director is of the opinion that his state's policy efforts are among the top three in the West. Oklahoma's respondent explains that the Oklahoma Water Resources Board has set clear goals and aims although its policy is in an early stage of implementation and enforcement is difficult in some areas. The picture is seen as most bleak in

Colorado, where some five years ago the legislature instructed the State Department of Natural Resources to develop a comprehensive water plan. Three years later the agency produced an inventory of resources that was not remotely related to policy. The effort was discontinued.[24]

AGENCY–TECHNICAL CAPABILITIES

Three issues were raised regarding the agency-technical capacities of southwestern states to handle a future water "crisis," including (a) existing incentives to conserve and (b) funding levels of the personnel within those agencies. The WRRB directors' assessments of these factors are likewise presented in Table 3.3.

As indicated, these water authorities are generally unimpressed with their states' conservation mechanisms (C grade over all), largely due to the region's orientation toward the beneficial use doctrine (which, some argue, encourages use rather than conservation). Those directors who cited any conservation incentives at all tended to mention price as a restraint, but often in a limited context pertaining only to the specific situation in their state.

The major exception to these skeptical responses was Arizona, one of the region's pioneering states in establishing a legal "framework for the comprehensive management and regulation of the withdrawal, transportation, use, conservation and conveyance of rights to use the groundwater. . . . "[25]

Although the directors from California (B+), New Mexico (A), and Utah (A) scored their states high on the funding of their management and planning agencies, the others were quick to point out perceived inadequacies due to the state–federal budget crunch on public dollars (B– grade over all). The funding situation, they emphasized, typically determines the adequacy of manpower and staff levels among the state water management agencies in the region (B– grade over all). Also, responses regarding the "expertise and skill of the leaders" of these agencies varied, with only one A grade assigned (B– grade over all). Specific concerns were voiced regarding the relatively low salary structures in some southwestern states (one or two references were made to the old adage that "you get what you pay for"), the reliance in some cases upon managers without adequate graduate-level training, the partisan (*i.e.*, unquestioning and uncritical) makeup of some agencies, and the potential for a generation gap due to the aging of the present leaders.

SOCIAL VALUE SYSTEM

During the discussion of the political factors relevant to the possible southwestern water "crisis," the author made the point that precrisis policy action is more likely to occur if water has emerged as a focal issue on the region's political agenda. Numerous writers on public policymaking have shown that changes in public policy are more likely to occur when public opinion on an issue has been aroused, particularly when a strong public consensus exists on the preferred policy alternative.[26] Examining the relevance of this dynamic for 1980s water policymaking, however, Ingram *et al.* cautioned that "if the direction of water politics is left to the residents of Western states and their elected representatives, we suggest that there will be little change from past policy."[27] With this admonition in mind, two questions were posed to the WRRB directors pertaining to the possible water "crisis" in the Southwest: 1) How would these authorities grade the level of public concern with water in their state? 2) Is there a consensus in their state on the direction of the state's real or needed water policy? Answers to these questions will help us understand the extent to which the social support and value systems are prepared to spur on the political leaders, water managers, and over-all political agenda to take appropriate precrisis action.

Returning to Table 3.3, the directors are in considerable agreement that water is a salient public issue in the Southwest (B grade over all). Only a single grade below B was given. The C+ Utah grade is that director's composite grade for flooding (A), quality (C), and supply (D). He based the C+, in part, on the public's fickle nature. We have a penchant, he suggested, to forget tomorrow what happened today.

Most knowledgeable observers would expect relatively little in these states in the way of consensus on the needs or direction of water policy. Too much has been said and written on the competitive, conflict-oriented nature of western water resources.[28] In fact, "water in the West is a different kind of resource, more important than other resources and overlaid with heavy symbolic meaning."[29] Although Mumme and Ingram are speaking specifically of a study of low income rural communities, their conclusion that water in the

Southwest is likely to be the natural subject of contention has much broader applicability. As they explain, southwestern water has

> . . . significance beyond its material value. Its social character is linked inextricably to political as well as economic power, to social welfare and equity, community security, cultural cohesion, and the nature of economic and social change within communities.
>
> The importance of water as a social resource, especially as a source of economic and political power, is well established. . . . [30]

It is no wonder, then, that with the stakes so high, rivalries between agriculture and industry, rural and urban areas, conservationists and developers are commonplace. Accordingly, consensus on the appropriate policy needs or directions is understandably difficult to achieve. This is the over-all view of these water authorities (over-all grade = C), although the states fall into two rather distinct categories. Arizona (B), Oklahoma (A–), Texas (B), and Utah (B) were depicted as having a more broadly based "commonality of purpose" than their counterparts in California (D), Colorado (F), Nevada (D), and New Mexico (C). The interviews concerning the latter four states brought repeated references to the traditional rivalries and disputes found in water policymaking efforts. The implication here is that the Southwest as a whole is as yet short of producing widespread agreement on the goals and priorities of water policy, although that process may be well under way in half of the states.

CONCLUSION

This chapter has raised the issues of whether a select group of authorities (directors of state water resource research bureaus) on water policy in the American Southwest (*a*) expect a pending water crisis to occur before the turn of the century—as is so widely feared and predicted—and which specific problems they most readily envision; and (*b*) believe the region is well prepared at present to deal with a pending crisis.

Although these authorities are not all taken with the use of the term *crisis*, they agree that their states and region face the realistic possibility of a serious water problem or problems within the next fifteen years. In this order, the directors envision the "crisis" in terms of quality (particularly groundwater), quantity, and institutional inadequacies (*e.g.*, legal roadblocks to water transfers, etc.). These responses are neither surprising nor unusual and are quite consistent with the broader literature predicting an American water crisis at large.

The more novel discussion here involves these authorities' perceptions of the region's present readiness to handle a future "crisis." Asked to assign letter grades as used in school, the authorities awared a series of B and C grades along four dimensions of readiness (legal, political, agency-technical, and social values). Acknowledging that differences certainly exist from state to state, the region as a whole scored a B for legal readiness, B– for political capabilities, C+ with regard to the adequacy of administrative agencies, and B– concerning their social values.

On the positive side, water is depicted as occupying a prominent position across the region's political agenda (B+), backed by a high level of public concern (B) and a well-entrenched (if not always admired or respected) legal system (B). On the negative side, however, there are apparent doubts and concerns about the farsightedness of southwestern legislatures (C+), the absence of existing policy (C+), the lack of incentives to conserve (C), and even sporadic "pockets of consensus" on what the region's policy needs, goals, and priorities ought to be (C).

But the over-all question still remains to be answered: "What are we to make of this?" In other words, what are we to make of B and C scores; are they to be considered high or low? After all, if Johnny is generally a poor student, his parents will be thrilled by a B or C. But if Johnny's parents expect their boy to be a surgeon, a single B or C might be seen as wholly inadequate. So how are these grades to be viewed?

The answer, the author believes, traces to the nature of the possible "crisis" and the hopes for Johnny's future. As depicted here, water in the Southwest is an issue with potentially devastating economic, social (i.e., human), and symbolic consequences. The region is not water dependent in the normal sense. According to Mumme and Ingram, the Southwest's water dependence is "different." And as Harvey Doerksen has said of water policy in general, "The highly diverse political and legal system for managing water resources," as suggested here, "creates uncertainties which defy comprehensive management."[31] But in the Southwest, B– readiness in the face of such a widely anticipated "crisis" may well be to gamble in extreme with "Johnny's" future. At the risk of sounding like Yogi Berra, adequate is "adequate," not "exceptional." If the region is in fact at B or C readiness, the future of the Southwest is unacceptably at risk.

NOTES

1. For a sampling of the writings on the pending water crisis, see H. Clyde Reeves, *Funding Clean Water*, Lincoln Institute of Land Policy Book (Lexington, Mass.: Lexington Books, 1984); Terry L. Anderson, *Water Crisis: Ending the Policy Drought* (Washington, D.C.: Cato Institute, 1983); Terry L. Anderson, ed., *Water Rights: Scarce Resource Allocation, Bureaucracy, and the Environment*. Pacific Institute for Public Policy Research (Cambridge, Mass.: Ballinger Publishing, 1983); "The Browning of America," *Newsweek*, February 23, 1981, pp. 26–37; Council on Environmental Quality, *The Global 2000 Report to the President*, vol. 1 (Washington, D.C.: Government Printing Office, 1980); U.S. Water Resources Council, *The Nation's Water Resources, 1975–2000*, (Washington, D.C.: Government Printing Office, 1978).

2. "Browning," *Newsweek*, February 23, 1981, pp. 26–37.

3. The Southwest as defined here is one of the most rapidly growing regions in the nation. In fact, between 1950 and 1980 the region's population more than doubled; by 1990, the U.S. Census Bureau estimates, its population will have tripled. Furthermore, each state in the region receives less than 20 inches of "normal yearly precipitation," except for Oklahoma (31 inches) and Texas (48 inches), and even those states have unusually arid regions. See *1985 Almanac and Yearbook* (Pleasantville, N.Y.: Reader's Digest Assoc., 1985), pp. 879–902, 963.

4. Actually, seven directors and one research professor were interviewed. The Nevada director deferred to one of his assistants, whom he cited as more familiar with these issues and better able to represent Nevada's view on the issues.

5. William Gormley, Jr., "Alternative Models of the Regulatory Process: Public Utility Regulation in the States," *Western Political Quarterly* 35 (September 1982): p. 299.

6. Harvey Doerksen, "Water, Politics, and Ideology: An Overview of Water Resources Management," *Public Administration Review* 37 (September/October 1977): p. 444.

7. Keith G. Baker, in review of *Water and the West: The Colorado River Compact and the Politics of Water in the American West*, by Norris Hundley, Jr., in *Western Political Quarterly*, 29(2) 1976, p. 318.

8. For a related discussion on this general theme, see John N. Barbour, "Municipal Water Supply Problems in the Southwest: Leadership at What Levels?" Paper presented at the annual meeting of the Southwestern Political Science Association, San Antonio, Texas, 19–22 March, 1986, p. 4.

9. Interview with Wayne Jordan, director of the Texas Water Resources Institute, Summer, 1986.

10. *Ibid.*

11. Walter A. Rosenbaum, *Environmental Politics and Policy* (Washington, D.C.: Congressional Quarterly Press, 1985), p. 146.

12. For discussions regarding these states and the pertinent issues, see: Zachary A. Smith, "Centralized Decisionmaking in the Administration of Groundwater Rights: The Experience of Arizona, California and New Mexico and Suggestions for the Future," *Natural Resources Journal* 24 (July 1984): pp. 641–88; Robert G. Dunbar, *Forging New Rights in Western Waters* (Lincoln: University of Nebraska Press, 1983); F. Andrew Schoolmaster and Bonnie C. Yates, "A Spatio-Temporal Analysis of Electorate Support and Water Development Fund Allocation in Texas," *Social Science Journal* 22 (July 1985): pp. 71–87; F. Andrew Schoolmaster, "Water Development Referenda and Planning in Texas," *Social Science Quarterly* 65 (1985): pp. 1147–56; Joe Holley, "The Politics of Water," *The Texas Humanist* 6 (July–August 1984); Charles T. DuMars, "New Mexico Water Law: An Overview and Discussion of Current Issues," *Natural Resources Journal* 22 (October 1982): pp. 1045–63; Susan Zeller, "New Mexico's Water Statute: Will It Float?" *Natural Resources Journal* 24 (April 1984): pp. 471–86; Robert F. Durant and Michelle Deany Holmes, "Thou Shalt Not Covet Thy Neighbor's Water: The Rio Grande Basin Regulatory Experience," *Public Administration Review* 45 (November–December 1985): pp. 821–31.

13. For a discussion of Arizona's Groundwater Management Act of 1980, see Smith, "Centralized Decisionmaking."

14. For a discussion of Colorado's legal format, see Dunbar, *Forging New Rights*, pp. 86–98.

15. Interview with Norman A. Evans, director of the Colorado Water Resources Research Institute, Summer, 1986.

16. Interview with Norman N. Durham, director of the Oklahoma Water Research Institute, Summer, 1986.

17. Chapter 2 in this volume makes a detailed examination of water law in the Southwest.

18. Under riparian systems (*i.e.*, Doctrine of Riparian Rights), which are popular among water-abundant states, all proprietors of land along the banks of a body of water have an equal property right to the use of the water, with certain restrictions on the diminution of the body of water. In states that follow the Doctrine of Prior Appropriation (popular in the arid West), property rights are determined on the basis of who put the water to beneficial use first. See James Kent, *Commentaries on American Law*, ed. Charles M. Barnes, 13th ed., 4 vols. (Boston: Little, Brown, and Co., 1884), 3: 439; Charles J. Meyers and A. Dan Tarlock, *Water Resources Management: A Coursebook in Law and Public Policy* (Mineola, N.Y.: Foundation Press,

1971), pp. 52–53, 117–19. For an excellent discussion of the particulars of these and other western states, see Dunbar, *Forging New Rights*.

19. It is possible, of course, that not all directors have had experiences with water shortages.

20. For an analysis of the reasons underlying the absence of legislative activity in formulating statewide water policies in the region (Arizona, Colorado, New Mexico, and Utah), see Helen Ingram, Nancy Laney, and John R. McClain, "Water Scarcity and the Politics of Plenty in the Four Corners States," *Western Political Quarterly* 32 (September 1979): pp. 298–306.

21. Evans interview.

22. Durant and Holmes, "Thou Shalt Not": p. 822. See Charles O. Jones, *An Introduction to the Study of Public Policy*, 2nd ed. (North Scituate, Mass.: Duxbury Press, 1977).

23. Everett Carl Ladd, Jr., *American Political Parties: Social Change and Political Response* (New York: W. W. Norton and Co., 1971), p. 2.

24. Evans and Durham interviews. Also, interview with Thomas G. Bahr, director of the New Mexico Water Resources Research Institute, Summer, 1986. Dr. Evans's comments deal specifically with water policy regarding water supply and quality, and do not pertain to other aspects such as flood control and recreation.

25. Ariz. Rev. Stat. Ann. s 45–451 (B), p. 466.

26. See, for instance, John W. Kingdon, *Agendas, Alternatives, and Public Policies* (Boston: Little, Brown and Co., 1984).

27. Helen Ingram, Nancy Laney, and John R. McCain, "Managing a Limited Resource: The Political Constraints on Water Policy in the Four-Corners States," *Utah Law Review*, no. 4 (1979): p. 719.

28. For a review of the literature on these conflicts, see: Helen Ingram, "Water Rights in the Western States," *Academy of Political Science Proceedings* 34 (1982): pp. 134–43; William B. Lord, "Conflict in Federal Water Resource Planning," *Water Resources Bulletin* 15 (October, 1979): pp. 1226–35; Dean E. Mann, "Water Planning in the States of the Upper Basin of the Colorado River," *American Behavioral Scientist* 22 November/December, 1978): pp. 237–76; and William M. Wolmant, "Selecting Alternatives in Water Resources Planning and the Politics of Agendas," *Natural Resources Journal* 16 (October, 1976): pp. 773–79.

29. Stephen P. Mumme and Helen M. Ingram, "Community Values in Southwest Water Management," *Policy Studies Review* 5 (November, 1985): p. 375.

30. *Ibid.*, p. 378.

31. Doerksen, "Water Politics and Ideology", p. 447.

II The Institutional Environment

4　The Importance of United States–Mexico Water Relations

Albert E. Utton

In order to assess the future of U.S.–Mexico water relations it is necessary to understand how we got to where we are. This chapter focuses on the historical background of water use in a large section of the Southwest (the border area and upper and lower Colorado River and Upper and Lower Rio Grande). The chapter will also examine the complex water diplomacy of the two countries in the past and suggest how this "hydro-history" affects the present, as well as laying a foundation for the future.

In spite of intense competition for a precious resource in an arid area the United States and Mexico have, through mutual agreement, settled amicably the sharing of the major rivers in the region. However, dramatic population and economic growth in the border region poses severe challenges for the future. The exploration of groundwater resources and the severe water quality problems to be faced in the near future will test the good will and creativity of the two countries. To solve these emerging problems amicably, the two neighbors will have to build on past patterns of mutual agreement and develop new concepts of cooperation.

There are two central realities that are essential to understanding the water politics of the major river systems shared by the United States and Mexico. First, there is intense competition for every drop of water in each river. Second, this competition has resulted in the rivers being allocated and reallocated in a complicated maze of intertwining laws, compacts, and treaties.

THE COLORADO RIVER

The water of the Colorado River is the lifeblood of the thirsty southwestern United States and the Mexicali Valley of northwestern Mexico. It presently meets the needs of fifteen million people by supplying water for their cities, irrigating their agriculture, providing water for mining and industrial enterprises within the basin, and permitting the recreational, fish, and wildlife uses of the river. In addition, the basin is being called upon to meet the nation's energy demands.[1]

The use of waters of the Colorado River is determined by the 1944 treaty between Mexico and the United States. Mexico is allocated 1,500,000 acre feet per year and deliveries under the treaty are carefully monitored by the International Boundary and Water Commission. The U.S. allocation from the Colorado is apportioned to the Upper Basin and the Lower Basin; this, again, is subdivided by allocating to each member state within the respective basins a position arrived at only after bitter negotiations. Then, within each state, individual users receive their water rights from the state or federal authority.

The U.S. portion of the Colorado River waters was divided by the Interstate Compact of 1922, which intended to divide the flow of the Colorado equally between the Upper and Lower Basins with the dividing point between the two being Lee Ferry in northern Arizona.[2]

The Compact was signed before a treaty with Mexico, but it contemplates that deliveries to Mexico will be borne out of waters surplus to the total of 16 million acre-feet (m.a.f.) allocated, and if no surplus is available, then "the burden . . . shall be equally borne by the upper basin and the lower basin, and whenever necessary the States of the Upper Division shall deliver at Lee Ferry water to supply one-half the deficiency. . . . "[3]

Although the Compact purports to allocate 16 m.a.f. between the basins, we now find that these figures are grossly inflated because they were based on one of the wettest periods in four hundred years. More recent estimates place the mean average flow per year far below the Compact figure of 16 m.a.f. In fact, tree ring records going back to 1570 indicate that the mean average flow is perhaps as low as 13.5 m.a.f. per year.[4]

Thus the delivery obligation of the 1922 Compact is a bone of contention with the Upper Basin states. They are required to deliver

Table 4.1   Surface Water Available for Consumptive Use in the
Upper Colorado Basin

Year Approx.	Approximate Projected Water Demands	LPRPG[a]	Conservative Hypothesis[b]	Department of Interior	Compact Share[c]
1975	3.8	5.25	5.8	6.5	7.5
1980	4.4	5.25	5.8	6.5	7.5
1985	5.2	5.25	5.8	6.5	7.5
1990	5.6	5.25	5.8	6.5	7.5
1995	6.0	5.25	5.8	6.5	7.5
2000	6.1	5.25	5.8	6.5	7.5

a. Estimate from the Lake Powell Research Project.
b. U.S. Dep't. of Interior's "conservative" estimate, *see* Weatherford & Jacoby,
   15 Nat. Res. J. 171, 184 (1975).
c. Estimate used at the time of the 1922 Colorado River Compact.
(*See* Cummings & McFarland, 17 Nat. Res. J. 82 (1977)).

75 m.a.f. per decade, a badly miscalculated figure. In addition the
Upper Basin has had to meet one half of the 1944 treaty obligation to
Mexico of 1.5 m.a.f. per year, because there has not been a surplus as
anticipated by the Compact since the treaty was signed. In other
words, the Upper Basin must deliver 8.25 m.a.f. per year for use below
Lee Ferry, not the 7.5 m.a.f. anticipated by the Compact.

This obligation, when combined with the fact that the mean
average flow is much less than estimated, means that the Upper
Basin has much less water than expected. Instead of the 7.5 m.a.f. per
year allocated by the Compact, the Upper Basin may have no more
than 5.25 m.a.f. This is a severe impediment to the potential for
growth in the Upper Basin. Depending on estimates, water requirements may exceed supply in the Upper Basin by 1990.

State Apportionment Within the Upper Basin
The federal government played the catalytic role in the negotiations between the Upper Basin states. The Upper Basin could not
utilize its allocation of the waters of the Colorado without the construction of expensive storage dams, and the federal government was
the only source that could fund these massive projects. But the

federal government gave notice in 1946 that it would provide the necessary funds only if the "states agree upon their respective rights. . . . "[5]

With this carrot before them, the states of the Upper Basin agreed upon the Upper River Basin Compact within three years, and the Compact was ratified by the U.S. Congress.[6] The principal purposes of the Compact as stated in the first Article are: 1) the equitable apportionment of the use of the waters of the river system, and 2) establishment of each state's obligation with respect to the delivery requirements of the 1922 Compact.

Article III apportions the use of Upper Basin water between the signatories to the Compact. Arizona, which is both an Upper and a Lower Basin state, is allocated 50,000 a.f. per year and all other states are allocated a percentage of the total consumptive use of Upper Basin flows after deducting Arizona's 50,000 acre-feet allocation. Each state's share is as follows: Colorado, 51.75 percent; New Mexico, 11.25 percent; Utah, 23 percent; and Wyoming, 14 percent.[7]

Consumptive uses are the net manmade depletions. Thus a state's percentage is not changed with nonmanmade depletions such as transpiration, evaporation, and seepage losses. Meyers provides some insight into the negotiations over the percentages: "Colorado delayed the final determination of percentages until the engineering committee reported on the production of water by the individual states. Wyoming and New Mexico then 'forced' Colorado to recognize that present and future consumptive uses were also relevant considerations."[8]

The Lower Basin and the Battle of the High Dam

The Lower Basin states could not reach agreement as to their respective allocations, and therefore there is no Lower Basin Compact.[9] Instead they had to resort to litigation. In *Arizona v. California*,[10] the U.S. Supreme Court looked to the Boulder Canyon Project Act of 1928[11] for congressional determination of the shares of the individual states. The Boulder Canyon Project Act was the legislation providing for the critical dam and storage works for taming the erratic flow of the Colorado River and providing reliable supplies in the Lower Basin, plus hydroelectric power. The Court held:

Congress decided that a fair division of the first 7,500,000 acre-feet of such mainstream waters would give 4,400,000 acre-feet to

California, 2,800,000 to Arizona, and 300,000 to Nevada; Arizona and California would each get one-half of any surplus. . . . Division of the water did not . . . depend on the States' agreeing to a compact, for Congress gave the Secretary of the Interior adequate authority to accomplish the division. Congress did this by giving the Secretary power to make contracts for the delivery of water and by providing that no person could have water without a contract.[12]

Reservoir Management

With the building of four new storage reservoirs in the Upper Colorado River—Glen Canyon, Flaming Gorge, Curecanti, and Navajo—combined with the complex mosaic of apportionments, Congress through the Colorado River Basin Act of 1968 mandated the Secretary of the Interior to develop operating criteria for these major storage works.[13] Congress established the priorities for releases from Glen Canyon Dam above the accounting point at Lee Ferry. The treaty obligation to Mexico, the 75 m.a.f. per decade obligation to the Lower Basin, and the carry-over storage needed to meet these obligations were given priority in that order. Guidelines for maintaining parity between Lake Mead and Lake Powell were also mandated, and the Secretary issued the operating criteria in 1970.[14]

Summary and Prognosis

Competition has been severe between Upper Basin and Lower Basin and between individual states within each basin. This competition led to an intricate legal architecture, which apportioned the use of the major rivers and, in so doing, provided security to water users in this arid region. Nonetheless, with the population and economic growth projected, competition will not abate. States and regions will continue to challenge these legal provisions and water accounting procedures in an attempt to increase or protect their share of a limited resource. Particularly, downstream states such as California will look thirstily upstream to sources in states such as Colorado for additional supplies.

At the international level the United States and Mexico have reasonably settled the distribution of the waters of the Colorado River and Rio Grande during normal flow conditions, but uncertainty still persists at the two extremes of the pendulum—i.e., shortage and surplus. In regard to times of shortage, the 1906 and 1944 treaties have provisions for reducing deliveries to Mexico. For example, the 1944 treaty provides that in case of "extraordinary drought" deliveries to Mexico may be reduced in the same proportion as is consumptive use in the United States. However, these treaty provisions are so vaguely written that conflict can be expected if the deliveries to Mexico are ever cut. In regard to surplus, the experience of 1983 and 1984 not only demonstrated that above-normal flows can cause severe damage downstream in Mexico, California, and Arizona, but also revealed that reservoir management arrangements had not adequately anticipated the problem. From this, we can conclude that:

1. The conservation of existing supplies will have to be intensified at all levels, including the use of new technologies in agriculture and energy production activities.
2. Many water-intensive uses, such as farming, will have to be reduced to accommodate new populations and economic growth. This is already happening at a substantial rate.
3. This growth will require constant review and vigilance so as to anticipate and avoid unacceptable increases in salinity as well as other contaminants.
4. Finally, we can anticipate that the intensity of competition between states, and between the Colorado Lower Basin and the Upper Basin, will increase.

THE RIO GRANDE

The Rio Grande is essentially two separate rivers: the Upper Rio Grande, and the Lower Rio Grande. The Upper Rio Grande begins in the Rockies of Colorado and ends at Fort Quitman, Texas, after flowing through New Mexico. Over the years there has been severe and often bitter competition between Colorado, New Mexico, Texas, and Mexico for the use of the flow of the Upper Rio Grande. Today, the flow is completely appropriated, and the population on the U.S. side is increasing rapidly. For example, the population of the New Mexico stretch of the Rio Grande is projected to double by the turn of the century.[15]

The situation in the Lower Rio Grande is remarkably similar to the situation of the New Mexico Upper Rio Grande Basin. The entire surface flow is fully appropriated; the population is projected to nearly double by 2000.[16] The management of water supplies is made more difficult by the fact that the river is divided by an international boundary. However, the preceding statement may be too gloomy. The Texas Rio Grande Basin situation is less than clear, in that the water use projection studies disagree.[17]

In spite of the ambiguity of the various forecasts, the Lower Rio Grande Valley presents a picture of a water-short area.[18] The Lower Rio Grande Valley of Texas, which includes Starr, Willacy, Hidalgo, and Cameron counties, has the capacity for significant economic growth and improvement in the quality of life of its residents, but water availability is a limiting factor.[19] More than eight hundred thousand acres of land in the Rio Grande Valley are irrigated, but more than five hundred thousand acres of additional, potentially highly productive irrigable lands exist in the valley and could be put into production if water were available.[20]

By the year 2000, municipal and industrial water requirements in the four-county area will have increased significantly and there will be water shortages 70 percent of the time for the 750,000 acres of land allotted irrigation water rights, with the average annual shortage approximately 253,000 acre-feet. Dr. Neal Armstrong of the University of Texas at Austin concludes that "maintaining the current level of irrigated agricultural acreage in the valley, as well as providing vitally needed supplies for additional prime irrigable lands, will require supplemental supplies over and above Rio Grande supplies which are fixed by International Treaty and court adjudicated decree."[21]

The Rio Grande is not only international, interregional, and interstate, but also its different basins are governed by different treaties. The Upper Rio Grande Basin is governed by the U.S.–Mexico Treaty of 1906, which allocates 60,000 acre-feet per year to Mexico[22]; the remainder is divided between Colorado, New Mexico, and Texas by the complicated obligatory delivery schedules of the 1938 Rio Grande Compact.[23] The Lower Rio Grande Basin is governed by the 1944 treaty, which roughly divides the flow of the Rio Grande equally between Texas and Mexico.[24]

Rapid increases in irrigated agriculture in the latter half of the nineteenth century began to pit state against state and country against country which led to the treaties of 1906 and 1944 and the Rio Grande Compact of 1938. In times of shortage, states have to strain to meet the delivery requirements of the Compact. Thirsty users have chafed at the restrictions, but by and large the Compact has worked with the help of the not infrequent prodding of the federal courts and careful monitoring. Among the conclusions we can draw concerning the Rio Grande are:

1. Continuing rapid growth in the borderlands will involve greater demands on water and the environment, not only because there will be more people, but also because per capita income will be higher.[25]

2. Successful management of the problems ahead will require greater transboundary cooperation.

3. The U.S. Water Resources Council study of the Rio Grande Basin pointed out the need for basin-wide planning. Because this basin crosses state lines in the United States and forms an international border, there is a tendency to view basin needs from the perspective of the state or county, rather than from the basin as a whole. Emphasis should be placed on basin-wide planning.[26]

4. The specific water shortages presently occurring or forecast will require continued attention from state, federal, and international institutions. The competing demands for groundwater in the El Paso–Juarez area invite international agreements.

GROUNDWATER IN THE U.S. BORDER STATES

The heaviest groundwater users in the United States are the states that are contiguous to Mexico[27] and yet, paradoxically, the laws and institutions of at least one half of these border states are inadequate to control the exploitation of their groundwater resources.[28] In addition, international competence over aquifers divided by the frontier is largely undefined; it is fair to say that the legal and institutional situation is chaotic.[29] (For a full discussion of surface and groundwater law in the border states see Wehmhoefer, Chapter 2 in this volume.)[30]

U.S.–Mexico International Groundwater Law:
A Nascent Beginning

Mexican Ambassador Cesar Sepulveda predicts that "one of the questions that can most affect diplomatic relations between Mexico and the United States in the latter part of the 20th century, if not corrected, will be the theme of the water resources shared by two countries in the frontier area, especially groundwater resources."[31]

This assessment takes into account the fact that the biggest ground-water users in the United States are those states adjoining Mexico and that the legal tools for securing groundwater rights are meager. The legal capability to control groundwater use and development runs from near zero in the case of Texas to near complete in the case of New Mexico, with Arizona struggling to gain control of its ground-water future, and California mired in a confusing and inadequate array of legal doctrines.

At the international level a modest first step has been taken. The International Boundary and Water Commission (IBWC) has a long and admirable history of dealing with the major international surface flows under the authority of the 1944 treaty, but its authority to deal with groundwater questions is limited to that given it by Minute 242 of the 1944 treaty to:

1. coordinate groundwater withdrawal in the Yuma area, and
2. consult and exchange groundwater data in the Border Region.

In this context of inadequate legal systems for providing security for water rights, there is substantial population and economic growth and growing demands for more withdrawals from transboundary aquifers in the border region.[32] This increased pumping, combined with the inadequacy of institutions for either resolving disputes or managing the resource, raises the potential for conflict in the region. (The following discussion centers on international conflict in the region. For a discussion of competition and conflict between New Mexico and Texas see Barilleaux and Bath, Chapter 5.)

The El Paso–Juarez Area: An Example of
Transboundary Groundwater Interconnection

The El Paso–Juarez area reflects the pattern of significant growth concentrating in urban centers.[33] A few figures will illustrate the trend and magnitude of this growth: In the United States as a whole, El Paso's birth rate was exceeded by only six nonborderland metro-politan areas.[34] The El Paso population has been projected to grow to between 479,000 and 792,000 by the year 2000. Between 1963 and 1979 manufacturing employment more than doubled in the El Paso metropolitan area.[35] In Cuidad Juarez the population increased 767 percent between 1940 and 1970. Between 1970 and 1980 the population increased another 44 percent.[36] Between 1980 and 2000 estimates vary from projecting a doubling to roughly a tripling of the population. One estimate projects a near quadrupling by 1990. The more conservative estimate projects a minimum population of 1,302,000 by the year 2000; the larger projection predicts a population exceeding 2,400,000 by 1990.[37]

Lloyd points out that these estimates vary greatly because of the volatile nature of the migration component and the uncertainty of actual population figures.[38]

All of the above figures are estimates only, but at the very least they indicate substantial growth in the area leading, therefore, inevitably to much greater demand on the available water resources.

Much of this growth occurs in an area that has one of the lowest rates of average annual precipitation in the entire border region and thus presents a collision course between rising demand and limited water resources in an arid region.

Water Supply in the El Paso–Juarez Area

The population of the metropolitan area of Ciudad Juarez, Chihuahua, and El Paso, Texas, is on its way to two million inhabitants. Both cities depend largely on shared groundwater reservoirs for their municipal water supplies. Studies indicate that both sides are now pumping water at a rate faster than the groundwater reservoir is being recharged. Day reports that:

> Between 1903 and 1976, water levels fell as much as 73 feet in the center of El Paso and 85 feet in Ciudad Juarez. Based on a digital model study, Meyer predicts extensive Hueco Bolson drawdown by 1991, concentrated in the center of Juarez and northeast El Paso. Annual recharge to Bolson aquifers may be as little as 5 percent of the annual withdrawal.[39]

He suggests that "indigenous Rio Grande groundwater supplies are already overdeveloped and serious doubts exist that there is sufficient water to support expected growth in total water demand.[40]

A report commissioned by the city of El Paso concludes: "Pumping of the Hueco Bolson is substantially greater than the rate at which the aquifer is normally replenished. For this reason, the water table is dropping at rates of up to three feet per year in El Paso." (Pumping in Juarez is causing up to ten feet per year drawdown in Mexico.) The net result is that the aquifer is being depleted (mined) at a rapid rate.[41] The report forecasts that Hueco Bolson supply "will be exhausted in the middle of the next century, if population increases as expected . . . "[42] or perhaps even earlier. In fact, the report concludes that the Hueco Bolson "may be effectively terminated by 2030," due to the circumstance that "as the storage declines, well yields will fall off and water quality will deteriorate due to the influx of salt water from adjoining parts of the aquifer."[43] This same report projects parallel gains of nearly 20 percent for both population and water demand from 1989 to 1999 for El Paso.[44]

Estimates of water demand in Juarez are even more arresting. Lloyd concludes that "dramatic increases" in population "are likely to produce a major surge in the aggregate demand for municipal water in Cd. Juarez."[45] He surveys estimates that project up to a quadrupling of the population by 1990 and suggests a "conservative" estimate of a doubling of the "minimum population" by the year 2000.[46] He then goes on to reduce the Juarez production targets of water service of "360 liters per capita per day and a direct serve target of 85 percent of the growing population" to "realistic figures" of 310 liters per capita per day and concludes that even this modest figure "would more than double production by the end of this century."[47]

Both cities largely depend on withdrawals from the Hueco Bolson, with perhaps 20 barrels of water being withdrawn for every barrel of recharge. Therefore, El Paso is looking upstream to the Mesilla Bolson in New Mexico to put in a large well field of 266 wells to withdraw nearly a quarter of a million acre-feet each year.[48] Ciudad Juarez is also considering the Mesilla Bolson for additional supplies.

This picture of greatly increasing competition for water is occurring in a complex and delicate situation both hydrologically and politically. The two cities in reality constitute one metropolitan area. Both cities rely on groundwater for most of their water supply. Both cities depend on and are looking to the same two aquifers. These aquifers, the Hueco Bolson and the Mesilla Bolson, are both transboundary and both are traversed by an international river, the Rio Grande, to which each is interconnected hydrologically. In this intricate hydrologic setting, the proposal of El Paso takes on important international dimensions including the following:

1. *Effects on Surface Deliveries* Since the Mesilla Bolson is interconnected with the Rio Grande,[49] and since deliveries to Mexico under the 1906 treaty are made in the bed of the river, and since withdrawals from the Mesilla Bolson can affect the surface flow of the Rio Grande, questions of when and how the

proposed withdrawals could affect the treaty obligations to deliver Rio Grande water to Mexico are relevant.

2. *Transboundary Aquifer Impacts*   The Mesilla Bolson is a large aquifer that runs in a north–south direction and extends well into Mexico. The general flow of water is from north to south. Therefore, the large withdrawals of El Paso adjacent to the border could well intercept flows into Mexico, and lower the water table levels there. The international impact is made even more stark when placed against the plans of Ciudad Juarez also to meet future water needs by looking west to the Mesilla Bolson for additional well fields.

Lloyd observes, "It does not take much imagination to envision an unregulated international drawdown in the Mesilla Bolson aquifers similar to that which is occurring in the Hueco Bolson, in the event El Paso secures access to New Mexico water.[50] He adds that "such an outcome is all the more likely given the inadequacies of international groundwater law, and the lack of jurisdiction over international aquifers by the International Boundary and Water Commission."[51]

The truth is that the exact opposite could be possible also—that is, significant withdrawals in Mexico could cause adverse transboundary impacts by lowering the water table and increasing lift distances in the Mesilla Bolson in the United States. This is very much a hypothetical scenario, and the hydrology would have to be much better understood, but nonetheless the possibility of unseen impacts caused in the territory of the other country by the pumping of either country in its own territory is a matter for serious consideration.

Mexico and the United States have, at best, limited protection from excessive pumping by the other under international law. The reasons are twofold: 1) Mexico and the United States have not reached agreement on their shared aquifers in the El Paso and New Mexico region, and 2) the general rules of international law are of limited utility because of the delays and uncertainties of international litigation.

First and most important is the fact that Mexico and the United States have not reached an agreement on transboundary aquifers. Minute 242 signed by the two countries more than a decade ago spoke of "pending the conclusion by the Government of the United States and Mexico of a comprehensive agreement on groundwater in the border areas." Minute 242 also provided that "each nation shall consult prior to undertaking any new development of surface or groundwater in its own territory in the border area that might adversely affect the other country."[52]

The two countries are cooperating and exchanging data, but as yet there is no "comprehensive agreement" on groundwater, and transboundary aquifers such as the Hueco Bolson and the Mesilla Bolson are subject to uncontrolled withdrawals under which neither country is assured of either a secure supply or a fair share.[53] Rather, we have the law of "he who pumps fastest," or the rule of "we'll race you to the bottom of the aquifer"[54] subject only to general principles of international law.

THE MEXICAN DIMENSION AND THE FUTURE

In retrospect we can, as two neighbors, look with justifiable pride at our handling of our principal shared surface waters. We have divided the waters of the Rio Grande and the Colorado Rivers by amicable agreement. Although there may be some latent discontent regarding the precise allocated share, we have been able to establish mutually assured shares for each country that each respectively can beneficially use in an environment of stability of expectations and tranquility.

However, looking into the future we must ask, what issues can we expect to face and what must be done about them?

Water Quantity

The biggest water quantity issue will be that of groundwater as illustrated by the El Paso–Juarez case. However, the groundwater pressure points are not limited to El Paso and Juarez. As we proceed westward through the arid reaches of the political boundary of New Mexico, Arizona, and California, other potential groundwater "critical zones" are developing. We would have to include the two Nacos of Arizona and Sonora and "ambos" Nogales of Sonora and Arizona. For example, the Santa Cruz River rises in Arizona, loops into Sonora and then flows northward past Nogales, Sonora, and Nogales, Arizona, en route to the Gila River and the sea. Both of the Nogales are growing rapidly, and both obtain water from wells recharged by the Santa Cruz River. As upstream Nogales, Sonora pumps water from its wells, the water levels in the wells of Nogales, Arizona are lowered causing concern to the downstream users. The surface and groundwater supplies are hydrologically linked, and withdrawals on one side of the border may well have detrimental impacts on the other side.

There is also growing concern in the Mexicali area that the lining of the All-American Canal in the Imperial Valley to prevent seepage will cut off the supply of water for wells on the Mexican side that supply water for farming in the border region.

As population increases at explosive rates, the withdrawals of groundwater, particularly in areas of population concentration, will become more critical. In the absence of the groundwater agreement that has been "pending" for more than a decade, uncontrolled drawdown is possible, and neither country has security in the transboundary groundwaters they share. The time has arrived when the long contemplated groundwater treaty should be consummated. It should be based on the concept that water rights must be determined by mutual agreement rather than by uncontrolled unilateral taking.

To minimize the intrusion into the sovereign sensitivities of both countries two concepts should be used: 1) rather than comprehensive administration along the entire border, control should be placed only in zones considered critical because withdrawals exceed recharge or contamination threatens groundwater quality; *and* 2) actual enforcement should be left to the internal administrative agencies of each country with oversight responsibility lodged in an international agency.[55]

In the case of the U.S.–Mexico border region the obvious candidate for the international agency is the International Boundary and Water Commission. The IBWC should be given authority to declare critical zones when water quality is threatened by uncontrolled withdrawals or water quantity is jeopardized. Within these declared international critical zones, measures such as regulating well capacity and spacing could be instituted to control withdrawals and thereby give each country security of water rights. The administration of these agreed-on measures should be left to the established administration of each nation within its own territory.[56]

The time is ripe to avoid "education by disaster,"[57] which often has characterized the development of water law and institutions. The two countries can and should build on their long and admirable tradition of amicable utilization of the waters they share.

Water Quality

A second major category of future U.S.–Mexico water issues is that of water quality. There are a series of important water quality issues along the border, and neither country has a monopoly on these problems. The sewage problems tend to flow northward from Mexico into the United States, and the salinity problems of the Rio Grande and the Colorado tend to flow southward from the United States to Mexico.[58]

There are serious sewage problems emanating from Nuevo Laredo on the Rio Grande; Naco, Sonora, and Nogales, Sonora, in the Arizona border area; and Mexicali, Baja California, and Tijuana, Baja California. They all result from population growth outstripping treatment facilities. Tijuana, for example, has doubled or tripled its population every decade since 1930, and collection and treatment facilities have chronically lagged behind. The two countries recently reached an agreement whereby the treatment facilities have been substantially expanded, but the continuing growth will still strain the ability of the system to cope.[59]

Nogales, Arizona, and Nogales, Sonora, are served by an international treatment plant of the International Boundary and Water Commission, but again population growth has overwhelmed the existing capacity.[60]

The new river flowing north from Mexicali, Baja California, into the Imperial Valley is notorious for its cargo of industrial and human waste. It is a continuing health hazard and a source of ill will between the populations facing each other across the international boundary.[61]

As grim as the catalogue of affronts to the health and esthetics of the border may be, the two countries now have in place institutions for dealing with the "sanitation" issues. In 1983 Presidents De La Madrid and Reagan signed the La Paz Agreement for protecting the environment in the border region. The agreement sets up consultative mechanisms for dealing with bi-national environmental problems.[62] The country representatives working with the International Boundary and Water Commission have made admirable progress in the case of Tijuana.[63] However, significant water contaminations at the New River, Nogales, Naco, and Nuevo Laredo continue to worsen and await solution. They will continue to pose difficult challenges, given the rate of population and economic growth and the disparity between the financial capabilities of the two countries.

Finally, we must not overlook the undoubtedly increasing contamination of groundwater supplies. Human activities in recharge areas are real threats, and in view of the near irreversible nature of groundwater pollution, the problem remains a serious one.[64]

Finally, on the salinity front, as we have seen, the trend will be toward increasing salinity on the Colorado River. Ongoing vigilance will be required far into the future.

In sum, the United States and Mexico have managed the dividing of major rivers well, but much remains to be done in the future in regard to groundwater quantity and surface water and groundwater quality.

NOTES

1. Bishop, *Impact of Energy Development on Colorado River Water Quality*, 17 Nat. Res. J., 649 (1977).

2. 70 Cong. Rec., 324 (1928); 46 Stat. 3000 (1929).

3. Art. III (c).

4. See Weatherford and Jacoby, *Impact of Energy Development on the Law of the Colorado River*, 15 Nat. Res. J., 171 (1975).

5. U.S. Dept. of Interior, *The Colorado River*, 13 (1946).

6. Meyers, *The Colorado River*, 19 Stan. L. Rev., 1, 27 (1966).

7. Art. III(a) (2), 63 Stat. 31, 32 (1949).

8. Meyers, *supra*, note 9, at 29.

9. Meyers, *supra*, note 9, at 41.

10. 373 U.S. 546 (1963).

11. 45 Stat. 1057 (1928), 43 U.S.C. s 617 (1964).

12. 373 U.S. 546, 565 (1963).

13. 43 U.S.C. s 1501 (1971).

14. See Criteria for the Coordinated Long-Range Operation of Colorado River Reservoirs Pursuant to the Colorado River Basin Act of Sept. 30, 1968 (P.L. 90–537) in Upper Colorado Commission Reports.

15. McDonald and Tysseling, *Water Availability in the New Mexico Upper Rio Grande Basin to the Year 2000*, 22 Nat. Res. J., 855, 865 (1982).

16. Hedderson, *The Population of Texas Counties along the Mexico Border*, 22 Nat. Res. J., 765 (1982).

17. Armstrong, *Anticipating Transboundary Water Needs and Issues in the United States–Mexico Border Region*, 22 Nat. Res. J., 877 (1982); and Charbeneau, *Groundwater Resources of the Texas Rio Grande Basin*, 22 Nat. Res. J., 957 (1982).

18. Armstrong, *supra*, note 17, at 896.

19. *Idem.*

20. *Idem.*

21. *Idem.*

22. Rio Grande Irrigation Convention with Mexico, May 21, 1906, 34 Stat. 2953, T.S. 455.

23. Rio Grande Compact of 1938, March 18, 1938; s 72–15–23 N.M. Stat. Ann. (1978).

24. Treaty with Mexico Respecting the Utilization of the Colorado and Tijeras Rivers and of the Rio Grande, Feb. 3, 1944, 59 Stat. 1219, T.S. No. 994 (effective Nov. 8, 1945) [hereinafter cited as Water Treaty of 1944].

25. Hansen, *Economic Growth Patterns in the Texas Borderlands,* Nat. Res. J., 805 (1982).

26. Armstrong, *supra* note 17.

27. Clark, *Institutional Alternatives for Managing Groundwater Resources,* 18 Nat. Res. J., 158 (1978).

28. Burman and Cornish, *Needed: A Groundwater Treaty between the United States and Mexico,* 15 Nat. Res. J., 385 (1975).

29. It has to be noted, however, that the International Boundary and Water Commission (IBWC) has done a remarkable job of resolving groundwater problems to date with a minimum of treaty mandate or international practice as precedent.

30. For a detailed examination of the groundwater law in these states, see Smith, *Centralized Decisionmaking in the Administration of Groundwater Rights: The Experience of Arizona, California and New Mexico and Suggestions for the Future,* 24 Nat. Res. J., 641 (1984).

31. Sepulveda, *Los Recursos Hidraulicos en la Zona Fronteriza Mexico–Estados Unidos: Perspective de la Problematica hacia el ano 2000.* 22 Nat. Res. J., 1081 (1982).

32. See Alba, *Condiciones y Politicas Economicas en la Frontera Norte de Mexico,* 17 Nat. Res. J., 571 (1971); Bradley and DeCook, *Groundwater Occurrence and Utilization in the Arizona–Sonora Border Regions,* 18 Nat. Res. J., 29 (1978).

33. Day, *International Aquifer Management: The Hueco Bolson on the Rio Grande,* 18 Nat. Res. J., 165, 168 (1978).

34. Hedderson, *The Population of Texas Counties along the Mexican Border,* 22 Nat. Res. J., 765, 791 (1982).

35. Hansen, *Economic Growth Patterns in the Texas Borderlands,* 22 Nat. Res. J., 805, 816 (1982).

36. *Idem* at 808.

37. Lloyd, *Growth of the Municipal Water System in Ciudad Juarez, Mexico,* 22 Nat. Res. J., 943, 945 (1982).

38. *Idem.*

39. See Day, *supra,* note 33.

40. *Idem*, p. 169.

41. Lee Wilson, Water Supply Alternatives for El Paso, A–8 (1981) (Prepared for El Paso Water Utilities Public Service Board, El Paso, Texas, by Lee Wilson & Associates Inc., Santa Fe, N.M.) [hereinafter cited as Wilson Report].

42. *Idem* at A–8.

43. *Idem* at A–10.

44. *Idem* at B–32.

45. Lloyd, *Growth of the Municipal Water System in Ciudad Juarez, Mexico*, 22 Nat. Res. J., 943, 945 (1982).

46. *Idem*.

47. *Idem*.

48. Wilson Report, *supra*, note 41, at B–14.

49. *Idem*.

50. Lloyd, *supra*, note 45, at 954.

51. *Idem*.

52. Text of IBWC Minute No. 242, in Dept. of State *Bull.* 69, paras. 5 and 6.

53. See Rogers and Utton, *The Ixtapa Draft Agreement Relating to the Use of Transboundary Groundwater*, 25 Nat. Res. J., 714 (1985).

54. Hansen, *supra*, note 35, at 805, 816.

55. Rogers and Utton, *supra*, note 53.

56. *Idem* at 767.

57. Clark, *Institutional Alternatives for Managing Groundwater Resources: Notes for a Proposal*, 18 Nat. Res. J., 153, 157 (1978).

58. For a good discussion, see Mumme and Nalven, Managing the Border Environment: Advances, Issues and Options (paper presented at PROFMEX Meeting, Santa Fe, N.M., April 16, 1986).

59. M. Jamail and S. Ullery, International Water Use and Relations Along the Sonoran Desert Borderland (1979).

60. *Idem*.

61. *Idem*.

62. Agreement between the United States of America and the United Mexican States on Cooperation for the Protection and Improvement of the Environment in the Border Area. La Paz, Baja California, Mexico, August 14, 1983.

63. Mumme and Nalven, *supra*, note 58.

64. Teclaff and Teclaff, *Transboundary Groundwater Pollution: Survey and Trends in Treaty Law*, 19 Nat. Res. J., 629 (1979).

5   The Coming Nationalization of Southwestern Water: A Cautionary Tale

Ryan J. Barilleaux and
C. Richard Bath

The American Southwest is noted for many things, not the least of which are its aridity and its independent spirit.[1] It is a land of wide-open, but quite dry, spaces. Water has been in the past— and promises to be in the future—a source of contention in the Southwest. Moreover, water is rapidly becoming a national issue.[2] At least one group, the National Water Alliance, has been formed to enter this fray, calling for a national water resource policy.[3] The controversy over water is one that pits cities against farmers, state against state, and even different regions of the same state against one another.

What is ironic about controversy over water in the Southwest is that aridity and conflict over water resources threaten to undermine the region's independence. Indeed, as this chapter will argue, the battle over southwestern water could lead to a future of decreased regional autonomy. Struggles over water in the future of the Southwest may ultimately result, we will argue, in the nationalization of southwestern water.

It is the purpose of this chapter to explain why the future holds the prospect of nationalization. The explanation lies in the nature of current and future water resource problems; the shape of current controversy, and the structure of American politics. We will focus on all these dimensions of the water resource issue, with particular attention to how one case, the El Paso–New Mexico water conflict, furnishes a number of lessons for the future of southwestern water. Finally, because this is a cautionary tale, attention will be paid to alternative courses of action that could protect the autonomy of southwestern states while dealing with the ever-growing demand for water.

FEDERALISM AND THE CONFLICT OVER WATER

In the Southwest, water controversy often takes the form of "haves" versus "have-nots": for example, in Colorado, "have-not" Denver seeks water from the state's less populated areas on the western slope of the Rockies[4]; Los Angeles is locked in a battle with northern California over diversion of northern water to the arid south[5]; and New Mexico is fighting an attempt by the west Texas city of El Paso to drill for water in southern New Mexico.[6] Nationally, water is increasingly a controversial subject: several states in the Great Lakes region have been exploring ways to protect themselves from what they believe will be a water grab from other regions; New York and Boston want federal aid to help them replace their antiquated water utility systems; and the National Groundwater Policy Forum has urged greater attention to water pollution problems around the country.[7]

One of the central issues in the water policy debate both in the Southwest and nationwide is that of jurisdiction and control: who does control and who should be responsible for water resources. It is an issue that has come to dominate many of the disputes over water, because it affects the resolution of other issues. It is an issue that goes beyond the question of who sets policy to involve the distribution of power in the American federal system. For controversies over water are increasingly framed in terms of state versus federal control of water resources.[8]

States such as New Mexico, joined by such groups as the National Groundwater Policy Forum, insist on state control, so as to protect themselves from the "have-nots" who want water. In contrast, "have-nots" such as El Paso want federal government limits on the power of the "haves" to deny them water. Those who favor state regulation maintain that water has always been subject to state control, and that such authority must continue if states are to protect their resources.[9] Their opponents respond that water crossing state lines is a commodity subject only to federal control or that water is such a precious resource that it is too important to be left under state authority.[10]

This issue of control has become a significant one largely because of the federal structure of American government. Natural resources regulation is a mixture of national and state government authority. States have historically, however, had broad discretion in water resource management: controlling usage, supplies, distribution, and water quality. Some states, notably Nebraska and New Mexico, have developed sophisticated water control regimes to regulate their water resources, while Texas and some other states have employed a more fragmented approach. Because of their aridity, however, all southwestern states have jealously guarded their powers over water resources. The question is then to what extent will states be able to maintain their discretion in water resources management in the future?

The federal government has been long and deeply involved in water policy. This is true in several respects. First, an enormous amount of land in the Southwest is owned by the federal government, and the water on or under it is subject to federal control.[11] Second, the national government controls more than 25,000 miles of inland waterways, including the Ohio, Mississippi, and Columbia Rivers.[12] Finally, and of great importance, the federal government has long been the main source of funds for the wide array of water projects throughout the nation. These projects have been instrumental to the growth and economic development of the Southwest.

The federal government has also been closely involved in water resource regulation through a variety of laws: the Land Reclamation Act (1902), the Federal Water Power Act (1920), and a variety of other water quality and usage laws. They all add up to extensive federal government involvement in controlling water policy.

The result of these combined federal and state activities is a confusion over the status of water control. It is not clear who has the upper hand, and of course there is disagreement about who should control water. Many, especially those interested in state control of water resources, recognize the overlapping areas of authority, but want to give states complete dominion over their water.[13] Others want a national water policy to establish federal coordination of efforts to develop a national water resources plan,[14] which will mean an effective end to state influence over water management and a *de facto* nationalization of water resources.[15]

What is ironic about this battle over federal versus state control is that the drive for greater state control is likely to eventually result in greater federal control. Why is this likely to be so? The answer can be found in the general trend of federal-state conflicts, the coalitions of interests involved in water controversies, and particularly in the experience of El Paso and the State of New Mexico in the dispute over water in the Rio Grande basin.

The Rio Grande Basin Dispute

In 1980, El Paso filed 326 applications with the state engineer of New Mexico asking permission to drill wells in the Mesilla Bolson[16] to appropriate some 300,000 acre-feet per year of water. To gain access to that water, El Paso sued New Mexico in federal district court on the grounds that a New Mexico statute prohibiting out-of-state transport of water violated the interstate commerce clause of the U.S. Constitution.

The city argued that it has consistently followed a policy of both conservation and water supply expansion.[17] El Paso employs a variety of ordinances and policies to encourage water conservation, although the effectiveness of these measures is questionable. At the same time, the city has energetically pursued new sources of water. For example, the city annexed surrounding areas with water potential, worked hard to expand the city's share in the distribution of Rio Grande water,[18] and even explored the possibility of importing water from other parts of Texas, including the far eastern areas of the state.[19] This last option proved both impractical and prohibitively expensive. Regardless of the options, officials in El Paso believe that the city will soon face a water shortage of dangerous proportions.

In 1978, the El Paso Water Utilities Public Service Board (PSB) retained attorneys to explore the best means of obtaining water from New Mexico. PSB attorneys argued that the constitutionality of the New Mexico export ban should be challenged. The U.S. Supreme Court had declared a similar Texas statute unconstitutional ten years before, and even an assistant attorney general in New Mexico had described his state's embargo as unconstitutional.[20]

As might be expected, officials in New Mexico regarded the 1980 El Paso suit as an attack on their well-constructed structure of water control and management. Within a week of the filing of the suit, the state engineer, S. E. Reynolds, declared the Mesilla Bolson a closed basin. This action meant that no water drilling could occur there without a permit from him. Permits cannot be issued until the El Paso case is resolved, and there are about 2,000 requests in sequence behind El Paso's permit application.[21]

New Mexico offers several arguments in defense of its position. First, it maintains that withdrawal of the water by El Paso would upset the delicate hydrological balance of the Rio Grande basin.[22] Second, New Mexico argues that it is being made victim of Texas's poor record in water conservation and regulation. Its reasoning is that states with careful water resource management should be protected from those that have squandered their resources, and that equity dictates that New Mexicans be allowed to benefit from New Mexico's scarce resources.[23] Finally, the state contends that El Paso has not given sufficient attention to the alternatives to groundwater from New Mexico: rigorous conservation, preempting irrigation rights around El Paso, desalinization of water from the Hueco Bolson near El Paso, recycling water, and other Texas sources of water.[24]

El Paso has responded with three basic arguments. First, pumping by El Paso will not be enough to damage the hydrology of the Rio Grande basin. Second, water from New Mexico will allow El Paso to avoid the expedient of condemning large tracts of agricultural land along the river. Thus, the PSB charges that New Mexico is willing to threaten Texas agriculture, but not its own. Finally, if El Paso does not take the Mesilla Bolson water, someone else will. One New Mexico farmer filed 1,034 well permit requests, three times the number of El Paso's applications. As state engineer Reynolds has admitted, there is no way to block other requests for water if El Paso's applications are denied.[25] In other words, the water will be pumped: the question is, who should benefit?

On January 17, 1983, U.S. District Court Judge Howard Bratton of Albuquerque ruled in favor of El Paso and declared the New Mexico embargo to be an undue burden on interstate commerce.[26] In his decision, he cited the 1982 U.S. Supreme Court decision *Sporhase v. Nebraska*, which struck down a similar Nebraska statute embargoing the interstate transportation of water without a permit from Nebraska. Judge Bratton ruled that water is an article of interstate commerce and, failing congressional regulation, states could regulate its movement only under certain conditions: state regulation must serve a legitimate local interest and have only incidental effects on interstate commerce. Furthermore, he noted that the Supreme Court had already established the principle that " . . . a state may discriminate in favor of its own citizens only to the extent that water is essential to human survival."[27]

New Mexico, of course, immediately appealed the decision. At the same time, the New Mexico legislature passed a new statute allowing groundwater to be exported if it was not contrary to state water conservation practices or detrimental to the welfare of the state's citizens.[28] The new law directs the state engineer to treat in-state and out-of-state well permit requests differently; the state engineer must consider alternative water sources available to out-of-state applicants in all deliberations. As a result of this change in the law, the federal appeals court vacated Judge Bratton's ruling, instructing him to undertake "fresh consideration" of "respective rights and obligations of the parties in light of whatever intervening changes of law and circumstances are relevant."[29]

In August 1984, Judge Bratton handed down a second decision. His new ruling was that New Mexico's statute imposing conditions on water exports was constitutional, but that a state moratorium on drilling permits was not.[30] He ruled further that New Mexico's conditions on groundwater exports could be applied only to new wells, but not to the transfer or sale of existing water rights. Both sides claimed victory and neither appealed the decision.

The courts have not been the only field of battle between the disputants, however. New Mexico's representatives in Congress introduced legislation guaranteeing state supremacy in water resource management.[31] At the same time, the New Mexico legislature explored a plan for the state to appropriate all unappropriated water within its borders. While the state's claim to control over the water may be somewhat shaky, there is little doubt on the part of New Mexico public officials that it should have complete control over water.[32]

As the legal battle continued, the voices of those actively involved became more shrill. An official of the Elephant Butte Irrigation District (in New Mexico) stated, "As far as we're concerned this [El Paso's suit] is nothing less than a well-planned invasion by a foreign country, and we'd rather spend our last dollar fighting El Paso than lie down."[33] There was also a much-heralded economic boycott of El Paso proclaimed by leaders in southern New Mexico, although its extent and effects were nugatory.

After the second court decision appeared in 1984, the Rio Grande basin dispute lost some of its urgency. Yet it is clear to those in the El

Paso–southern New Mexico region that the issue is not dead. A final answer was not provided, and lingering animosities have not dissipated. At some point in the future, there is likely to be another explosion of the controversy into the open public arena.

More significantly, this case is important because it illuminates many aspects common to other controversies that will shape the future of water in the Southwest: (a) the central issues that will be debated in other water disputes, (b) the responses and tactics employed by the parties involved, and (c) the battlegrounds where these disputes will occur. In short, this case is a foreshadowing.

THE FUTURE

The dispute over water in the Rio Grande basin illuminates some important lessons about the development, issues, and resolution of water conflicts.

First, the Rio Grande case illustrates the sensitivity and controversy of water politics. As this case demonstrates, the participants often look upon the struggle for water as something analogous to outright war. Any battleground is considered appropriate in conducting that war: the courts, state legislatures, the U.S. Congress, and the public forum. Economic boycotts, publicity campaigns, and a "battle of experts" are all tactics to be used. No matter the specific circumstances, future disputes over water will quickly broaden into wide-ranging conflicts.

Second, resolving such controversies will entail some hard choices. The Rio Grande basin dispute not only pits a city against agriculture, but also the agriculture of Texas against that of New Mexico. Moreover, there is a conflict between state water control and economy: if El Paso is unable to obtain water from New Mexico, its alternatives involve significantly higher costs. The city would effectively face a choice between 1) buying out local irrigators with the attendant disruptions to the agricultural economy, 2) desalinating available groundwater resources, or 3) importing water from other regions of Texas.[34]

Each of these choices would be very expensive. So New Mexico's control over water competes with economical water management. If El Paso were forced to resort to such options, the city would probably have to seek financial help. Considering intergovernmental trends in the twentieth century, help is likely to be sought from the national government.[35] In a time of federal budget deficits the national government is not likely to respond with costly solutions. To the extent that the national government officials feel a need to act they may be left with a choice between state control over water resources (*i.e.* state sovereignty over water) and economies in water resource management (*i.e.* choosing the possibly less expensive option of mandating interstate transportation of water). Clearly the incentives in this or a similar situation would lead the national government to choose the latter option.

These kinds of choices are apparent in other water controversies. The battle between northern and southern California presents such difficult choices, as the thirst of the south is weighed against economic and environmental considerations in the north. Other cases will arise as development continues in the Southwest.[36]

These considerations point to a final lesson of the Rio Grande basin dispute: the inevitability of a growing federal role in the resolution of water disputes. The national government, whether in its courts or its representative institutions, will be an important scene of conflict. That it will be so is a fundamental reason why the nationalization of southwestern water is likely to occur.

The Rio Grande basin case contains a number of implications for the future of the Southwest, and they all point to nationalized water in the region. That development will not come immediately, but it will come.

As is clear from the Rio Grande basin case, states will not quietly surrender control over water within their borders. Thus, just as New Mexico has done, states will attempt to circumvent federally imposed solutions to water problems by revising embargo statutes, declaring moratoria on well-drilling, and appropriating water resources for state control. Already, several states, including Nebraska and Wyoming, have acted to secure their control.

Even advances in state control over water as the result of state or congressional activity are likely ultimately to induce greater federal involvement. With that involvement will come greater federal control. As water in the Southwest becomes scarcer and long-range transportation schemes grow more costly, the national government will have to choose among competing objectives. Federal control over water resources will be increased in order to protect population centers, even if such a move undermines state prerogatives.

The current situation of fiscal stress in national budgeting has induced the federal government to reduce the amount of money it gives to state and local governments. Some observers believe that this reduction will result in a smaller federal role in southwestern water controversies as federal funding shrinks. In the short term, less federal control may well be an accurate prediction. In the long run, however, the dynamics of interstate and intrastate water conflicts will inevitably invite a larger federal role.

Lessons for the Future

The logic of nationalization is apparent only in an environment that allows no other choices. Only if states insist on pressing their prerogatives to the limit, forcing the "have-nots" to turn to the federal government, can nationalized water become a serious option. And yet that is the direction in which the Southwest is headed.

If nationalization is to be avoided, then southwestern states should accommodate themselves to the legitimate needs of the growing Sun Belt cities. These cities are changing the character of the region and fueling its rapid development. The future of the Southwest is largely an urban one, and political power is rapidly shifting to places such as Phoenix and Tucson.

In an age in which the national government mandates a national speed limit by manipulating highway funds, and in which the Supreme Court rules that state and local government employees are subject to federal minimum-wage provisions, states cannot be complacent about the protection of their prerogatives. But that protection is not best advanced by intransigence. It is promoted by skillful accommodation to reality.

NOTES

1. The aridity of the Southwest is unquestionable. On its independent-mindedness, see Smith, Chapter 1 in this volume, and Daniel Elazar, *American Federalism: A View from the States*, 3rd ed. (New York: Harper and Row, 1984), especially Chap. 5.

2. See, for example, Norris Hundley, Jr., *Dividing the Waters* (Berkeley: University of California Press, 1966); *idem, Water for the West* (Berkeley: University of California Press, 1975); "War Over Water," *U.S. News and World Report,* October 31, 1983; and Robert Durant and Michelle Deany Holmes, "Thou Shalt Not Covet Thy Neighbor's Water: The Rio Grande

Basin Regulatory Experience," *Public Administration Review* (November/December 1985): pp. 821–31.

3. *Christian Science Monitor*, March 24, 1984.

4. "War Over Water," p. 59.

5. See *op. cit.* and "Cost of Irrigating California Farms to Rise Steeply," *New York Times*, November 21, 1984.

6. See Ryan J. Barilleaux, *The Politics of Southwestern Water*, Southwestern Studies No. 73 (El Paso: Texas Western Press, 1984); Durant and Holmes, *op. cit.*, and Albert E. Utton, "The El Paso Case: Reconciling *Sporhase* and *Vermejo*," *Natural Resources Journal* 23 (January 1983): pp. ix–xv. A considerable amount has been written about the El Paso-New Mexico controversy. The three citations just listed are exemplary and serve as a good introduction to the issue.

7. See "Protection for Water in Ground Urged," *New York Times*, November 15, 1980; "War Over Water"; Terry L. Anderson, *Water Crisis: Ending the Policy Drought* (Baltimore: Johns Hopkins University Press, 1983); and Rochelle L. Stanfield, "The Water Crisis," *National Journal*, August 17, 1985, pp. 1876–87.

8. For a summary of legal and political reasons federal involvement in the management of groundwater resources may increase, see Zachary A. Smith, "Federal Intervention in the Management of Groundwater Resources," *Publius: The Journal of Federalism*, 15 (Winter 1985): p. 145.

9. See Leonard U. Wilson, *State Water Policy Issues* (Lexington, Ky.: The Council of State Governments, 1978), p. 5; "West Watches Water Battle, Roots for New Mexico," *El Paso Times*, January 4, 1982; and *The City of El Paso v. Reynolds*, Mem. Op., U.S. District Court of the District of New Mexico (1983).

10. *El Paso v. Reynolds; Christian Science Monitor*, March 24, 1984; and Douglas M. Wrenn, "Water Will Be to the 1980s What Oil Was to the 1970s," *El Paso Times*, August 21, 1983.

11. Richard D. Lamm and Michael McCarthy, *The Angry West* (Boston: Houghton Mifflin, 1982), pp. 235–37. Federal land ownership in the Southwest (as a percentage of state territory): Arizona, 42.7%; California, 44.6%; Colorado, 35.9%; Nevada, 86.0%; New Mexico, 33.1%; Oklahoma, 3.6%; Texas, 2.0%; Utah, 64.1%. (*Source:* Public Land Statistics, 1981. U.S. Bureau of Land Management.)

12. T. R. Reid, *Congressional Odyssey* (San Francisco: W. H. Freeman and Co., 1980), pp. xii–xiii, and p. 4.

13. "Congress Interested in Water Tug of War," *El Paso Times*, December 8, 1983; H.R. 1207, 98th Cong., 1st sess. (1983); and Lamm and McCarthy, *op. cit.*

14. Wrenn, *loc. cit.; Christian Science Monitor*, March 24, 1984.

15. See, for example, Wilson, pp. 5 and 53.

16. The term *bolson,* referring to an aquifer, is derived from the Spanish word for "purse." The Mesilla Bolson lies under southern New Mexico, west Texas, and part of northern Mexico.

17. *El Paso Times,* October 2, 1983. See also Barilleaux, *op. cit.,* and Christopher Wallace, *Water Out of the Desert,* Southwestern Studies No. 22 (El Paso: Texas Western Press, 1969).

18. Wallace, pp. 28–30; *El Paso Times,* August 2, 1983.

19. Interview with John Hickerson, general manager, El Paso Water Utilities Public Service Board, El Paso, November 10, 1983. The interview was conducted by Professor Barilleaux.

20. *Ibid.*

21. Chapter 2 in this volume has a summary of New Mexico water law. For a more detailed examination of New Mexico groundwater law, see Zachary A. Smith, "Centralized Decisionmaking in the Administration of Groundwater Rights: The Experience of Arizona, California and New Mexico and Suggestions for the Future," *Natural Resources Journal* 24 (July 1984): p. 641.

22. *El Paso Times,* August 21, 1983; and Leo Eisel (engineer with Wright Water Engineers, Denver), public lecture in Las Cruces, N.M., October 1983.

23. Charles T. Du Mars, "New Mexico Water Law: An Overview and Discussion of Current Issues," *Natural Resources Journal* 22 (October 1982): p. 1058.

24. Eisel lecture.

25. Hickerson interview.

26. *El Paso v. Reynolds.*

27. *Ibid.*

28. *El Paso Times,* August 21, 1983.

29. *El Paso Times,* January 1, 1984.

30. See Durant and Holmes, pp. 823–26; and, "Judge: NM Can Limit Water Export," *El Paso Times,* August 4, 1984.

31. See *El Paso Times,* December 8, 1983.

32. See *El Paso Times,* January 31, 1984.

33. "War Over Water," *loc. cit.*

34. See Barilleaux, pp. 29–30.

35. There has already been some interest displayed by the Federal Government in helping to fund a solution to water problems in the region. See Lee Wilson and Associates, Inc. *Water Supply Alternatives for El Paso* (El Paso: El Paso Water Utilities Public Service Board, 1981), p. B–5.

36. See "El Paso Water Fight Sends Ripples across the West," *El Paso Times,* August 22, 1983. New Mexico, Nebraska, Colorado, Nevada, Montana, Wyoming, Utah, and Texas all had or have some form of water export ban.

6 The Future of State–Federal Relations in Water Resource Policy in the Southwest

R. McGreggor Cawley and
Charles E. Davis

Politics in the allocation of monies for western water projects is increasingly complicated by confusion and uncertainty over the appropriate policy positions to be adopted by the federal government and the states. It is evident that the political consensus that has long supported a dominant federal role in water resource development is threatened by changing policy priorities and growing fiscal pressure. On February 21, 1977, President Jimmy Carter sent political shock waves throughout the West by announcing the de-authorization of nineteen federal water projects. He subsequently put forward a five-point plan designed to tighten up eligibility criteria for project authorization decisions and to enhance both policy-making and managerial authority of state water resource officials.[1] Some of the water policy reform objectives—notably the provision that called for a greater emphasis in cost-sharing by recipient governments and project beneficiaries—have been continued by the Reagan administration.

Presidents Carter and Reagan sought to promote the decentralization of water project decision-making, but the attainment of this objective requires not only the support or acquiescence of other federal administrators and legislators but also the willingness of state officials to assume greater responsibility as well.[2]

To assert that federal support for and control of water project development is on the wane does not necessarily mean that states have the institutional capacity to take over decision-making responsibilities. State institutional capacity means the ability and willingness of public officials within a given jurisdiction to develop and administer governmental policies. It encompasses three dimensions—political, fiscal, and managerial.[3] Policymakers in states characterized by high political capacity are able to articulate needs, weigh conflicting demands, establish priorities, and allocate resources. Fiscal capacity is closely associated with the maintenance of a productive and stable revenue base to fund public services. Managerial capacity involves the development of sufficient organizational resources and administrative talent to design and execute governmental programs. A state that is prepared to combine all three of these components within a particular area of policy is indeed well positioned to assume a more autonomous role in the management of water resources in the future.

Whether the decentralization of water policy is embraced by various states is dependent upon the nature of their relationship with the federal government as well as the availability of resources. Some states may choose to partially sever the Washington umbilical cord by developing their own sources of funding to cover resource needs. Federal monies could then be sought as a useful supplement to state-initiated projects rather than as the sole or even primary basis of ensuring an adequate water supply.

California is in the forefront of states choosing to use federal funding as a means of augmenting their own resources in ways that contribute to state water plans and program priorities. This state developed a water plan in the 1930s that was designed to move excess waters from the northern part of the state to the more arid (and populous) areas in the south. Subsequent projects involving the cooperative efforts of both state and federal officials (such as the Central Valley Project) have been based on this plan, and state officials have assumed a major share of construction responsibilities.[4]

Moreover, the state of California has constructed numerous facilities through financing provided by the State Water Fund. Project revenues are acquired from a variety of sources including the sale of revenue bonds, state general obligation bonds, and, to a lesser extent, from legislative appropriations, user fees, and tideland oil and gas revenues.[5] However, California has been more active than most other western states in developing policies and financial infrastructure to meet future water needs.[6]

Other western states are inclined to promote the development of water projects that are restricted in terms of financial commitment. The Idaho Legislature created the Revolving Development Loan Program in 1969 to provide low interest loans for the construction of small projects; the rehabilitation, expansion, or improvement of existing facilities; or the financing of feasibility studies. In administering the program, which received an initial appropriation of $500,000 from the State's General Fund, the Idaho Department of Water Resources was also authorized to distribute grants of up to $50,000 for any project judged to be in the public interest.

In 1980, the state legislature provided additional support for projects through the creation of a revenue bond program. This permitted state policymakers to encourage the financing of larger projects without a significant increase in the expenditure of general revenues. According to a report issued by the Western Water Council, the acquisition of funds involved a rather innovative partnership between government and industry:

> The Idaho Water Resources Board borrows the money from private lenders through the issuance of bonds and loans with the proceeds of the bond sale going to the project sponsor. Any interest paid on bonds and notes issued by the Board is exempt from state and federal income taxes. Therefore, in essence, the Board's assistance provides a "double exemption" enabling projects to obtain more favorable terms than conventional financing.[7]

While Idaho legislators seek to maintain a lid on the amount of state funds spent on water projects, policymakers in Oregon have focused on a rather limited set of objectives for resource development. Loans are provided for projects designed to drain or irrigate agricultural lands or to provide water supplies for communities with fewer than 30,000 residents. Outlays from the General Fund are limited, as in Idaho, and project financing is obtained through the issuance of bonds. Since developers must repay these loans from the Oregon Department of Water Resources over a designated period of time, state taxpayers bear little or none of the cost.

The state of Arizona is in a favorable position of meeting the short-term water needs of its citizens through the infusion of substantial federal funding for the Central Arizona Project (CAP). Approximately $2 billion will have been authorized for the project, some of which will be covered by cost-sharing arrangements with project beneficiaries. Accordingly, state officials have not taken strides to develop a financial capability for project development within Arizona other than a policy adopted in 1973 to help local interests meet nonfederal cost-sharing requirements on federal flood control projects. On the other hand, progress has been made in the development of legislation to better manage existing water supplies. The passage of the Arizona Groundwater Management Act of 1980 placed emphasis upon conservationist practices as the key to preserving declining groundwater resources and divided the state into four active management areas to ensure correspondence between legislative intent and varying hydrologic conditions. In short, state lawmakers have yet to agree on a financing mechanism to address future water project development needs, but should be able to meet existing requirements for water use following the completion of CAP and the continuing implementation of the groundwater conservation program.

Other states, such as New Mexico and Nevada, are less prepared to chart an independent path in water resource planning and development. Nevada is the most arid state within the United States and is also experiencing the most rapid population growth.[8] According to the Western States Water Council, Nevada has no special development account or program, but does occasionally appropriate funds for the construction of specific water projects or to meet the matching requirements for federally sponsored projects.[9]

New Mexico created the Water Research Conservation and Development Fund in 1975, but the statute was amended two years later to prohibit the use of funds for the construction of dams, reservoirs, and distribution system. The state has occasionally authorized the expenditure of monies for smaller projects and did issue severance tax bonds for the initial construction phase of the state-owned Ute Dam and Reservoir Project. However, the tendency thus far has been to rely upon Washington-based funds for larger projects; approximately 96 percent of water development project costs in New Mexico have been federally financed.[10] Under these conditions, stronger resistance to federal decentralization and defunding of water project decision-making can be anticipated.

While the states vary in their degree of dependence upon Washington for funding and, in some cases, managerial expertise, the development of sufficient institutional capacity to handle water resource needs requires a delicate balancing act between the political will of state legislators and the commitment of resources. Clearly,

California has led the way in achieving this balance. However, the usefulness of lessons to be drawn from California's experience for other states is restricted by its lack of demographic, political, and industrial representativeness within the region. No other state approaches California in terms of population size, level of industrialization, or economic muscle.

As a consequence, other states share two critical characteristics not found in California—a dependence upon the natural resource base as the key to economic survival and a historic reliance upon the federal government for water project funding and technological expertise. In the following section, we present a case analysis of efforts to develop the necessary resources for water project construction and management in one of these jurisdictions, the state of Wyoming.

WATER POLICY DECISION-MAKING IN WYOMING

A cursory glance at the history of relationships between Wyoming and the federal government over water resource issues reveals a decidedly ambivalent quality. On the one hand, state officials have not been timid in seeking federal funding for development purposes. However, the willingness of Wyoming officials to participate in the water policy subgovernment has not been accompanied by a corresponding appreciation for federal reclamation efforts. State political leaders have consistently expressed frustration with the manner in which Washington authorities handled western resource needs.

In his 1909 message to the state legislature, Governor B. B. Brooks observed, "Unfortunately, the present policy . . . seems to be to accomplish all reforms through federal agencies whose meddlesome activity frequently acts as a hindrance to our development, and hence irritates our people."[11]

In 1978, Governor Ed Herschler stated: "I have been frustrated, annoyed, infuriated, exasperated, bewildered, appalled, alarmed, and disgusted in my dealings with the federal government."[12]

One interpretation of this discontent is that it reflects the tension common to fiscal federalism. The states desire, if not need, federal funds but rail against stipulations placed upon their use. However, there is also a substantive argument associated with the dissatisfaction of Wyoming officials. Wyoming is in the unique position of having contributed more to the Federal Reclamation Fund than it has received in project monies.[13]

Federal officials may argue, with some justification, that their efforts are intended to ensure that a degree of accountability is associated with the expenditure of federal funds. To paraphrase Banfield, the pleasure of spending federal dollars should be associated with the pain of raising them. However, the mismatch between funding source and decision-making authority may have a darker side as well. A recent study concludes that an unfortunate consequence of federal policies has been the inability of states to develop the necessary policymaking and organizational apparatus to administer water programs. According to Harrison, the generosity of federal subsidies, coupled with a lack of emphasis on the provision of planning assistance, has encouraged states to become overly dependent while substituting state and local priorities for Washington-based initiatives.[14]

Developing State Institutional Capabilities

The years of frustration with federal reclamation efforts have produced several attempts to create a state water planning and development agency in Wyoming. As early as 1939, the State Planning and Water Conservation Board was created to promote the "orderly and planned development" of Wyoming's water resources.[15] But the state's slow population growth in combination with the dearth of financial resources served to tie project efforts to the availability of federal funds. However, this historical pattern underwent dramatic change in the 1970s.

Several forces converged during the past decade to help stimulate state water development efforts. First, the emergence of the environmental movement created demands on the states through federal policies to build planning capacity. Second, the national "energy crisis" led to the accelerated exploitation of Wyoming's fossil fuel reserves. On the one hand, the increased energy production and resulting population growth promoted the greater use of—as well as conflicts over—the state's limited water resources. On the other hand, the legislature responded with the passage of a rather hefty severance tax on energy resources, thereby providing a new and significant source of revenue. A third factor was the realization in the 1970s that federal water subsidies were likely to decline.

The state reaction to all these forces is reflected in the legislative evolution of water planning and development efforts. In 1967, the legislature gave the state engineer responsibility for the coordination of water resource plans.[16] An Act passed in 1973 changed the state engineer's responsibility to the "formulation" of state water plans. In addition, it created the Governor's Interdepartmental Water Conference (GIWC) consisting of the governor, the state engineer (who served as chairman), and representatives from the other major state agencies. The primary function of the GIWC was to provide coordination in the development of state water plans.[17]

It is interesting to note that although the 1973 Act went a long way toward establishing a water resource planning development mechanism, the language of the statute continued to refer to proposed actions as "water plans." This was changed by a 1975 amendment which called for the creation of a state "water development program." The wording of the latter enactment clearly suggests that the water development program was to be viewed as a comprehensive state plan that would provide guidance for project decisions.[18] In short, the state of Wyoming had created the basic organizational machinery for water resource development by 1975.

The piece still missing was a source of revenue for financing future projects. This problem was addressed in 1977 when the state legislature increased the severance tax on coal to 10.5 percent. A portion of these monies (1.5 percent) was used to create the Wyoming Water Development Account (WWDA). This Act marks the first time that the state legislature authorized funding for the construction of state water projects.

In 1979, criticism of existing administrative institutions and the lack of progress toward the initiation of water projects brought further changes. The GIWC was replaced by a new collectivity entitled the Wyoming Water Development Commission (WWDC). It is composed of nine members appointed by the governor on the basis of recommendations from the state water superintendents and subject to the approval of the state senate. In addition, the state engineer, the water division administrator of the Department of Economic Planning and Development, and one representative from the University of Wyoming serve as nonvoting advisors to the WWDC.[19] The design of the WWDC suggests that every effort was made to exclude direct access by environmental interests and to impose a developmental bias upon the commission.

From 1979 to the present, two additional changes have been adopted to improve the state's ability to assume financial and programmatic responsibility for the development of water projects. In 1981, the state legislature increased the severance tax on oil and gas.

By this action, it arrived at the unusual figure of 1/12 of 2 percent of this revenue to be deposited in the WWDA.[20] The following year, Governor Herschler called for a comprehensive state water program that included: (1) a four-level study process for water projects; (2) a list of twenty-seven prospective projects to be examined by the commission; and (3) annual appropriations of $100,000,000 over a six-year period for water development planning and construction.[21] The legislature approved the plan with a slight financial modification. A one-time appropriation of $114,600,000 was okayed, but no specific guarantees for future expenditures were included.[22]

In addition, the legislature also established a select water committee composed of five members from each house to provide oversight on the WWDC and to develop policy and decisional criteria for the selection of water projects. Since legislative action is required at each step of the four-level process (see Appendix), political representatives can presumably maintain a watchful eye over project developments. Less charitably, this can also be interpreted as a political ploy by the Republican-controlled legislature to prevent the governor from receiving full credit for the policy.

Wyoming officials have thus made considerable progress in developing both the institutional and financial capacity to administer water resource programs. On paper, a number of significant policy objectives have been achieved. Unfortunately, it is difficult to venture a prediction about the probable correspondence between legislative intent and subsequent efforts to implement the program by state officials. In the following section, the political/economic opportunities and constraints affecting future water resource decision-making options are analyzed.

Opportunities and Constraints

One area of encouragement for proponents of greater state autonomy in the development of water resources lies in the apparent acceptance of responsibility for state-funded projects by Wyoming political leaders in both parties. The water development issue received considerable emphasis in the 1982 gubernatorial election without disagreement between Democrat Ed Herschler (the incumbent) and Republic Warren Morton on the question of who administers. Both candidates campaigned on the basis of nonfederal solutions, differing primarily on their approaches to project financing.

However, optimistic assessments of current political resolve must be tempered by the effect of changing economic conditions on the state's policy priorities. The "oil glut" and the declining price for crude oil have taken a significant toll on Wyoming's energy industry. At present, forecasts for state revenues from energy-based severance taxes are not encourgaging. Moreover, rising unemployment and related economic dislocations associated with a depressed energy industry have intensified the competition for general fund revenues.[23] To these factors can also be added the negative impact of present and future reductions in federal funding.

Serious as these economic constraints are, they may not be insurmountable. More recent trends suggest that state policymakers are beginning to reassess state water needs in an attempt to balance future development efforts with current economic realities. For example, the Wyoming Heritage Foundation published a position paper in 1985 that questioned the efficacy of large-scale water storage projects in Wyoming. At least one of the state's major conservation groups, the Powder River Basin Resource Council (PRBRC), praised the report as a realistic assessment of future water development efforts.[24]

Given the fact that the Heritage Foundation and the PRBRC have traditionally advocated opposing positions in water policy conflicts, this development may portend the emergence of a new political coalition. One tangible measure for the potential strength of such a coalition is that the Wyoming Legislature, which provided no water development funds during the 1983 and 1984 sessions, authorized $65 million for two municipal water projects in 1985.[25] Whether or not this action signals an authentic trend toward greater state independence, a more important question is what lessons the Wyoming experience might provide other states. In the concluding section we attempt to answer this question.

CONCLUSION

The current state of water policy may be more accurately portrayed as a period of reassessment and realignment than simply being the end of the federal era.[26] If this is in fact the case, then state policymakers must confront the difficult question of where water development needs fit within their overall policy agenda. Although the diversity of needs and experience among southwestern states denies a "single-solution" approach, we believe Wyoming's situation offers insights regarding the future for decentralized water resource decision-making.

The first and perhaps the most important of these insights centers on the fiscal dimension. Wyoming's abundant energy resources combined with its substantial severance taxes gives the appearance of ability to chart an independent path. Upon closer examination, however, this turns out not to be the case. On the one hand, the water development plan crafted in 1981 required $600,000,000 from general funds in addition to the revenues generated by severance taxes. On the other hand, the traditional "boom/bust" cycle associated with extractive industries can be counterproductive to the long-range planning needed for an effective water resource program.

Uncertainties about financial resources accentuate the importance of the political and managerial dimensions of state institutional capacity. The most recent developments in Wyoming suggest that financial barriers might be overcome by moving from the large-scale project mentality characteristic of the earlier water policy era to an emphasis on smaller, and therefore less costly, projects. The ability of other states to follow a similar path, however, is dependent on each state's water needs and the willingness of state political leaders to forge new coalitions.

Viewed in this light, future state-federal relations in water resource policy may be more similar to the past than is generally recognized. Financial resources for water development have always been scarce. Nevertheless, previous policymakers were able to mobilize needed resources by constructing effective coalitions. The process of building new coalitions is hampered, of course, by the resiliency of past efforts and expectations. However, as future coalitions begin to take shape, state leaders may well discover both new subnational institutional capacity and more persuasive arguments for continued federal assistance.

NOTES

1. Council of State Governments, *State Water Policy Issues* (Lexington: Council of State Governments, 1978).

2. Warren Viessman, Jr., and Claire Welty, *Water Management: Technology and Institutions* (New York: Harper and Row, 1985).

3. Charles Warren, "State Governments' Capacity: Continuing to Improve," *National Civic Review,* May 1982, pp. 234–58.

4. Theodore M. Schad, "Water Resources Planning—Historical Development," *Journal of the Water and Resources Planning and Management Division,* March 1979, pp. 9–23.

5. Anthony G. Willardson, *State/Federal Financing and Western Water Resource Development, 1984 Update.* (Sacramento, Calif.: Western States Water Council, 1984).

6. See also Dean E. Mann, "California Water Policies: Future Options," Western Political Science Association Conference Paper, 1983.

7. Western States Water Council, 1984.

8. Viessman and Welty.

9. Western States Water Council, 1984.

10. *Idem.*

11. T. A. Larson, *History of Wyoming* (Lincoln: University of Nebraska Press, 1978).

12. Tim Miller, *State Government and Policies in Wyoming* (Dubuque: Kendall–Hunt, 1981).

13. U.S. Dept. of Interior, Bureau of Reclamation, *Water and Land Resource Accomplishments, Statistical Appendix II* (Washington, D.C.: U.S. Government Printing Office, 1976), pp. 65–68; and ——, *Wyoming* (Washington, D.C.: U.S. Government Printing Office, 1976).

14. David C. Harrison, "Institutional Barriers to National Water Policy," *Water Spectrum,* No. 2: (1982), pp. 1–7.

15. Wyoming Compiled Statutes, 18–2105 (1945).

16. Session Laws of Wyoming, Chapter 138 (1967).

17. Session Laws of Wyoming, Chapter 233 (1973).

18. Session Laws of Wyoming, Chapter 180 (1975).

19. Session Laws of Wyoming, Chapter 59 (1979).

20. Session Laws of Wyoming, Chapter 49 (1981).

21. Enrolled Acts No. 35 and 44, House of Representatives, 46th Legislature of the State of Wyoming, 1982 Session.

22. Enrolled Act No. 26, House of Representatives, 46th Legislature of the State of Wyoming, 1982 Session.

23. P. L. Blair, "Wyoming's Water Plan Hits a Drought," *High Country News,* November 25, 1985, p. 2.

24. Bruce Farling, "Wyoming Water Makes Strange Bedfellows," *High Country News,* February 4, 1985, p. 2.

25. S. G. Jones, "The Wyoming Legislature Heads Home After a Low-Key 38 Day Session," *High Country News,* March 18, 1985, p. 6.

26. Henry P. Caulfield, Jr., "Financing Water Projects: Where Do We Go from Here?" Paper presented at *Western Water Law in Transition,* conference sponsored by the Natural Resources Law Center, University of Colorado

School of Law, June 3–5, 1985. ——, "Let's Dismantle (Largely But Not Fully) the Federal Water Development Establishment," in U.S. Water Resources Council, *Proceedings of the National Water Conference* (Washington: Government Printing Office: 1975), pp. 180–84.

APPENDIX

Four-Level Process of the Wyoming Water Development Program

Level I —— *Reconnaissance Study:* These studies are generally intended to provide the basis for a preliminary assessment of project feasibility and constraints to development.

Level II —— *Feasibility Study:* These studies are generally intended to provide a detailed analysis of project feasibility, impacts, constraints, and benefits.

Level III —— *Development Plans:* These plans include final design, cost estimates, financing plans, and identification of necessary acquisition of land and water rights.

Level IV —— *Construction and Operation Plans:* These plans are implemented under the direction of the Department of Economic Planning and Development.

At the completion of each level prior to construction, the legislature would evaluate the results and determine whether the project merits further state funding. If it does, the legislature may authorize the next level.

Source: 1982 Annual Report of the Wyoming Water Development Commission.

7 Water and the Future of Non-Indian Federal Lands in the Southwest

Daniel McCool

Eighty years ago the federal government began to realize that publicly held lands in the American West contained vast amounts of timber, minerals, wildlife, and scenic resources. With the intent of conserving these resources in the public interest, the government gradually began withdrawing specific tracts of land from the public domain. As a result, the federal government is now the owner of a complicated network of federal land reservations. But despite the government's early foresight in reserving land, it has only recently begun in earnest to clarify and solidify rights to water for that land.

Recent years have witnessed a concentrated effort on the part of both state and federal governments to sort out the complexities of water rights for federal lands, which include national parks and monuments, national forests, fish and wildlife refuges, and the remainder of the public domain (federal lands also include military and Indian reservations, which are covered in other chapters). The impetus for this effort came in part from the Reagan administration's policy of stressing quantification of federal water rights. Both the president and his western allies hoped to establish a specific limit on federal water rights in order to end the uncertainty created by potentially open-ended federal claims. Resolving the conflict over federal water rights promises to be a contentious and complex process, and the issue is presently in such a state of flux that predictions are exceedingly hazardous. Nevertheless, several important trends have been set in motion that offer some indication of future water allocations for federal lands in the Southwest.

This chapter will examine the water policies of four agencies that manage federal lands in the Southwest: the National Park Service, the U.S. Forest Service, the U.S. Fish and Wildlife Service, and the Bureau of Land Management (BLM). The first section explains the geographic, judicial, statutory, and political parameters of the issue. These parameters, established in the past and presently in force, will help determine the likely path of future policymaking activity. A second section discusses how each agency employs a variety of strategies to gain legal recognition of existing water uses or obtain new sources of water. A final section offers some concluding observations.

PARAMETERS OF WATER POLICY
FOR FEDERAL LANDS

Geographic Limitations

There are three important geographic factors that will affect future water policy for federal lands: 1) the amount and distribution of water, 2) the amount and distribution of federal lands, and 3) the relationship between the two.

As pointed out in earlier chapters, the Southwest has serious water problems. The Second National Water Assessment noted that problems of inadequate surface water supply for the Southwest "will be severe by the year 2000."[1] The report also warned of serious groundwater shortages due to overdraft.[2] A recent analysis of western water found that the Lower Colorado River Basin, southern California, and parts of New Mexico, Texas, and Colorado face the most severe problems of supply.[3]

The second geographic factor concerns the amount of federal land in the Southwest. Federal land management agencies control nearly 700 million acres nationally, most of it in the western states. On average, about 46 percent of each western state is federal land (excluding Indian reservations).[4] This leads us to the third geographic factor: on the average, 60 percent of the annual water yield in the eleven western states comes from these federal lands. In the Southwest, the figures are even higher; 96 percent of the Upper Colorado River Basin water originates on federal lands. The comparable figure for the Rio Grande Valley is 77 percent.[5]

Together, these three geographic factors constitute the physical reality that frames all policy decisions concerning water and federal lands. This framework of inadequate supply, intense competition, and a large federal presence greatly limits the number of alternatives available and complicates the search for solutions. To a great extent, the three parameters discussed in the following sections are a result of this geographic reality.

In the future these geographic parameters will change, but most likely the changes will exacerbate the problem. Population growth in arid regions will intensify the competition for water and create greater concern over water scarcity. And while the size of federal land holdings will probably remain fairly constant, the use of that land will probably increase. This expanded usage will encompass a broader range of activities as well as larger absolute numbers of users. As a result of this increased competition for water, the relative geographic location of federal lands and other principal water claimants will become critically important to the issue of in-stream flows. Most federal water claims are for nonconsumptive in-stream water uses such as fish and wildlife, watershed protection, or aesthetic needs. Federal lands that happen to lie downstream from major consumptive water users will have greater difficulty maintaining an adequate stream flow. Conversely, those federal reservations that straddle headwaters will be more successful in protecting their water resources as long as they do not consume significant amounts.

Case Law

The courts have been intimately involved in water rights issues since the founding of the republic. In the American West the role of the courts is especially interesting because the case law has, on many occasions, been contrary to perceptions of prevailing congressional policy. The conflict revolves around a long series of cases, often referred to as the Winters Doctrine, that established a federal reserved water right.[6] In *Winters* and subsequent cases the courts held that the federal government implicitly reserved water rights when establishing federal reservations, even though no mention of water was made in the enabling legislation.

In recent years the courts at both the state and federal levels have retreated somewhat on the definition, scope, and intent of federal reserved rights.[7] Several recent Supreme Court decisions have served to "illustrate the continued deference shown by the courts to state water laws when they conflict with federal statutes."[8] The case of *U.S. v. New Mexico*[9] is particularly significant for the management of non-Indian federal lands because it limited Forest Service reserved water claims to "primary purposes," meaning those that were explicitly delineated in the legislation that established the federal reservation.[10]

In sum, the case law that applies to the federal reserved rights doctrine is inconsistent on several levels: (*a*) state and federal courts have often offered contradictory interpretations of the doctrine, (*b*) the federal courts have altered their interpretation over time, and (*c*) the doctrine is at odds with prevailing congressional policy. This creates obvious problems for the federal land manager. There is no clear policy in regard to federal reserved water rights, yet there is no doubt that the Congress has a constitutional right to override state water law if necessary. Federal agencies can exercise a reserved right, but the unknown extent of such rights and their questionable security limit the value of the reserved rights approach. This may force federal agencies to look for other methods of securing dependable (from a legal standpoint) sources of water.

Statutory Guidelines

Federal water policy in the Southwest has been characterized to a great extent by a combination of federal money and deference to state water law. The Winters Doctrine of federal reserved rights represents an important exception to this deferential policy, but it is based on case law, not statutory law.

The congressional preference for state control over water rights is evident in numerous statutes. The policy was first enunciated in a series of western land laws passed in the mid-nineteenth century that recognized "local laws and customs, thereby validating, in effect, state appropriation water laws."[11] Deference to state law was recognized again in the Reclamation Act of 1902 (Section Eight). In the ensuing years Congress passed at least thirty-seven statutes that contain language similar to Section Eight of the Reclamation Act.[12] An example of such language can be found in the organic Act for the National Wildlife Refuge System, which stipulates that "nothing in this act shall constitute an express or implied claim or denial on the part of the Federal Government as to exemption from State water laws."[13] Another example is provided by the 1972 Water Pollution Control Act: "It is the policy of Congress that the authority of each

State to allocate quantities of water within its jurisdiction shall not be superseded, abrogated or otherwise impaired. . . . "[14]

Although it is clear that Congress prefers to defer to state water law, there is also evidence of congressional tolerance, if not support, of the federal reserved rights doctrine. Since the *Winters* case was handed down in 1908, Congress has been presented with bills designed to emasculate the reserved rights doctrine. But despite the avowed reverence for state law, none of these "water rights settlement acts" has been approved. This is due to the realization on the part of many legislators that federal agencies need some control over water to carry out their congressionally mandated missions. In essence, Congress has passively accepted reserved water rights, but has remained unwilling to recognize statutorily the doctrine upon which they are based. There is no doubt that the federal government has the right to supersede state water law, but Congress has left it up to the courts to exercise that right.

Congress' inability to establish a consistent policy in regard to western water rights has created considerable ambiguity. A case in point is the 1976 Federal Land Policy and Management Act (FLPMA).[15] That law contains several clauses dealing with water rights, including a savings clause stating the Act neither expands nor diminishes federal or state control over water.[16] In effect, the law creates new responsibilities, principally for the Bureau of Land Management, but provides no grant of power to obtain water to meet those responsibilities: "FLPMA contains no specific grant of authority to appropriate water for management needs either in accordance with state law or in defiance of it. The needs for and uses of water on the public lands to support assigned management functions are not mentioned in FLPMA, except in passing reference. . . . "[17]

Another statute that reflects congressional ambivalence over federal water rights is the 1968 Wild and Scenic Rivers Act.[18] Meyers and Tarlock note that it is "one of the few apparent congressional assertions of the reserved rights doctrine."[19] Yet even this statute carries a disclaimer identical to the savings clause in the National Wildlife Refuge System Act quoted above. It also stipulates that compensation will be provided if a water right vested under state law is confiscated.[20]

In short, there is some implicit congressional support for federal reserved water rights, but for the most part statutory guidelines defer to state prior appropriation law. In the words of the Supreme Court, national water policy has been characterized by a "consistent thread of purposeful and continued deference to state water law."[21] The Congress, and in recent years the courts, have "disfavored" the federal reserved rights doctrine,[22] and instead have permitted states to retain control over most of the water within their borders.

Political Reality

In addition to limited congressional and judicial support for federal reserved water rights, federal land management agencies are also influenced by political considerations. These agencies are sensitive to local support and often are hesitant to antagonize constituents at the state and local levels. As a result, federal agencies tend to abide by state water law as a matter of policy, departing from such policy only when absolutely necessary.

In recent years this necessity has become more apparent due to the issue of in-stream uses. All western states now recognize some form of in-stream use associated with recreation and fish and wildlife, but efforts to protect in-stream flows still face "formidable legal obstacles."[23] And in some states, such as Colorado, in-stream rights are held by the state, a condition that is unacceptable to some federal agencies. In such situations the agency may have no choice but to rely on federal reserved rights. This often antagonizes some regional and local political forces.[24]

An example of the difficulties encountered when an attempt is made to expand federal water rights is the much maligned Krulitz Opinion. Interior Department Solicitor Leo Krulitz issued an opinion in 1979 that established a "federal non-reserved right" to water.[25] It was a significant expansion of federal control over western water, and provoked an immediate and sustained outcry from western states. The political pressure was so great that an amended opinion was issued by Krulitz's successor,[26] and Secretary of the Interior Andrus agreed not to implement the opinion.[27] When the Reagan administration took office the new Solicitor, William Coldiron, quickly disavowed the "nonreserved rights" claims of the Krulitz Opinion.[28] Reagan's assistant interior secretary for land and water resources assured westerners that the new administration was "very pro-state water rights."[29]

In sum, federal land management agencies are constrained by the realities of western water politics. Although a federal reserved right exists, agency claims based on that doctrine must be tempered by the limitations imposed upon them by state and local policymakers. In the case of in-stream rights, federal agencies face potential problems because some state laws do not recognize all such claims as a beneficial use. But consumptive claims face formidable opposition also since they would deprive downstream users of their water supply. Federal agencies must finesse their way through a quagmire of contradictory case law, an unclear statutory mandate (what one writer called a "national water nonpolicy,"[30] and potentially hostile water policymakers at the regional, state, and local levels.

LIKELY SCENARIOS

This section will examine the four federal land management agencies, and attempt to determine how their policies will affect future allocations of water for federal lands.[31] These agency policies are built upon five different approaches to obtaining rights to water for federal lands.

First, federal agencies can file for unappropriated water under the auspices of state law. In this manner they approach the problem just like everyone else; they obtain the proper legal paperwork from an office of the state government, usually the state engineer's office. This approach minimizes federal-state conflict, does not usurp water from existing users, and helps to maintain a comprehensive and coordinated system of use permits. However, it requires that unappropriated water be available, and that the contemplated federal use is recognized by state water law. In the case of in-stream use this latter point sometimes creates a problem.

A second approach is to obtain water appurtenant to newly acquired lands. When the agency buys a parcel of land, the water comes with it in most cases. Since this approach also relies on state law, it has the same advantages and disadvantages of the first approach.

A third approach is useful when all water sources have been appropriated. Under such conditions the federal government can purchase rights to water from private parties. This approach also follows the dictates of state law. But in many states there are prohibitions against transferring water from one use to another, and that limits the utility of this strategy. It also assumes that existing users are willing to sell, and that the federal government has the necessary funds to purchase the rights. In an age of extremely limited budgetary resources, it may be difficult for federal agencies to fund this approach.

A fourth method of obtaining water rights is to rely on the Winters doctrine of federal reserved water rights. Most federal agencies limit this type of claim to reserved land that was created from the public domain and has never been state or private land. In theory this approach is the most attractive to federal agencies; it is not limited by the precepts of state law, it is potentially open-ended, and it can be applied to any primary use for which the reservation was created. As noted above, however, in actual practice claims for reserved water create serious problems.

A fifth and final method of obtaining water rights is through negotiation with state agencies. This approach avoids long and costly litigation *if* all parties can agree to a compromise solution. The basic concept is to get the state to recognize the federal government's right to a specific amount of water. In return, the federal government agrees not to press for additional reserved rights.

In short, there are advantages and disadvantages to each of these approaches. The first method—filing under state law—is simple and straightforward, but cannot be applied to all situations. The second approach can provide water for purchased lands, but most federal lands are principally public domain lands, not purchased tracts. The third and fourth approaches can be utilized when other methods cannot, but both create substantial costs, either in budgetary expenditures or in political capital. The fifth method—negotiation—is desirable, but not realistic in many cases. Because of these relative advantages and disadvantages, the choice of strategies is a critical element in each agency's effort to obtain water rights.

Interior Department Agencies

In the early 1980s the Interior Department initiated an effort to solidify its water rights for federal reservations. These activities involve nearly every western state, and are a mixture of all five of the approaches described above. Most of the activity is taking place in the solicitor's office, rather than at the agency level, to produce a comprehensive coordinated strategy. Nevertheless, each agency's situation is unique in some respects.

The National Park Service has embarked on an ambitious program to identify its water needs and then obtain legal rights to the necessary amount of water. The impetus for this effort came in part from the Reagan administration's push for quantification, but it is also a result of Director William Mott's Twelve Point Plan, which established basic policy guidelines for the national parks. The plan lists water as one of the critical park resources that must be protected through a "creative land protection initiative."[32] A water resources division was created within the agency in 1983, and was recently expanded to help implement the water-related elements of the Mott plan.

The agency's approach to reserved rights is fairly typical in that it recognizes the needs of the states. The agency manual requires that whenever a claim for reserved water is made, "the proper state agency may be notified, as a matter of comity, of current and foreseeable future water requirements in a manner to be developed with each state."[33] Claims for reserved water for national parks were, until recently, quite rare. A spokesman for the service noted: "We are not actively pursuing reserved water rights except when we are joined in a McCarran action (*i.e.* state–federal joint adjudication of a watershed). The number of these actions has increased significantly over the last two years." Although the service has filed several reserved claims as a result of the McCarran litigation, most of them involve fairly modest amounts of water.

State resistance to National Park Service reserved claims has been mitigated by two factors. First, as noted above, the claims usually do not involve large amounts of water. And second, many of the claims are for in-stream flows at or near river basin headwaters. Since in-stream flows are nonconsumptive, and nearly all other water users are downstream, the reserved claim does not usually threaten existing state-granted water rights. This condition is referred to by some as "highority," meaning that federal rights can achieve priority just by virtue of being at the highest point in a watershed. Politically, this geographic fact of life is critically important; claims that would otherwise be bitterly contested have a much greater chance of being accepted by all interested parties. Rocky Mountain, Glacier, Yellowstone, and Yosemite are all examples of national parks that potentially benefit from this fortuitous good fortune.

The service has avoided litigation over reserved rights in some areas by relying upon negotiation. According to one Interior Department official: "Negotiations are a definite possibility, even more so than for Indian lands. The sides in many cases are not that far apart, and state people recognize the economic importance of national parks." This approach holds particular promise in Montana, where a state agency, the Reserved Water Rights Compact Commission, was established in 1979 to negotiate with federal agencies. Considerable progress has been made in the negotiations over water for Glacier National Park. However, these negotiations also demonstrate some of the potential pitfalls of this approach: after reaching a preliminary agreement with the state, the Park Service began to worry that the park's long-term needs might be compromised by the agreement. In its zeal to avoid costly litigation, the service may have been too willing to compromise. Now, a new agreement may have to be negotiated.[34]

Nearly all the water claims presently being pursued by the Park Service involve water that has been used by the parks since their inception. A completely different situation arises when a new park is proposed, especially if the new park cannot take advantage of "highority." A case in point is the proposed Black Canyon of the Gunnison National Park Complex. Upstream water users oppose the creation of the park because they fear it will require minimum in-stream flow levels. This could interfere with plans to build hydropower dams just above the site of the proposed park.

The Park Service's Division of Water Resources faces a formidable task. Although the agency's claims are relatively modest, it will still be difficult to achieve legal recognition of the water needs for all parks. These efforts will undoubtedly lead to considerable conflict in the future.

The policy of the Bureau of Land Management (BLM) in regard to water is different from the Park Service's policy in several respects. Most BLM claims are for site-specific consumptive uses such as wells, watering holes, and springs. According to an agency spokesman, very little water is diverted or claimed by BLM for in-stream flow.

The bureau also takes a minimalist approach to reserved rights. The agency manual provides a policy statement that clearly illustrates federal deference to state water law:

> The water policy of the BLM is that the States have the primary authority and responsibility for the allocation and management of water resources within their own boundaries, except as otherwise specified by Congress on a case-by-case basis. . . . In order to imple-

ment the BLM water policy of state water resources primacy, Bureau personnel shall . . . cooperate with State governments under the umbrella of State law . . . [and] . . . comply with applicable State law, except as otherwise specifically mandated by Congress.[35]

Furthermore the BLM, during the Reagan administration, encouraged private lessees on BLM lands to file for water rights with the state government. Although deference to state water law is the predominant theme in BLM water policy, the agency still recognizes the existence and potential application of reserved rights. However, the definition of reserved rights, as outlined in the manual, is fairly restrictive; such rights reserve "only the minimum amount of appurtenant water then unappropriated to accomplish the primary purpose of the reservation."[36]

Also, reserved rights are not applicable to most BLM lands. In 1980 the Sierra Club sued the BLM, arguing the agency had failed to claim reserved rights for some of its holdings in southern Utah. But an appeals court ruled that public domain lands not specifically reserved by statute or presidential order are not entitled to reserved rights.[37]

Much of the argument in the Sierra Club case, and also in the controversy over the Krulitz Opinion cited earlier, revolved around various interpretations of the 1976 Federal Land Policy and Management Act (FLPMA), the enabling legislation for the contemporary BLM. The official policy of the Department of Interior is that the Act did not create any new reserved rights for the agency: "FLPMA does authorize appropriation of water for land management uses but does not give an independent statutory basis for claims for water uses inconsistent in any way with the substantive requirements of state law."[38] However, the Act did create new management responsibilities that can conceivably be viewed as primary purposes for which certain BLM lands are reserved. At least one authority has argued that this creates a potential for applying the reserved rights doctrine to such purposes.[39]

Even though the BLM manages about 340 million acres of land, and most of it is in the driest sections of the most arid states, it is doubtful that the agency will demand large increases in its water allocation in the future. According to an agency spokesman, there are no plans to claim significant amounts of water under the reserved rights doctrine. Like present uses, future water allocations will consist principally of small, isolated sites. However, there is a potential for future conflict due to the uncertainty surrounding FLPMA and reserved rights. Future interpretations of the Act may be more amenable to reserved claims in order to meet the increased management responsibilities mandated by the legislation.

To a great extent the Fish and Wildlife Service has avoided many of the water rights problems that plague other federal agencies. This is because most of the agency's lands have been purchased with appurtenant water rights. Thus, their rights are, for the most part, already quantified and in congruence with state water law. However, there have been a few cases in which the Fish and Wildlife Service has filed claims for reserved rights. The amount of water involved is quite small, but these claims are unique because some of them are for purchased land. As a matter of policy the other federal land management agencies generally file for reserved rights only for lands that were part of the public domain when the agency obtained the land and have never been privately held. In this respect the reserved claims of the Fish and Wildlife Service, although modest, are based on a more expansive definition of the reserved rights doctrine.

Two examples of this approach are the Adair case in Oregon and Lake Havasu on the Colorado River. The former involves lands that were once part of the Klamath Indian Reservation, including parcels that were allotted private holdings.[40] The service is presently negotiating with the relevant parties in an effort to establish an acceptable priority date for the federal reserved rights. In the Havasu case the Fish and Wildlife Service was awarded reserved rights for wildlife refuges that included purchased holdings.

Despite the agency's willingness to claim reserved rights for purchased lands, it still adopts a conservative policy in regard to reserved rights and their impact on state appropriation systems. The agency manual states: "The Service's policy of following State law in appropriating water should be carried out to the greatest practicable extent."[41]

In the future the Fish and Wildlife Service may have its greatest impact on water rights through the Endangered Species Act, which, as Professor Tarlock notes, "creates de facto regulatory water rights."[42] A significant number of proposed water development projects may be halted or altered due to the threat posed to endangered species. Since it is the Fish and Wildlife Service that must evaluate the potential for such threats in many cases, the agency could have a significant impact on future water development.

In sum, the land management agencies in the Interior Department are presently pursuing a fairly rigorous effort to quantify their water rights. Potentially, this is a very contentious issue, but the conflict will be mitigated by the federal government's deference to state water law. As former Secretary of Interior James Watt put it, federal agencies "will have to take their place in line like any other citizen" when seeking water.[43] While this strategy will help alleviate conflict in some areas, it will mean that in the future Interior agencies will be restrained in the amount of water that they can realistically expect to obtain.

The Forest Service

In recent years the Forest Service has been actively involved in acquiring water rights for national forest lands. In many cases these claims have been based on federal reserved rights, and this has resulted in considerable litigation and conflict. Four important court cases have dealt with the Forest Service and its water claims.

In *U.S. v. New Mexico* (1978) the U.S. Supreme Court ruled that the Forest Service's 1897 organic Act did not create reserved instream rights for so-called "secondary uses" such as wildlife and aesthetic preservation, and that the 1960 Multiple–Use Sustained Yield Act did not create additional reserved rights for such purposes.[44] This case is often cited as an example of the court's recent tendency to narrow the reserved rights doctrine, but the actual impact of the decision on the Forest Service's ability to claim reserved rights for in-stream flows remains uncertain.[45] Several spokesman for the Forest Service described the case as fact-bound and applicable to only certain clauses in the relevant statutes. According to their interpretation there is still sufficient statutory justification for in-stream flow claims under the reserved rights doctrine if state law provides no possible relief and such in-stream waters are necessary to maintain favorable conditions of water flow.

A second and related case was decided in 1983 by the Supreme Court of Colorado. In *U.S. v. City and County of Denver* the court relied extensively on the *New Mexico* decision, and held that the agency's reserved rights did not include instream flows because they were not "primary uses" established by statutory authority.[46] But the

Denver decision concerned specific statutory clauses, and thus left open the possibility of reserved in-stream rights based on alternative statutory language. Four years later the Forest Service returned to the Colorado Supreme Court to press its claim once again. This time, however, the agency met with at least partial success. The court agreed that the Forest Service has a reserved right for uses established under the 1960 Multiple Use/Sustained Yield Act. This opens the possibility of federally reserved water rights for in-stream flows to benefit recreation, grazing, and wildlife.[47]

The fourth case involves reserved rights for wilderness areas. Although the decision involved Forest Service lands it is potentially relevant to other agencies that manage statutory wilderness (*i.e.* the National Park Service and BLM). In *Sierra Club v. Block*[48] a U.S. District Court judge found that wilderness areas do indeed have reserved water rights. The judge noted that he was "dismayed by the federal [government's] benign neglect of this issue of federal reserved water rights in the wilderness areas."[49]

Both the Forest Service, which is opposed to applying reserved rights to wilderness, and the intervenors, including the Western States Legal Council, have appealed the decision. The Reagan Administration supported their contention that water in wilderness areas is not subject to the reserved rights doctrine. Former Attorney General Edwin Meese claimed that "no legally sufficient basis exists for an implication of federal reserved water rights for wilderness purposes" (see: *U.S. Water News*, September, 1988: p. 6).

The issue of water rights for wilderness areas has been salient in political as well as judicial arenas lately. In 1984 Congress passed wilderness bills for eighteen states, but the Colorado wilderness bill failed due to opposition to water rights for the new wilderness areas. Senator Armstrong of Colorado was so concerned over wilderness water rights that he introduced his own wilderness bill that specifically disavowed any water rights associated with wilderness designation.[50] Conflict on this point has thus far prevented the passage of any wilderness bill for Colorado. Concern over water rights in wilderness areas has now spread to other states. Several wilderness bills in western states are encountering opposition from state officials who fear that wilderness designation could lead to more reserved water rights.

The official water management policy of the Forest Service, as reflected in the agency manual, is similar to that of the Interior Department agencies. As a matter of comity agency personnel are required to inform state-level officials of any action affecting water rights. And, the manual notes, water rights must be obtained "with due consideration for the needs of other water users."[51] But the manual appears to reflect the view that recent cases have not eliminated the agency's right to claim reserved rights for in-stream flows. It instructs agency personnel to "use the Organic Administration Act of 1897 authority to claim reserved water rights for consumptive or nonconsumptive needs on reserved lands directly related to securing favorable conditions of water flow or to furnish a continuous supply of timber."[52] The manual also cautions personnel to consult with the Chief Forester and the General Counsel before filing reserved claims due to the "legal complexities" involved.[53]

In sum, the water management policy of the U.S. Forest Service reflects the characteristic mix of deference to state water law and, when necessary, reliance on reserved rights. In the future the Forest Service, probably more than any other non–Indian federal land management agency, will be involved in long-term contentious struggles to obtain legal recognition of water rights. The agency manages about 190 million acres of land, most of it heavily timbered, well watered, and aesthetically pleasing. With so many resources at stake, serious conflicts will undoubtedly continue to arise well into the future.

CONCLUSION

The push to quantify federal water rights began with the Carter Administration, and continued with increased fervor during the Reagan years. The *raison d'être* of this policy is to reduce uncertainty regarding the ultimate scope of federal water use. In the future, both the costs and the benefits of this policy will become more evident. The certitude of quantified rights will remove the cloud of doubt that presently hangs over western water rights. This is expected to contribute to the economic development of the area and encourage the full utilization of all water resources. However, there is a price to be paid. Once federal water rights are quantified, it will be much more difficult for federal agencies to obtain additional quantities of water. If it is discovered in the future that the quantified amount is insufficient, the number of realistic options available to the agencies will be limited, and the expense of exercising those options will probably be substantial.

Of course there is no guarantee that quantification will remain the predominant policy. In the future other imperatives might become more salient. For example, if problems of water quantity become severe throughout the Southwest—not an unlikely possibility—there will be pressure to manage federal lands for their water production capabilities. Marion Clawson argues that " . . . the possibility of managing federal land primarily for water yield is likely to emerge as one major policy issue."[54] Elements of this approach can be seen in some contemporary activities, such as defoliating certain areas to increase their runoff. In any event, the future will almost certainly bring increased competition for the waters that arise on federal lands.

Another major issue of the future concerns the ultimate impact of the Winters Doctrine of federal reserved water rights. Reserved claims that have the advantage of "highority" and do not disrupt existing economic development will have the greatest potential for success. This assumes the reserved rights are for the "primary purposes" recognized by the courts. But the reserved rights doctrine has never been a very effective approach: political, statutory, and judicial parameters limit the potential substantive impact of the doctrine. The Forest Service manual alludes to some of the practical problems that arise when claims are based on the Winters Doctrine: "Reserved rights cannot be lost for nonuse. However, they can be made ineffectual if associated water sources are diverted, polluted, impounded, or otherwise made unavailable or unusable."[55] As competition for water becomes more intense in the future, the potential for successful reserved rights claims will diminish.

To an extraordinary extent Congress has been unwilling to face the issue of water for federal lands. On the one hand, laws are passed that create enormous management responsibilities for federal land management agencies. But, on the other hand, Congress has been exceedingly deferential to state control over water rights. This places federal agencies in a predicament when state law cannot adequately respond to their water needs. As a result, many crucial water management decisions have been left to the courts, and are the subject of prolonged conflict between the various interests. It is not a simple case of federal-state conflict, however. Involved are interstate disputes, clashes between different elements in the federal government, and bitter splits in the clientele of some of the agencies. The lack of comprehensive congressional action may be remedied in the future; there are many calls for such a statutory solution. But the stakes are high, conflict and competition are increasing, and any resolution of the problem will create substantial costs. Reaching a consensus on this issue poses a significant challenge for the future.

NOTES

1. U.S. Water Resources Council, *The Nation's Water Resources* 1975–2000 (U.S. Government Printing Office, 1978): p. 56.

2. *Ibid.:* pp. 58–59.

3. John Bredehoeft, "Physical Limitations to Water Resources." In *Water Scarcity,* Ernest Engelbert and Ann Foley Scheuring, eds. (Berkeley: University of California Press, 1984): pp. 22–25.

4. Broken down by state, the percentage of federally owned land is: Arizona, 44%; California, 46.6%; Colorado, 35.5%; Nevada, 86.1%; New Mexico, 33.3%; Utah, 63.6%. See Robert H. Nelson, "The Public Lands," in *Current Issues in Natural Resource Policy,* Paul Portney, ed. (Washington, D.C.: Resources for the Future, 1982): pp. 16–17.

5. See *U.S. v. New Mexico* 438 U.S. 696 (1978): p. 699.

6. *Winters v. U.S.* 207 U.S. 564 (1908). See Daniel McCool, *Command of the Waters: Iron Triangles, Federal Water Development, and Indian Water* (Berkeley: University of California Press, 1987), chaps. 3 and 7.

7. The most important cases are: *U.S. v. New Mexico, California v. U.S.* 438 U.S. 645 (1978); *Sierra Club v. Watt* 659 F. wd 203 (1981); *U.S. v. The City and County of Denver* 656 P. 2d 1 Colo. (1983); *Arizona v. California* 103 S. Ct. 1382 (1983); *Nevada v. U.S.* 103 S. Ct. 2906 (1983); *Arizona v. San Carlos Apache Tribe* 103 S. Ct. 3201 (1983).

8. Evan Delgado and Jon Vaught, "Hydroelectric Power, the Federal Power Act, and State Water Laws: Is Federal Preemption Water over the Dam?" *University of California Davis Law Review* 17 (Summer, 1984): p. 1192.

9. *U.S. v. New Mexico* (1978).

10. These cases are discussed in greater detail in the second section of this chapter.

11. Leo Krulitz, "Federal Water Rights of the National Park Service, Fish and Wildlife Service, Bureau of Reclamation and the Bureau of Land Management." *Decisions of the United States Department of Interior* 86 (U.S. Government Printing Office, Jan.–Dec., 1979).

12. See *Sporhase v. Nebraska* 102 S. Ct. 3456 (1982): p. 3461, and *U.S. v. New Mexico* (1978): p. 702.

13. Sec. ddii of the National Wildlife Refuge System Act of 1970. 16 U.S.C. 668.

14. 33 U.S.C. sec. 1251 (g) (1982).

15. 43 U.S.C. pp. 1701–1784 (1982).

16. *Ibid.*, sec. 701 (g).

17. John Shurts, "FLPMA, Fish and Wildlife, and Federal Water Rights." *Environmental Law* 15 (Fall, 1984): p. 125.

18. Wild and Scenic Rivers Act, 16 U.S.C. sec. 1273 (1982).

19. Charles Meyers and A. Dan Tarlock, *Water Resource Management,* 2nd ed. (Mineola, N.Y.: The Foundation Press, 1980): p. 232.

20. Wild and Scenic Rivers Act, sec. 13b.

21. *California v. U.S.* (1978).

22. A. Dan Tarlock, "The Endangered Species Act and Western Water Rights." *Land and Water Law Review* 20 (1985): p. 15.

23. William Goldfarb, *Water Law* (Boston: Butterworth Publishers, 1984), p. 89. Also see, Corinne C. Sherton, "Preserving Instream Flows in Oregon's Rivers and Streams." *Environmental Law* 11 (Spring, 1981): pp. 381–419.

24. Frank Trelease, "Uneasy Federalism—State Laws and National Water Uses," *Washington Law Review* 55 (1980): p. 769.

25. Krulitz Opinion, *Decisions of the United States Department of Interior,* 86 (U.S. Govt. Printing Office, Jan.–Dec., 1979).

26. Clyde O. Martz, "Supplement to Solicitor Opinion No. M-36914, on Federal Water Rights of the National Park Service, Fish and Wildlife Service, Bureau of Reclamation, and the Bureau of Land Management." *Decisions of the United States Department of Interior* 88 (U.S. Government Printing Office, Jan. 16, 1981).

27. Shurts (1984): p. 146.

28. William Coldiron, "Nonreserved Water Rights—United States Compliance with State Law" in *Decisions of the United States Department of Interior* 88 (U.S. Government Printing Office, Sept. 1981).

29. *National Journal,* Aug. 14, 1982: p. 1421.

30. Edward Schwartz, "Water as an Article of Commerce: State Embargoes Spring a Leak under *Sporhase v. Nebraska." Environmental Affairs Law Review* 12 (1985): p. 163.

31. I am indebted to David A. Watts, Assistant Solicitor for Parks and Recreation, Department of Interior, for his help in obtaining information from the relevant Interior Department agencies.

32. "12 Point Plan: the Challenge," National Park Service, U.S. Department of Interior, private printing, 1985.

33. National Park Service manual, mimeograph (2–78): IV–16.

34. *U.S. Water News* 2 (June, 1986): p. 1. Also see David Ladd, "Federal and Interstate Conflicts in Montana Water Law: Support for a State Water Plan." *Montana Laws Review* 42 (1981): pp. 299–300.

35. Bureau of Land Management manual, mimeograph (Mar. 19, 1984): sec. 7250.06A and 7250.06B.

36. *Ibid.*, Glossary: p. 3.

37. *Sierra Club v. Watt (1981).*

38. See the Martz Opinion (1981): p. 257.

39. See Shurts (1984).

40. *U.S. v. Ben Adair*, D.C. #75914, U.S. Dist. Ct., Ore. (1981), and No. 80–3257, 9th. Cir., filed Nov. 15, 1983.

41. U.S. Fish and Wildlife Service manual, mimeograph, Part 13, sec. 13.2A.

42. Tarlock (1985): p. 13. A recent report by the U.S. General Accounting Office concluded that there has been very little conflict between western states and the Endangered Species Act ("Endangered Species: Limited Effect of Consultation Requirements on Western Water Projects". GAO Report, March, 1987). For an opposing view see the 1987 *Annual Report* of the Western States Water Council (Salt Lake City, Utah): pp. 37–38.

43. *The New York Times*, June 18, 1982: A18.

44. *U.S. v. New Mexico* (1978).

45. Hank Meshorer, "Federal Reserved Water Rights Litigation," *Rocky Mountain Mineral Law Institute Proceedings* 28 (1983): pp. 1298–1305. Also see A. Dan Tarlock and Sally Fairfax, "No Water for the Woods: A Critical Analysis of *United States v. New Mexico*," *Idaho Law Review* 15 (1979): p. 509, and Constance Boris and John Krutilla, *Water Rights and Energy Development in the Yellowstone River Basin* (Baltimore: Johns Hopkins Press, 1980): pp. 35–39.

46. *United States v. the City and County of Denver* (1983). See S. D. Emery, "Water Law—The Limits of Federal Reserved Water Rights in National Forests," *Land and Water Law Review* 19 (1984): pp. 71–82.

47. *U.S. v. Robert W. Jessee*, Supreme Court of Colorado, 1987.

48. *Sierra Club v. Block* civ. A. No. 84–K–2, U.S. District Court, D. Colorado, Nov. 25, 1985: p. 842. See: Hugh Dangler, "*Sierra Club v. Block*, Wilderness Water Rights Protected Were Not in Conflict with Purposes of National Forest in Colorado," *Natural Resources Journal* 27 (Spring, 1987): pp. 441–456.

49. *Ibid.*, at p. 865.

50. S. 2097, sec. 8. Introduced on Feb. 24, 1986, 99th Congress, 2nd. session: p. 18.

51. U.S. Forest Service manual, mimeograph, Title 2500, chapter

2541.02.

52. *Ibid.*, chapter 2541.21.

53. *Ibid.*, chapter 2541.12.

54. Marion Clawson, *The Federal Lands Revisited* (Washington, D.C.: Resources for the Future, 1983): p. 105.

55. Forest Service manual, chapter 2541.4.

8   Weapons and Water in the Southwest

Lauren Holland[1]

The military forces of the United States have had a major role in the history and development of the Southwest. During World War II facilities were built and/or expanded throughout the region, and after the war the military presence continued to grow. Given the large number of installations in the area, many of them near cities, it is crucial to understand the role of the military in the Southwest's water future. A number of questions spring to mind: For example, what happens when water needs and military activities converge—that is, when military decisions raise concerns about the status of water availability and quality? Can the states use their water rights and powers to intrude upon or otherwise influence military decisions in ways favorable to their interests? Under what conditions are states likely to play a significant role in military policymaking? Finally, what is the nature of that role likely to be? These questions, which form the basis of the following analysis, are explored from both a theoretical and practical (case study) perspective. The last section of the paper relays some thoughts about the role of water in future military activities in the Southwest.

CAN THE STATES PLAY A ROLE IN MILITARY POLICY?

The role of the American states in military affairs has been traditionally a limited or indirect one. Although the U.S. Constitution does reserve to the states some powers in military affairs and self-defense, it clearly establishes the federal government's authority as paramount, particularly in matters concerning wars and treaties.[2]

As with most constitutional declarations, however, the actual impact of subnational actors in influencing the nature and direction of military policy has been somewhat greater than is anticipated by the formal expressions of power and authority. This has been particularly true of issues with domestic implications such as installations and military bases, which activate more of a state's residual powers. One of these residual powers is state water rights. Despite the constitutionally superior status of federal water rights, states and communities still exercise primary (statutory) responsibility over the control of water flowing within their jurisdictions.

The states in the arid southwestern region of the United States have a considerable stake in retaining their control over water. Any project, public or private, that jeopardizes the availability or quality of water is likely to precipitate considerable interest and concern, given the distributive and redistributive nature of water decisions, and a predicted future condition of full appropriation in the region.[3]

However, since the states are essentially precluded from a direct policy role in military decisions, the nature of the influence they exercise is linked to the procedural channels in policymaking. Yet, in influencing the medium, the states may indirectly influence the message. It is important, then, to consider the extent to which the policymaking process for both water and military decisions afford opportunities for state input. For, through these channels, the states may affect the manner in which military questions and solutions are framed, the range of policy options, program implementation and, ultimately, policy decisions themselves.

According to the literature, there are two dimensions to the policymaking process that are important.[4] One, the policy system must be an open one in which power is sufficiently dispersed to facilitate and even encourage state input. Two, the states must have at their disposal some degree of formal and informal power that justifies their performing a role in the military policy process.

To what extent do these factors have explanatory value in anticipating state involvement in military projects in the Southwest that threaten to drain water? First, while the military policy process represents a solid, impermeable front, water policy is porous and fragmented and presents points open to influence. In cases where military policy has to come to grips with water policy, the holes in water policy make for holes in (or opportunities to influence) defense policy. This occurs when the military needs to acquire water for the success of a particular project. Unless the military is able to confine its base operations and activities to federally reserved land, it will be compelled to tap into state and private water systems.

Second, the states do have some potential formal power in military politics through their control over water. Although the federal government's control over water, which extends primarily from its commerce and land powers, is predominant, it has delegated considerable power to the states. In so doing, the national government has facilitated the devolution of actual power to the states—at least in the area of water allocation.[5] Additional political influence can be exerted through the representatives who serve their constituents on critical congressional committees. According to Helen Ingram, the national legislature is structured in ways to facilitate the representation of state interests in water policy issues. Currently, the legislative committee system for water is dominated by western states, advancing direct regional influence at the policy formulation stage, with state political–lobbying activity.[6] However, at the implementation stage, the ability of the states to exercise an indirect impact on national security issues that involve water concerns also exists. Here the federal government relies upon, and in some cases is obligated by statute to seek out, the states to assist them.[7] In either case, the nature and degree of state power is contingent upon its organizational capacities. In short, the states may influence military policy as it impacts on water, not military policy as military policy.

Given the stressed condition of water in the Southwest, we can anticipate that the states will employ their water rights powers to influence the nature and direction of military decisions in cases where the threat to water is critical, or where states perceive that concessions can be derived from doing so. Let us turn now to a discussion of the nature and degree of state and military water rights and power.

THE STATUS OF MILITARY WATER RIGHTS

The military, by virtue of its control over millions of acres of public land in the southwestern region of the United States,[8] exercises considerable power over water appurtenant to land withdrawn or reserved.[9] Because of the reservation doctrine (Winters Doctrine), which has its constitutional basis in the property clause, the military has the power to reserve the rights to unappropriated surface and groundwater sufficient to accomplish the primary purpose of the reservation when it withdraws land from the public domain, irrespective of state law. (See Burton, Chapter 9, for a detailed discussion of the Winters Doctrine.) Additional regulatory authority over surface water derives from the commerce clause, the welfare clause, and the war and treaty powers of the U.S. Constitution.[10]

On the other hand, state laws control cases involving nonreserved water rights, unless Congress provides otherwise.[11] In these cases, the military is expected to acquire water rights as any public or private appropriator. As we have seen in Chapter 2, in most of the southwestern region both surface water and groundwater are regulated according to the prior appropriation doctrine. This means that a military claim to water will be weighed against the priority rights of others ("first in time, first in right"). Therefore, a water right may not be appropriated for speculative reasons. Additional limitations exist in California and Texas, which have retained elements of the riparian doctrine wherein water rights accrue to land ownership. (See Wehmhoefer, Chapter 2, and Templer, Chapter 14, for a further discussion of the California and Texas laws.)

Further restrictions exist by virtue of the U.S. Supreme Court's decision in *U.S. v. Mexico*[12] limiting the reserved rights doctrine to the original purpose for which the land was withdrawn. This prevents the federal government "from legislatively changing the purpose of previously reserved land to reflect usage for (a new project or program such as) the MX missile system. . . . "[13]

Furthermore, the McCarran Amendment of 1952[14] gives state courts the power to adjudicate and administer water rights in cases involving the federal government in state water adjudications. In *Colorado River Water Conservation District*, the Court found a "presumption that when both federal and state actions are pending for adjudication of federal reserved water rights, the federal action should be dismissed," if the state has a comprehensive system for water rights adjudication.[15] At a minimum, these cases constitute a "first step toward allowing the states to determine federal reserved water rights."[16]

As discussed in Chapter 7, additional statutory powers exist in cases where the National Environmental Policy Act (NEPA)[17] and/or the Federal Land Policy and Management Act (FLPMA)[18] are operable.

Most of these constraints now apply to groundwater as well. As we saw in Chapter 2, the Supreme Court extended the reservation doctrine in *Cappaert v. U.S.*, and the Court's recent decision in *Sporhase v. Nebraska* found groundwater to be an article of commerce subject to federal regulation under the commerce clause.[19] This provides the basis for federal control over groundwater on nonfederal lands. Moreover, even in cases where state law prevails, the military may be able to purchase water rights.[20]

For their part, the states may regulate the purchase of groundwater from private owners, creating additional practical constraints. According to the federal courts, a state's policy powers allow it to regulate or diminish private rights for the public good.[21]

Finally, and perhaps most significantly, "[I]t may not be politically feasible for the United States to assert (either ground or surface) water rights in the western states where water is scarce. If the Federal Government does claim reserved rights, it may well be met with disapproval, if not open hostility."[22] In fact, while there is no written policy, most military bases try to defer to state water procedures as well.[23] According to one author, this is the stated intention of the Reagan administration.[24] What happens when this policy comes in conflict with the Reagan administration's current view of water as a "strategic material . . . as critical to our military strength as other more obvious strategic materials used in weapons development"?[25] Do the states have the means to protect their rights? What is the nature of these rights? As a corollary question, to what extent is the national government reliant on state administrative implementation programs and the direct input of state personnel on both policy and technical matters for the success of its programs? These questions are addressed by examining actual situations in which the military and states have come into conflict over the issue of water. In particular, the MX and Midgetman missile systems and several military base operations will be considered to capture the full range of activities—from exotic to routine military activities—affecting water availability and quality.[26]

IMPACTING MILITARY DECISIONS[27]

From MX to Midgetman

In September of 1979, President Carter announced a plan to place the new generation of Intercontinental Ballistic Missiles (ICBMs) in a multiple protective shelter (MPS) configuration on public lands in

Utah and Nevada. Two years later (October 1981), Ronald Reagan announced that the MX system would not be deployed in the Great Basin region, citing strategic and political factors as influential in his decision. The primary strategic difficulty, the system's vulnerability to Soviet attack, even today has not been surmounted, although the missiles now are being deployed in retrofitted Minuteman silos in Wyoming. Of the political factors cited as crucial in Reagan's decision, the inconvenience of a lengthy public legal battle with the states was paramount. A Reagan administration official admitted that "while it is not the determining factor, it should be noted that MPS basing has strong environmental opponents who would use every available tactic, and there are many, to delay MX deployment."[28] One of the legal tools the states had at their disposal to challenge the military's decision to deploy MX multiple protective shelters in the Great Basin was state water rights. Given the enormity of the proposed weapons system,[29] and its extraordinary need for water (190 billion gallons of water over a twenty-year period), the states were brought into the fray both as water appropriators and as legal critics by virtue of certain critical statutory provisions of NEPA and FLPMA.

Nevada and Utah both regulate and manage surface and groundwater according to the doctrine of prior appropriation. Thus, in all cases where the reservation doctrine is not applicable, the military is treated as any other prospective water user. Both states provide for hearings to allow for public reaction to, and comment on, water requests, thus enhancing the dilatory potential of state water rights as a land management tool. Legally, a state may invoke its right to regulate the supply of water, and deny a permit request if (1) the use to which the water will be put is not viewed as being a "beneficial" one; (2) water is fully appropriated; or (3) appropriation would not serve the "public interest." Other permit owners also may challenge the federal government's rights to preempt their use, forestalling action.

During preliminary survey work in the Great Basin region in advance of an MX site selection decision (fall of 1978), the Air Force itself concluded that "while water (in the Great Basin) may be physically available, legal impediments may hamper routine acquisition in other than narrowly prescribed applications."[30] However, by the time of the official release of the Site Selection and Land Withdrawal/Acquisition Environmental Impact Statement (EIS) in winter of

1981,[31] the water situation was being classified as a "problem" of availability: "the annual recharge capability of most valleys in Utah and Nevada is fully appropriated." In their own study, the Utah Division of Water Resources concluded that the planned deployment of MX multiple protective shelters in the Great Salt Lake Desert, Servier River, and Cedar-Beaver hydrologic areas would raise additional problems of water quality since groundwater already was being mined.[32] The prospect of having their water rights preempted by the military provoked several hundred private challenges of Air Force applications. Litigation of only a fraction of the claims could have delayed the water permit process for as long as two years. Efforts by the military to circumvent state permit procedures for water and land-use rights persuaded the legislatures in both states to take statutory action. In neither case did opponents expect to defeat the missile project. However, postponing the weapon system long enough to make it obsolete was a practical albeit not deliberate consequence. Yet in the fast-changing sphere of weapons technology the delays ensuing from the tangle of federalism and prospects of legal opposition amounted to a sort of sword of Damocles. Thus, timing is a source of leverage for the states. Military policy is time-bound and because the process is porous, it is time-consuming. Military policy has to be time-saving to be timely.

The intent of Utah Senate Bill 123 and Nevada Assembly Bill 383 was to compel those federal agencies responsible for the MX missile project to comply with FLPMA requirements for intergovernmental cooperation and consultation. Toward this end state agencies were authorized to withhold state water and land-use permits from federal agencies that failed to comply; and the state attorneys general were empowered to take legal action to block the project. After passing the Senate by a vote of 17 to 3, the Utah bill fell victim to the House's "sifting" process. However, the Nevada bill did become law on March 26, 1981, with questions of its constitutional validity immediately being raised.[33]

Despite the clear legal vulnerability of the Nevada bill on constitutional grounds,[34] the dilatory potential of statutory state action was still in play. This point was not lost on the Air Force, which sought fast-track legislation from Congress to allow the federal government in the case of MX multiple protective shelters to circumvent the relevant provisions of FLPMA.[35] The fast-track bill, called Draft 22, would also allow the military to expedite the public review and litigious aspects of the environmental impact statement process mandated by the National Environmental Policy Act (NEPA). Draft 22 was withdrawn under pressure from the congressional delegation and citizens groups from Utah and Nevada.

Not unexpectedly, the deployment schemes subsequent to MPS basing recommended by the Reagan administration appear to have been designed in part to circumvent the more burdensome and possibly obstructive provisions of FLPMA and NEPA. Neither the current plan of deploying the missiles (now called "Peacekeepers") in retrofitted Minuteman silos (silo basing) nor the previous Dense Pack/closely spaced basing (CSB) schemes would necessitate the large withdrawals of land from the public domain that MPS basing required. In each case the missiles would be deployed either on private lands currently being employed for military purposes or on exclusive military lands. In either case, the reservation doctrine would control.

Similar efforts are being made to deploy the newest in a series of ICBMs, the single warhead Midgetman missile system, in ways that do not raise "public interface problems." While the current scheme to deploy 1,000 Midgetmen could consume 12,000 to 38,000 square miles of area, tentative plans are for its placement on land currently owned by the military. Most of the sites identified by the military as suitable are in the southwestern region of the United States, however, and in areas where the stress on water is considerable. The most widely endorsed basing scheme is the MPS configuration, once again raising questions of water availability and quality. Presently, the amount of unappropriated water in this region is small.[36] The states have the power to quantify water and to control groundwater. In the future, these powers will become even more important as continued competition for water in the Southwest reduces further its availability, accessibility, and quality.

Military Base Activities

The impact of a large military project on the availability and quality of water in the southwestern region of the United States, where missile deployment is most likely to occur, provides a case study of one extreme of the military and water issue. By contrast there are the routine activities the military conducts on its bases and its operations, which utilize water daily in regular ways. Given projected increases in military spending, we can expect expansions in

conventional military activities. In areas where water is fully appropriated or nearing full appropriation, will water policy act as a constraint on projected military functions?

Kirtland Air Force Base (AFB) is located within the Rio Grande
Basin (RGB) of New Mexico, a designated groundwater management
area. Since 1982, the state has regulated the conservation and exploitation of groundwater in the RGB according to strict guidelines. In
1972, Kirtland attempted to drill several small wells within the
perimeters of its base for the purpose of providing irrigation for the
base golf course. The matter, while seemingly insignificant, was
viewed by the state as having serious enough implications that it
filed suit against Kirtland. The matter was resolved through a stipu-
lated agreement between New Mexico and the base.[37]

Several factors combined to provoke New Mexico into this action. For one, the state argued that in drilling the wells, Kirtland AFB
would be exceeding the annual quantity of acre-feet of water it had by
right under the reservation doctrine. As such, Kirtland was obligated,
but failed, to apply for additional water rights under state law. The
state authorities felt that allowing the base to proceed with its action
would set an unfavorable precedent in an area where groundwater is
being mined and surface water resources are fully appropriated.

In its suit, the state asserted that the wells were being drilled on
lands acquired after the original land withdrawal. Moreover, using
water to irrigate a golf course was not compatible with the original
purpose for which the base was established. (It could also be argued
that the purpose for which the water was being put was neither a
"beneficial" one nor one advancing the "public interest.") The matter
was resolved when the state and Kirtland AFB agreed to a stipulation
that Kirtland would file for permits on the wells and the state would
approve the applications.

The point is not that denying the U.S. Air Force a golf course will
undermine military operations of a strategic or routine logistical
nature. Rather, the case points up the tools that can be invoked by
states in situations involving conflicts over water between the military and a state. In this case both sides compromised. However, Dave
Stone of the New Mexico Department of Water Rights contends that
the potential for other disputes in the future exists. Today, there is no
surplus water to support new uses or the expansion of existing uses.
Moreover, groundwater is being mined, also threatening water qual-

ity. Thus, any additional water use on federal lands will require a transfer of use. Currently, both Kirtland AFB and the White Sands Missile Range, which are possible Midgetman deployment sites, have pending applications filed under state water law for lands acquired by the bases subsequent to the initial reservation. According to Stone, these filings are second in line after the City of El Paso (see discussion below). Given the state water patterns, conflict is imminent.

In Texas, where aquifer depletion is estimated in some areas by the year 2000,[38] the preeminent water problem in El Paso is one of quality. Heavy reliance upon groundwater in the area is contributing to the increasing pollution of this source as the water reserves are drawn down. Processing this water and removing minerals and particles in the aquifer is expensive, thus raising groundwater costs. John Hickerson, managing director of El Paso Water Utilities, estimates that in ten to twenty years, groundwater will exceed minimum acceptable levels of "total dissolved solids."[39] Currently, El Paso is mining new wells and seeking alternative well locations, including beneath Fort Bliss (U.S. Army post). (See Barilleaux and Bath, Chapter 5, for a detailed examination of the El Paso situation.)

Forty to forty-five percent of the underground formation that supplies El Paso's groundwater is located beneath the Fort Bliss reservation. Presently, El Paso draws water from the four wells on the reservation in return for supplying one third of its "take" to the base. (This one third constitutes more than 60 percent of the total base requirements. Fort Bliss also uses groundwater in El Paso County.) Thus a reciprocal but potentially contentious relationship exists. The situation is complicated by the proximity of El Paso to Mexico, which also draws upon some of the same water sources; most notably, the Hueco Bolson deposits. (See Utton, Chapter 4, for a discussion of this international water management situation.)

For twenty years, El Paso has been involved in attempts to gain access to groundwater beneath the expanses of the Fort Bliss reservation. Recent attempts by El Paso to gain additional wells on Fort Bliss land have been denied because the base asserts that drilling activities would interfere with its routine operations and conflict with the "purpose of its mission." Subsequently, El Paso has filed applications with the New Mexico state engineer for permits to drill wells on Department of Defense (DOD) lands there. According to Hickerson, while DOD cannot deny the city the right to drill for groundwater, it can deny rights of ingress and egress. Since El Paso acted without consultation with DOD, that department also has filed a vigorous protest with the New Mexico state engineer against the city's filing. At the same time, Fort Bliss has filed for water rights under state law for acquired lands over groundwater sought by El Paso. The New Mexico state engineer has yet to act on the filing and will not discuss the case. The sheer complexity of the legal entanglement implies some intriguing future encounters.

Arizona presents an example of limited cooperation between a state and the military over water rights. Arizona's water situation is considered to be extremely critical by most observers. The state relies to a large extent on groundwater, which is being overdrafted by more than 2 billion gallons annually. In the Phoenix and Tucson areas alone, groundwater overdraft is projected to reach respectively 450,000 and 50,000 acre-feet annually by the 1990s, even with the completion of the Central Arizona Project (CAP). Currently, groundwater constitutes 53 percent of water withdrawals; although surface water is also completely appropriated.[40] Existing and continued high levels of growth in the state suggest that the overdraft problem will continue unless remedial and preventive actions are taken.

Arizona does have a comprehensive groundwater management and conservation measure. This legislative Act establishes Active Management Areas (AMAs) in portions of the state that are experiencing the most severe overdraft problems. (See Wehmhoefer, Chapter 2, for a further discussion of AMAs.)

Three aspects of the Act are important as they relate to the military bases. First, the Act allows for "grandfathered rights." All three bases applied for, and were denied, such rights after the Act's passage. Therefore, they are subject to a second provision of the Act, which calls for a determination of the beneficial use and a classification of users. Under this section, the bases have been classified as having a "Service Area Right"—a right in the same category as any other municipal water district or private provider. The region does not have enough water to meet present uses. In the event that the bases need more water, which they invariably will with their projected expansions, a transfer of uses would need to occur. "Even the smallest application for transfer of water from one use to another [will] meet a series of complex and often expensive conditions before being legally permitted if, indeed, it is permitted at all."[42] Currently, Luke AFB and Williams AFB each uses water at a rate of about 383 gallons per capita/per day.[41]

To qualify for a "Service Area Right" classification, each base was required to formulate special management plans with specified conservation goals. The bases complied. However, they refused to pay pump taxes on their wells, citing immunity from state action interfering with federal activities as a constitutional cloak. Here again we find a contentious situation with likely resolution favorable to the federal government, but only after considerable delay.

An analysis of the probable outcome of conflicts over water involving the federal and state governments in which standard base operations and activities are involved raises issues similar in nature to those we considered in our discussion of major weapon systems, with some important exceptions. One exception concerns a state's power to determine whether the proposed water use is one that is beneficial or advances the public interest. Another is the ability to quantify rights. Maintaining a base golf course is an extreme example. More realistically, in a fully or nearly appropriated situation—a condition that is predicted to come about in the not-so-distant future—expansion of base operations, ranges, and so on, could fall victim to prior and/or more important civilian needs. Here too the permit process can be employed as a bargaining tool by the state to forestall military action. In New Mexico and Arizona, for example, the permit systems for both surface and groundwater provide for an administrative process of notice and hearing.

A potential for future conflicts exists in other areas throughout the Southwest. According to a supplemental 1983 Final Environmental Impact Statement, space shuttle launch and recovery facilities at Vandenberg AFB in California will strain local water supplies and efforts to meet anticipated growth in the region. In Nevada, according to Mike Turnipseed of the state engineer's office, the military often disregards state water law and asserts the reservation doctrine in the fulfillment of its water needs. In a case involving the Hawthorne Ammunition Depot, for example, the federal district court refused to grant Nevada a standing to sue. Since then, Nevada has not sought legal redress.

Finally, the likelihood of similar future conflicts can be demonstrated by considering the geographic location of the major Air Force bases and operations in areas of the Southwest where water problems are recognized as being severe.[43] Table 8.1 portrays the nature of this relationship.[44]

THE FUTURE OF WATER AND WEAPONS

Having discussed the theoretical, practical, and legal dimensions of the states' water rights and powers, and presented several cases in which conflict is either real or imminent, it remains to speculate on both the future nature of state/federal (military) water conflicts in the Southwest, and the conditions under which such conflicts are likely.

How significant are the variables we identified at the beginning of our discussion in predicting future patterns? Unless there are major improvements in weapons technology along with arms control negotiations significant enough to improve Soviet–U.S. relations, national defense is likely to continue to command a sizable portion of the federal budget, with deterrence being the primary national security objective of future administrations, and the nuclear triad of land-, air-, and sea-based missiles to garner the support of defense experts. We have already seen how the military provisionally has "downsized" two weapon systems—the MX and Midgetman. In both decisions the availability of water was a consideration. Unless expanses of public or military land large enough to support even reduced land-based weapon projects can be found in the water-rich East, the arid Southwest will continue to be an attractive site. Given this prospect it is likely that military demand for water in the Southwest will increase in the future. If this is true, then the military will need to operate within state water systems—systems that provide for multiple points of access.

Second, unless there are major improvements in water technology, the depletion of and competition for both surface and groundwater is likely to continue; thus sustaining the interest the states have in confining the thirst of the military for water. Third, unless Congress and the courts decide to reverse an eighty-year pattern of increasing support for state water rights, some degree of formal and informal state power in this area is likely to continue. Fourth, unless Congress undergoes yet another major reorganization of its committee system and pattern of decision-making, and/or reverses its statutory support for the democratization of the federal administrative process, there will continue to exist formal linkages tying the mili-

Table 8.1   Military Base Location/Water Situation

Arizona	Davis-Monthan AFB	SE of and adjacent to Tucson	Located in Tucson Active Management Area; severe ground water overdraft area.
	Luke AFB	8 mi W of Glendale	Major problems include inadequate surface and ground water supplies for present and future users and increasing costs associated with ground water depletion.
	Williams AFB	8mi E of Chandler	Located in Phoenix Active Management Area; ground water overdraft area.
California	Edwards AFB	100 mi N. of L.A.; 35 mi NE of Lancaster	No critical water issues identified.
	George AFB	8 mi NW of Victorville	Ground water quantity and quality are issues of growing concern as urban growth puts increasing pressures on fixed quantities of water; also a concern to agriculture in the area is the increasing salinity of the Colo. R., a major source of irrigation water.
	March AFB	10 mi SE of Riverside	Refer to George AFB.
	Norton AFB	4 mi E-SE of San Bernadino	Refer to George AFB.
	Vandenberg AFB	10 mi NW of Lompac	Area dependant upon ground water for nearly all water supplies, particularly agriculture; overdraft presently occurring and the need for importation may arise in the next 25 years.
Nevada	Nellis AFB	N-NE of Las Vegas	Severe water and land resource problems related to surface water quantity, ground water overdraft and land subsidence; water quality problems with Lake Mead, a major water resource.

New Mexico	Cannon AFB	6 mi W. of Clovis	Located in area of ground water overdraft; approaching level where remaining supplies will be uneconomically recoverable for irrigation; although potable ground water is available, quality is growing increasingly poor in some areas.
	Holloman AFB	6 mi W. of Alamagordo	Located in Rio Grande Basin; surface water scarce and fully appropriated; ground water overdraft and mining occurring, despite poor quality; actively managed by state.
	Kirtland AFB	SE of and adjacent to Albuquerque	Water supplies fully exploited for present uses; new supplies available only through retirement of agricultural uses.
Texas	Goodfellow AFB	4 mi SE of San Angelo	No critical issues identified.
	Laughlin AFB	7 mi NE of Del Rio	No critical issues identified.
	Reese AFB	6 mi W. of Lubbock	Located in the Ogallala Aquifer, one of the most intensely developed aquifers in the U.S.; will not support economic irrigation for the long term; area of increasing concern to agricultural and municipal interests.
	Webb AFB	SW of and adjacent to Big Spring	Surface water of the Colo. R. Basin of Texas affected by serious salinity problems due to gas and oil operations in the area.
Utah	Hill AFB	5 mi S. of Ogden	Favorable water supply, major problem with assuring adequate quality.

Sources: Water Resources Council, 1978, and Mueller, 1982. Prepared by Marc Young.

tary and water policy processes together.

While these conditions anticipate continued state/federal inter-actions over the water and military issue, what about the nature and degree of such interactions? Here the type of program has explana-tory value. Military projects or activities that will have a distributive or redistributive effect on a state's water source will most likely elicit state and private interest and reaction. In short, "[t]he more interna-tional processes concentrate on activities that are distributive, the more they resemble traditional domestic political process."[45] This suggests that foreign or defense issues that impact domestic-distrib-utive ones will bring into the fray subnational actors, and the policy process will conform more to a pluralistic one.

CONCLUSION

Water is the major natural resource issue of the 1980s. Deter-rence, or avoiding a nuclear exchange, is the major defense issue of the 1980s. When the two issues converge, the states gain some influ-ence over the way in which defense policy is made. Perhaps through the control the states exercise over the nature of the decision-making process, they may ultimately affect the substance of policies them-selves. At the very least, water policy may be a tool for bringing citizen initiatives to military decision-making through the side doors; doors that are proliferating and widening. This may lead to a better balance between the needs of the states in the region, and the needs of the federal government. It may even forestall the premature deployment of some weapons or the expansion of conventional mili-tary operations.

Should the states be allowed to interfere with U.S. national se-curity policy? Or should defense policy objectives be allowed to override domestic state considerations? Regardless of how one an-swers this question, in the future students of defense policy will need to recognize the role the states will play in military decisions that threaten to consume the "lifeblood" of the southwestern region—its water.

NOTES

1. I wish to acknowledge the indispensable assistance of my research assistant Marc Young and my colleague Robert C. Benedict.

2. U.S. Constitution, Art. 1, secs. 8 & 10; Art. VI, amendment II. See also

John Norton Moore, "Federalism and Foreign Regulations," *Duke Law Journal* (Spring, 1965): pp. 248–321.

3. See Smith, chapter 1, in this volume.

4. Stephen P. Mumme, "State Influence in Foreign Policymaking: Water Related Environmental Disputes Along the United States–Mexico Border." *The Western Political Quarterly* 38 (December 1985): pp. 620–640; and John M. Kline, *State Government Influence in U.S. International Economic Policy* (Lexington, Mass.: D. C. Heath and Co., 1983).

5. Helen Ingram, "Water Rights in the Western United States," *Proceedings of the Academy of Political Science* 3 (1982): pp. 134–43.

6. Kline, *supra*, note 4.

7. See, *e.g.*, National Environmental Policy Act, 42 U.S.C. sec. 4321–4347 (1976); and Federal Land Policy and Management Act, 43 U.S.C., sec. 1701–1782 (1976).

8. The amount of land (in 1000-acre units) administered by the U.S. Department of Defense and U.S. Department of Energy for military purposes is as follows: New Mexico (2564), Arizona (3590), Utah (1872), Nevada (3936), California (3875), and Texas (471). See H. Thomas Frey, *Major Uses of Land in the United States: 1978* (Washington, D.C.: U.S. Department of Agriculture, 1982).

9. *United States v. Grand River Dam Authority,* 363 U.S. 229 (1960). See also Wehmhoefer, Chapter 2, in this volume.

10. For a summary of these powers, see Zachary A. Smith, "Stability Amid Change in Federal–State Water Relations," 15 *Capital University Law Review* 6 (Spring 1986): pp. 479–91.

11. Federal efforts to establish a federal nonreserved water rights doctrine have not proved fruitful. Unlike reserved rights, which are based on legislative intent (*i.e.*, what the statute says about the purpose for which the land was withdrawn and water reserved), nonreserved powers would be based on prior appropriation and beneficial use, allowing the federal government to claim a prior right to water contingent upon the date of land withdrawal. In 1982 the solicitor general determined that the theory had no legal basis.

12. 436 U.S. 645 (1978).

13. Kirk S. Samelson, "Reserved Water Rights on Air Force Property," *The Air Force Law Review* 22 (1980–81): pp. 302–17.

14. Affirmed and clarified in *U.S. v. County of Eagle,* 401 U.S. 520 (1971) and *Colorado River Water Conservation District v. U.S.,* 424 U.S. 800 (1976).

15. See also *Arizona v. San Caros Apache Tribe of Arizona,* 103 S. Ct. 3201 (1983).

16. Todd A. Fisher, "The Winters of Our Discontent: Federal Reserved Water Rights in the Western States," *Cornell Law Review* 69 (1984): pp. 1077–93.

17. 42 U.S.C. sec. 4332–33.

18. Frank J. Trelease, "Uneasy Federalism—State Water Laws and National Water Uses," *Washington Law Review* 55 (1980): p. 755.

19. For an examination of the prospects of increased federal involvement, see Zachary A. Smith, "Competition for Water Resources: Issues in Federalism," *Journal of Land Use and Environmental Law* 2 (Spring 1987).

20. *Idem.*

21. See *Town of China Valley v. City of Prescott,* 102 S. Ct. 2897 (1982); Ellen K. Wheeler, "The Right to Use Ground Water in Arizona after *China Valley II* and *Cherry v. Steiner*," *Arizona Law Review* 25 (Spring 1983): pp. 473–90; and Zachary A. Smith, "Centralized Decision-making in the Administration of Groundwater Rights: The Experience of Arizona, California and New Mexico and Suggestions for the Future," *Natural Resources Journal* 24 (July 1984): pp. 641–88.

22. Samelson, *supra,* note 13, at 302.

23. Author's interviews.

24. Zachary A. Smith, "Federal Intervention in the Management of Groundwater Resources: Past Efforts and Future Prospects," *Publius* 15 (Winter 1985): pp. 145–59.

25. Clifford I. Barrett, "The Decision Process in Allocating Water Resources," in *Water and Energy: Technical and Policy Issues,* eds. Fritz Kilpatrick and Donald Matchett (N.Y.: American Society of Civil Engineers, 1982): pp. 555–60.

26. For a future discussion of the Winters Doctrine and federal-state relationships, see Chapters 10, 2, and 9.

27. This section draws upon Lauren H. Holland and Robert A. Hoover, *The MX Decision: A New Direction in U.S. Weapons Procurement Policy?* (Boulder, Colo.: Westview Press, 1985).

28. *New York Times,* 3 October 1981.

29. The proposed system would consist of 200 advanced ICBMs each weighing about 190,000 pounds and carrying 10 Multiple Independently Targetable Reentry Vehicle (MIRV) warheads each, shuttled among 4,600 concrete shelters in a deployment area encompassing 6,000 to 15,000 square miles of mostly public land.

30. U.S. Department of Air Force, Final Environmental Impact Statement, MX: Milestone II (Washington, D.C.: Government Printing Office, 1978), pp. 159–60.

31. U.S. Department of Air Force, "Deployment Area Selection and Land Withdrawal Draft EIS" (Washington, D.C.: Government Printing Office, 1980).

32. Utah, Division of Water Resources, *State of Utah–1980* (1981), pp. 25–35.

33. Statutes of Nevada, 1981, chap. 409.

34. *McCulloch v. Maryland,* 4 Wheat 316, 4 L.Ed. 579 (1819).

35. U.S. Congressional Record, 1979: 3510 1f.

36. Of the forty-five military installations that constitute the current list of candidate basing areas, nine are in Arizona; thirteen in southern or south central California; five in New Mexico; six in Nevada; two each in Texas, Florida, Washington, and North Dakota; and one each in Missouri, Montana, Wyoming, and South Dakota. In New Mexico (including Kirtland AFB), Arizona (including Luke AFB, Williams AFB, and Davis–Monthan AFB), and Texas (including Ft. Bliss, near El Paso), states (and military installations) discussed in this chapter, the water situation is serious. In Arizona, for example, groundwater, which currently constitutes 53% of annual water withdrawals, is being overdrafted by two billion gallons a year. Surface water is completely appropriated. In New Mexico, surface water, which constitutes 46% of annual water withdrawals, is fully appropriated, and ground water is being mined. In Texas, El Paso's need for water is so great that the city is trying to import it from New Mexico. In the High Plains area where another Texas site has been identified (Reese AFB near Lubbock), heavy agricultural use is already causing substantial water-level declines. For data on other states, see U.S. Geological Survey, *National Water Summary 1983—Hydrologic Events and Issues* (Washington, D.C.: Government Printing Office, 1984). [Hereinafter cited as USGS, 1984.]

37. David Stone, Department of Water Rights, State of New Mexico, telephone interviews, January, February, and March 1986.

38. USGS, 1984.

39. Telephone interviews, January, February, and March 1986.

40. USGS, 1984; and Smith, *supra,* note 21.

41. Author's interview. Both Luke AFB and Davis–Monthan AFB are undergoing expansion and construction worth $10 million each. See FY 1985 Construction Funds. Microfiche.

42. Allen V. Kneese and F. Lee Brown, *The Southwest Under Stress: National Resource Development Issues in a Regional Setting* (Baltimore, Maryland: Resources for the Future, Inc., 1981).

43. Comparable information for other military bases and operations was not readily available.

44. Special thanks to Marc Young for the preparation of this table. Sources used include Robert Mueller, *Air Force Bases* (Washington, D.C.: Simpson Historical Research Center, 1982); and U.S. Water Resources Council, *The Nation's Water Resources: 1975–2000,* vols. 1–4 (Washington, D.C.: Government Printing Office, 1978).

45. Wolfram F. Hanrieder, "Dissolving International Politics: Reflections in the Nation State," *The American Political Science Review* 72 (1978): pp. 1276–87.

9 American Indian Water Rights in the Future of the Southwest

Lloyd Burton

In 1952 the U.S. Congress adopted a policy favoring the dissolution of American Indian tribes and the sale of the reservation lands to non-Indian interests. When asked if such an approach would not violate existing treaties between the tribes and the United States, the Utah senator who authored the policy said "It is like treaties with Europe. They can be renounced at any time . . . [and] . . . disappear."[1]

The question of treaties did not disappear, however, and with the emergence of the civil rights era in the 1960s came new federal legislation reaffirming tribal sovereignty and Indian self-determination. Through that decade and the one that followed, many tribes also asserted rights to land and other resources, which (they charged) old treaties had awarded them, but which the federal government had allowed to pass into non-Indian hands. In the area of water rights alone, nearly fifty such disputes are now being adjudicated in state and federal tribunals throughout the western United States.[2] About half of these major water rights cases involve tribes living in the Southwest, and the total amount of water being sued for exceeds that now being used by any one state in the region.

When Congress was trying to strip some tribes of their resource base and their governmental existence during the 1950s, legal scholar Felix Cohen wrote:

The Indian plays much the same role in our American society that the Jews played in Germany. Like the miner's canary, the Indian marks the shifts from fresh air to poison gas in our political atmosphere; and our treatment of Indians, even more than our treatment of other minorities, reflects rise and fall in our democratic faith.[3]

All this provides two important reasons why no study of the future of the Southwest is complete without a look at the Indian water rights dilemma. One reason is that the tribes in this arid region are alleging senior rights to a *lot* of surface and groundwater—some of which is already being used by non-Indians in accordance with state water laws. Indian gains in this latest round of western water wars will mean non-Indian losses in both legal entitlements and wet water. Furthermore, nobody makes money but the lawyers when water rights are in dispute; neither public nor private investors in the southwestern states are eager to plunge capital into taking water that the courts may later rule was not theirs to take. So presently unused water may stay unused until some fundamental legal questions have been answered.

The second reason a consideration of Indian water rights is important is that as so often has happened in the past, the way in which these issues are handled will reflect quite directly on the moral character of the American people and the government that represents them. Official federal policy toward indigenous Americans during the last two centuries has ranged from generosity to genocide; from respect for cultural diversity and independence to its brutal suppression. Historically, American governmental leaders and their supporters have been most honorable in their dealings with indigenous peoples at times when they were least covetous of resources the tribes controlled. Conversely, some of American history's sorriest chapters have been written during periods when the dominant culture demanded what the Indians did not wish to relinquish.

In evaluating the influence of tribal water rights on the future of the Southwest, the first step will be to identify some of the variables that have governed the creation and evolution of Indian rights. Next we will review the principal issues in current disputes and the various methods being used in an attempt to settle them. The final step will be an application of the variables identified through historical analysis to current issues and dispute-settling methods, to come up with scenarios for alternative future conflict resolution outcomes. And since there is an undeniable moral dimension to this subject, our concern will be not only with forecasting what *might* happen, but with finding the ingredients for a future in which both Indian and non-Indian cultural groups in the Southwest may have some sense that justice has been done.

HISTORICAL OVERVIEW

At the heart of the conflict over Indian water rights lies the fact that the Indians' claims and those of the non-Indian majority in the Southwest are based on two entirely different systems of law. Tribal water rights emanate mostly from *federal* court interpretations of treaties and other agreements made between Indian tribes and the U.S. government during the latter half of the nineteenth century. But the predominant means of water rights allocation throughout the Southwest is some variation on the doctrine of prior appropriation, adopted by each of the state legislatures and enforced in *state* courts. To understand how these two essentially incompatible water rights doctrines came to exert so much influence over the parceling of water requires that we briefly trace them back to their respective historical roots.

Early Developments

When the U.S. Constitution was first drafted, Indian tribes east of the Mississippi were a military force to be reckoned with—as populous and nearly as well armed as the American revolutionaries themselves. The tribes' original status in the Constitution is therefore somewhat akin to that of foreign nations: Congress was empowered generally to regulate commerce with the tribes; the president was authorized to negotiate treaties with them, subject to senatorial advice and consent; and the supremacy clause held that such treaties are the "supreme law of the land," overriding state law whenever the two might come into conflict.[4]

However, none of these constitutional provisions were tested in court until thirty years after they were ratified, by which time Euro-American society had grown rapidly in population, military power, and appetite for arable land. When tribes in the Southeast tried to legally prevent encroachment on their lands on the theory that they were a sovereign nation, the Supreme Court ruled instead that they were "domestic dependent nations," and that the relationship between the tribes and the federal government was as that between a "ward" (an orphaned child, for example) and his guardian.[5] In another

155

decision,[6] which to this day remains a rationale for federal control of Indian lands, the court ruled that actual legal title to all lands inhabited by Indian tribes was held not by the Indians but by the U.S. government, with the tribes retaining a "right to occupancy."[7]

To the states, this seemed an invitation to also exercise their own jurisdiction over the behavior of tribal members and the management of their lands. But once having unequivocally subjugated Indian sovereignty to the federal will, Justice Marshall and the federalists on the Supreme Court then proceeded with equal vigor to bar the state governments from asserting any authority over the Indians without congressional assent. By 1832, the courts had consigned the tribes to the enigmatic legal niche they still occupy today. Indian tribes are subordinate to the will of the United States but not to individual states (except with congressional permission); unable to protect their resources effectively if Congress decides to sell them, and unable to market their resources if Congress decides to conserve them.

During the latter half of the nineteenth century and the early years of the twentieth, new states and Indian reservations were carved out of federal territories in the West—the states by Act of Congress and the reservations by treaty, congressional enactment, or executive proclamation (which the courts have upheld as having the force of a treaty). As the states came into being, their legislatures adopted policies to foster orderly economic development, including procedures for distributing their water. Since the limited, erratic precipitation and undependable surface water supplies in most southwestern states made equal distribution to all would-be users impractical and inefficient, the doctrine of *prior appropriation* was developed.[8] (See Chapter 2 for a discussion of the prior appropriation doctrine.)

Congressional recognition of the prior appropriation doctrine came first in the Desert Land Act of 1877, but more explicitly in the 1902 Reclamation Act, which called for federal compliance with state water rights doctrine in distributing federal project water. Only when state law directly conflicted with congressional instructions in a specific reclamation project would the state doctrine be overruled.

Conflict between state water law and federal treaty rights finally came to a head around the turn of the century, on the Fort Belknap Reservation in Montana. In 1888 Congress enacted an agreement with the Gros Ventre and Asssiniboin tribes, in which the Indians relinquished all but 600,000 acres of their 17.5-million-acre range in return for the supplies and support necessary to transform the Fort Belknap Reservation from buffalo range to productive farmland. But a year later upstream white settlers dammed the Milk River (the reservation's principal water supply) and started diverting water away from Indian lands—in full compliance with state water laws.

By 1905 the tribes hadn't enough water to raise a crop, and were near starvation. At the reservation superintendent's urgent request, the U.S. attorney secured an injunction in federal court against further non-Indian diversions from the Milk River upstream from the reservation. Asserting (correctly) that their diversions were entirely legal under state law, the settlers in 1908 appealed the lower court rulings to the U.S. Supreme Court.

But in its seminal decision, the high court not only upheld the reservation's right to a minimum flow, but laid the foundation for an entirely new structure of federal water rights doctrine at the same time. In *Winters v. United States*,[9] the Court first reasoned that Congress would not have made an agreement to establish Fort Belknap as an Indian agricultural preserve unless it concomitantly intended to provide enough water to ensure that agriculture would be feasible.

It then held that 1) whenever the federal government creates an Indian reservation it also impliedly reserves enough previously unappropriated water to fulfill the purposes for which the reservation was established; 2) in keeping with prior appropriation doctrine, the date a reservation was established is the date on which the waters were reserved (making the Indians senior appropriators on most western streams); but 3) contrary to appropriative doctrine, the Indians' "reserved right" is not liable to extinction through nonuse; and 4) the Indian right need not be quantified in absolute terms, as long as waters withdrawn are used to fulfill the reservation's purpose. Since this ruling was a federal court interpretation of a congressional enactment, the decision held state prior appropriation doctrine to be unenforceable against the Indian right.[10]

State's rights advocates throughout the West bitterly assailed this "reserved rights" or "Winters Doctrine" as a federal imposition of uncertainty and inhibition of development on state allocation systems that prize maximal use and certainty of supply above all else.

Political leaders from every western state containing an Indian reservation did their utmost to see that the Winters Doctrine was rarely enforced, and, for the most part, they succeeded.

They succeeded because of a deep-seated institutional ambivalence (some say "conflict of interest") within the federal government concerning its status as guardian over and titleholder to Indian resources. For example, over the last eight decades Congress has authorized the Interior Department's Bureau of Reclamation to build billions of dollars' worth of federal water projects, and to distribute the waters to western farmers and ranchers in keeping with state prior appropriation doctrine. But also within the Interior Department is the Bureau of Indian Affairs, which is responsible for protecting Indian natural resources against non-Indian predation.

So far, the record shows the federal government to have been much more successful in fulfilling its former responsibility than its latter one. From 1908 to 1963 the U.S. government built the most extensive system of agrarian water distribution in the history of humankind, parceling out the waters of the West to agricultural interests in conformance with state water law; during this same fifty-five-year period, it obtained federal court decisions enforcing Indian reserved rights against state prior appropriation doctrine only four times.[11]

Later Cases

In 1963 the situation changed dramatically, with the U.S. Supreme Court's ruling in *Arizona v. California*.[12] This decision made history for a couple of reasons. It was the first time the U.S. Attorney had sought and the federal courts had granted a "Winters" right for federally controlled property other than Indian reservations (in this case, a wildlife preserve),[13] and it was the first time the Court had set forth generalized criteria for the quantification of reserved rights. The five Indian bands living on either side of the lower Colorado River whose rights were in dispute had traditionally been farmers, and agriculture was among the reasons their reservations had been established. In deciding how much water they should get, then, the Supreme Court ruled that they be awarded enough to raise crops on all the *practicably irrigable acreage* within the boundaries of their respective reservations.

Even by southwestern standards, the lower Colorado Basin is arid and sparsely populated; only 3,500 Indians lived on the five reservations in question. Yet in keeping with the Court's practicably irrig-able acreage criterion, the tribes were awarded over 900,000 acre-feet of water a year—three times that allocated to Nevada and nearly a third of the amount apportioned to the entire state of Arizona. More-over, the Court ruled that each tribe's share of the river water was to be deducted from the award to the states in which the reservations were located. This aspect of the ruling made an already antagonistic relationship between the tribes and the neighboring state govern-ments even worse.[14]

The Supreme Court made it clear in these findings that Indian water rights were a claim to be taken seriously. In the wake of *Arizona v. California* and several lower court decisions to follow, the legal and economic significance of these rights became "front burn-er" topics on the southwestern policy agenda. Then in 1976 the Supreme Court stirred new ingredients into the pot with two more water rights decisions. In *Cappaert v. U.S.,*[15] the Court for the first time extended federal reserved rights to groundwater whenever a "hydrological connection" between surface and groundwaters can be shown. The other case was as deleterious to the Indian cause as *Cappaert* was encouraging. In *Colorado River Conservation District v. U.S.,*[16] the high court ruled that in many circumstances Indian water rights claims must be initially adjudicated in state courts—a serious jurisdictional defeat for the tribes. The implications and effects of this ruling (popularly known as the *"Akins* decision"] are covered in more detail below.

In sum, a review of Indian water rights development in the South-west is the story of two systems in conflict: chronologically hier-archical state allocation doctrines that award specific annual quan-tities of water to be devoted to specific "beneficial uses," with nonuse as a grounds for forfeiture of the right; contrasted with federal reserved rights (which may or may not be quantified) based on the purposes for which a federal reservation has been established, and with no extinction of unused rights. The state systems place max-imum value on complete, continuous, current use of water resources and certainty of expected supply based on seniority of appropriation; while the federal reserved right foresees the need to conserve for specified future uses, and therefore represents a more "open-ended" claim on water supplies in the Southwest.

Because of serious institutional ambivalence regarding its guard-ianship role, the federal government now finds itself in the paradoxical position of trying to restore to Indian tribes some of the water it earlier impounded in federal reclamation projects and distributed to non–Indian westerners in compliance with state water laws. As we shall see, the theme of federal-state relations will be no less significant in the future development of Indian water rights issues than it has been historically.

SETTLING DISPUTES

In adversarial advocacy, the first procedural issue is often the choice of a forum or setting for resolving the dispute. Different institutions play by different rules, usually to the benefit of one disputant and the disadvantage of another. This explains in large part why most Indian tribes have a distinct preference for federal court litigation, while state governments and other non–Indian interests in the Southwest are urging either a comprehensive federal legislative remedy or a negotiated settlement of Indian water rights claims. Until recently, Indian advocates have enjoyed remarkable success in getting federal judges to see things their way.

Litigation and Legal Issues

Legal questions raised by Indian water rights suits vary from region to region, tribe to tribe, and time to time.[17] Detailed below are issues that are now the subject of litigation between tribes, state governments, and other interested parties in the Southwest. Given the rate at which some of these cases are moving through the legal system, these same issues will probably still be in dispute at the end of this century.

As we entered the 1980s, the Southwest was the setting for 19 major Indian water rights cases,[18] in Arizona, 6; in southern California, 1; in Colorado, 1; in Nevada, 2; and in New Mexico, 9. At the time of this writing only one of these cases has been settled out of court. All of them raise at least one or more of the following questions:

Should state or federal courts hear Indian water rights cases? The Indians' early-nineteenth-century legal skirmishes before the Supreme Court were essentially jurisdictional disputes with state governments, and jurisdictional conflict is no less a problem today than it was in 1832. Since it is the states that compete most directly with the tribes for the economic benefits resulting from resource control and development, it should come as no surprise that these two entities are in direct conflict over water throughout the Southwest. When a court decision grants additional control over water resources to an Indian tribe, it is inevitably at the expense of control formerly exercised by state government. Many aspects of American Indian policy, including the controversy over water rights, are most easily understood as a contest between states' rights and federal guardianship authority.

Those periods in American history during which federal governmental institutions were paying maximum deference to states' rights were also the periods when the Indians suffered the most egregious resource losses. At the same time, however, the federal judiciary has traditionally been more rigorous in its assertion of trust responsibility for the Indians' welfare than has Congress. For this reason, Indian advocates always try to make sure their cases are heard in federal courts rather than in state courts.

But in 1952 a states' rights-oriented Congress enacted legislation mandating that under certain circumstances the federal government's water rights must be adjudicated in state courts. Popularly cited as the "McCarran Amendment" to the Reclamation Act,[19] this policy holds that whenever a state water rights commission or state court is engaged in a "general stream adjudication"—a proceeding in which all the water rights claims in a given watershed are adjudicated simultaneously—the water rights of any Federal property in that watershed must be determined in that forum. (Indian reservations were nowhere specifically mentioned in the amendment.)

Since its passage, the McCarran Amendment has been applied mostly to water rights determinations involving federal preserves like national forests. However, in 1976 the Supreme Court held in the *Akins* decision that the policy applied to Indian reservations as well. In 1983, when the Navajos and the San Carlos Apaches tried to get the high court to reconsider or at least narrow the *Akins* ruling, the Court thoroughly rejected the Indians' arguments and reaffirmed its earlier decision.[20]

The Court did hold that state adjudicators must adhere to Winters Doctrine principles in determining the extent of Indian rights (by allocating enough water to fulfill the purposes for which the reservation was established). But tribal advocates suspect that an unfriendly

forum might construe either reservation purposes or quantities necessary to fulfill them much more narrowly than a federal trial court,
which bears guardianship responsibility for Indian interests.

How can the Akins *and* San Carlos *decisions be reconciled with
the assertion earlier in this chapter that one of the federal court
system's traditional functions has been to shield the tribes from
state jurisdictional intrusions?* The answer lies mostly in the changing composition and orientation of the Supreme Court. At the risk of
oversimplification, the more deferential an individual justice tends
to be toward the traditional powers of state government, the more
likely will he or she be to vote in favor of the states and against the
Indians whenever a jurisdictional conflict between the two occurs.
And just as the Court has become markedly more states' rights-
oriented over the last decade (beginning with the appointment of
Justices Burger and Rehnquist), so has it become correspondingly less
supportive of the Indian position in jurisdictional disputes. Thus
since 1970 the Indians have lost five of the last six water rights cases
to come before the high court—mostly on jurisdictional grounds.[21]

The issue of general stream adjudication jurisdiction appears to
have been clearly decided in favor of the states. Federal jurisdiction is
still being asserted by the tribes and the federal executive branch,
though, in cases involving groundwater resources and all water
rights disputes not subject to general stream adjudication. Thus, the
jurisdictional question is by no means closed.

*How much water does the Winters Doctrine reserve for Indian
use?* Finding appropriate quantification methods has proved to be an
elusive undertaking. The special masters who have been trying to
implement *Arizona v. California* for the last twenty years have been
using classic cost-benefit analysis in determining which lands along
the lower Colorado are and are not "practicably irrigable." But analysts familiar with the use and misuse of this technique have been
quick to point out that in the hands of a hostile or untrained fact-
finder, an Indian right could be quantified at drastically reduced
levels through a failure to distinguish between economic and financial feasibility, an insufficiently narrow consideration of costs and
benefits, or the choice of an inappropriate discount rate.[22] On the
other hand, erroneously large awards could result from making these
same mistakes in reverse. The same problems apply whether it be
surface or groundwater that is the subject of litigation (since *Cappaert,* most suits now involve both).

For Indian reservations in mountainous or heavily forested terrain, agriculture will never have the primacy in tribal economies that logging, mining, grazing, or recreation might enjoy. In these circumstances, the courts will eventually have to devise some alternative means of quantifying tribal entitlements on those reservations that have little or no "practicably irrigable acreage." This issue is also closely related to the following question, having to do with permissible uses of reserved waters.

What are the allowable uses of reserved waters? Since the general purposes stated in creating nearly all Indian reservations included assistance in learning the "arts of civilization" and otherwise becoming economically self-sustaining, analysts for minerals developers have concluded that the courts will probably construe activities such as timber production, minerals extraction and processing, and recreation as among the legitimate uses to which a tribe can devote water resources acquired under the Winters Doctrine.[23] But since efficiency of use is a continuing concern in the West, there will no doubt be continued controversy over what technologies the tribes use to apply water to these purposes, since method of use affects quantities needed.

The Supreme Court addressed the issue of allowable uses of reserved waters on agriculture-based reservations in an unsigned supplemental decree implementing *Arizona v. California* in 1979.[24] It held that even though "practicably irrigable acreage" was the criterion for quantifying the Indian right, and agricultural development was among the primary purposes of the reservations concerned, the tribes were *not* restricted in the use of their waters to irrigation or other agricultural applications.

Can reserved waters be sold to non-Indian users? This question bears on the preceding issue of the allowable uses of reserved waters. Indian advocates assert that there should be no restrictions on their freedom to sell water to any interested buyers. Critics of this expansive approach charge that water marketing is nowhere mentioned as a purpose for which any Indian reservation was created, and that Indian tribes should therefore not be allowed to use the Winters Doctrine first to take water away from their non-Indian neighbors, and then to sell it back to them.

Neither Congress nor the courts have made a definitive ruling on the freedom of all Indian tribes to sell water they gain control of through the Winters Doctrine. In settling the groundwater dispute between the San Xavier Reservation of the Tohono O'odham (Papago) tribe and its Tucson-area neighbors, Congress both authorized tribal members to sell water if they wished to, and specifically disclaimed extension of that permission to other southwestern tribes.[25]

As the population of the Southwest continues to grow, there will certainly be no shortage of willing non-Indian customers for Indian water. The San Xavier Reservation, for instance, lies along the city of Tucson's southwestern growth corridor, adjacent to interstate (and international) highway and rail systems. Tribal members are now being offered long-term leases on their land and water rights by non–Indian residential and commercial land developers, triggering some-times bitter disputes between those tribal members who do and do not favor intensive commercial exploitation of their land and water resources. As urban sprawl in other southwestern cities continues apace, this same conflict situation will no doubt be replicated throughout the region, wherever Indian reservations lie in the path of impending metropolitan development.

What is the extent of tribal jurisdiction over water resource management and water quality control? As southwestern tribes become more insistent on controlling water resources the Winters Doctrine had formerly granted them only in theory, more attention is being drawn to the question of how responsibly and effectively the tribes can manage more water if they are awarded it. In a series of cases arising in the Pacific Northwest in 1981,[26] the 9th Circuit Court of Appeals (whose decisions are binding federal law in much of the Southwest) ruled that it is within the power of a tribal govern-ment—not the states—to regulate water rights on private lands owned by non-Indians within reservation borders. The court charac-terized tribal authority to adopt and enforce its own water codes as an "important sovereign power," unabridged by the McCarran Amend-ment.

In keeping with these 9th Circuit rulings, the Interior Depart-ment in the same year published tribal guidelines for adopting water codes and otherwise assuming broader management authority.[27] But as of mid-1986, the department had refused to endorse the enforce-ment of any of these codes as official federal policy; the issue is a highly controversial one at the state level, and the breadth of tribal management jurisdiction remains legally indistinct.

Further, the Supreme Court does not share the 9th Circuit's per-spective on some management jurisdiction issues. In 1981 the high court ruled that state governments—not Indian tribes or the federal government—own the beds of navigable rivers flowing through Indian reservations, and state governments are therefore empowered to manage aquatic wildlife on and in those waterways.[28]

The questions of tribal rights *and* responsibilities in the area of water quality control is one that is emerging as an important southwestern policy concern. Several federal statutes governing water pollution control—the Clean Water Act, Safe Drinking Water Act, and Resource Conservation and Recovery Act (RCRA)—provide for a very substantial devolution of enforcement authority to state government. But state governments are now implementing their own enforcement programs at the same time that many tribal governments are trying to lure increased industrial activity onto reservation lands; and (over tribal objections) some states have been asserting authority to enforce their environmental programs on the reservations.

Precisely this issue arose in a case before the 9th Circuit between the State of Washington, the U.S. Environmental Protection Agency, and the Colville Confederated Indian Tribe in 1985, over whether the state should be empowered to enforce its RCRA implementation program on the reservation, or the E.P.A. should work directly with the tribe (as a sovereign government) in developing an implementation program. The court ruled in favor of the E.P.A. and the tribe.[29]

But this case represents only the tip of the iceberg. A survey commissioned by the E.P.A. and published in the same year as the *Colville* decision found nearly 1,200 hazardous waste dump sites on or proximal to Indian reservations, mostly in the western states, with some of them posing immediate and serious public health hazards.[30]

If non–Indian neighbors of southwestern Indian reservations suspect the Indians of trying to attract polluting industries without adequately regulating the discharge of effluents, the tribes may face stiff legal opposition to any future development. Likewise, the tribes are becoming more sensitive to the effects of non-Indian development on reservation water quality, and are becoming ever more willing to take legal action when they perceive a water quality threat.

Legislation
Proposals considered by Congress for the settlement of Indian water rights conflicts may loosely be organized into three categories: 1) bills submitted by western states' rights advocates to legis-

latively terminate the Winters Doctrine and extinguish all Indian claims to waters now in non–Indian use; 2) bills submitted by civil rights-oriented advocates for the federal adjudication of Winters Doctrine claims, with—where necessary—termination of non–Indian rights and reassignment of those rights to the tribes; and 3) case-by-case legislative settlements of disputes between specific southwestern tribes and their non–Indian neighbors. As yet, no proposals in categories 1 and 2 have been enacted; the two settlements in category 3 deserve our attention, and are covered in the following subsection on negotiation.

From 1955 to 1979, western members of Congress and senators submitted more than fifty bills for the termination or diminution of Indian reserved water rights.[31] Rather than reallocate already appropriated water to the Indians, under most of these bills the federal government would estimate the amount of water due the tribes that non–Indians had already appropriated under state law, then give the Indians a one-time cash payment for this water rather than giving them the water. Payment of these funds would terminate all future Indian claims. None of these proposals ever became law; opponents charged that such an approach was an effort to legitimize retroactively the federal government's complicity in giving away Indian water to non–Indians.

Unfortunately, the effect of "category two" proposals could be just as harsh for some non–Indian southwesterners as "category one" policies would be for the Indians. In 1973 the National Water Commission recommended that 1) Congress should designate the federal district courts as having primary jurisdiction over the adjudication of all Indian water rights claims, to avoid the "suspicion of bias" involved in state court adjudication; 2) all Indian reserved rights should be quantified, and 3) when Indians can prove under the Winters Doctrine that water already appropriated under state law is rightfully tribal water, the non–Indian right should be terminated, with damages payments made to the non–Indian appropriators (rather the reverse of "category one" damages proposals).[32]

Whatever the rational merit of these ideas, they proved to be quite unpalatable politically. In the fifteen years since these policy recommendations were made, not one of them has been enacted into law. To many legislators, eastern and western alike, terminating the water rights of non–Indians who acquired these rights in good faith under state law is no more just a solution than terminating Indian rights. In short, at this time Congress appears at a deadlock in its efforts to enact a fair and comprehensive program for resolving the Indian water rights conflict.

Negotiation

Congress has played a more limited but effective role in settling such disputes in the Southwest by using federal reclamation project water as an inducement for Indian and non–Indian disputants to reach negotiated agreements rather than to engage in litigation.

Just after the 9th Circuit Court of Appeals ruled that the Winters Doctrine applied to groundwater, the San Xavier Reservation of the Tohono O'odham (Papago) filed suit against the city of Tucson, several neighboring mines, ranchers, and farmers for depletion of the groundwater underlying the reservation.[33] Had the suit ultimately been successful, the tribe might have acquired rights to almost half the annual recharge of the entire Tucson-area groundwater basin, using the practicably irrigable acreage criterion. Since the city of Tucson and its neighbors are withdrawing groundwater about three times faster than it is being recharged, the tribe could theoretically have brought to a halt all but a fraction of current groundwater pumping in the upper Santa Cruz Basin.

However, the Indians were amenable to negotiation, and the defendants were quite eager to settle out of court. The defendants resolved to experiment with self-regulation of groundwater withdrawals, and to seek new sources of water. The former task was made easier by the Arizona legislature's 1980 enactment of strict new groundwater regulation legislation,[34] and the latter was facilitated by modifications in the as-yet-uncompleted Central Arizona Project.

What Congress essentially did in this dispute was to "make the pie larger." Under the leadership of Tucson-area Congressman Morris Udall—who chairs the House Committee with legislative jurisdiction over Indian affairs *and* reclamation—a settlement was fashioned in which the Indians would abandon all Winters Doctrine claims to Santa Cruz Basin surface and groundwater in return for deliveries of specified quantities of agricultural-grade water from the Central Arizona Project (CAP). When this bargain was struck, the Tucson Aqueduct portion of the CAP had not yet been built, nor the location of its Tucson terminus decided. As a result of Congressman

Udall's mediatory efforts, in the water rights settlement legislation the terminus was located above the city at the reservation border. Congress ratified the agreement in June of 1982.[35]

When the San Xavier Papago negotiations were first getting under way, the Ak Chin Indian Community (an agricultural reservation of Pima and Papago Indians located between Phoenix and Tucson) informed the Interior Department that neighboring non–Indian groundwater withdrawals had caused a 300-foot drop in the reservation's water table. A bill obligating the federal government to replace the Ak Chin Community's water was cleared in Congress in 1978.[36]

Both the Ak Chin and Tohono O'odham (Papago) bills contain provisions in which the Indians agree to abandon all Winters Doctrine claims in return for the federally guaranteed delivery of specified quantities of water. If the federal government does not deliver the water, it must pay money damages to the tribes instead.

Unfortunately, the Interior Department initially failed to uphold the federal government's end of the Ak Chin agreement. The original 1978 Ak Chin Act called for the drilling of new wells, which ultimately proved infeasible. When in 1982 the Interior Department failed to ask Congress for more money to find other water supplies for Ak Chin, the Indians threatened to invoke the damages clause of their agreement (calculated at about $50 million). Instead, the Interior Department did two things: It arranged for grants and loans equaling the damages amount to help the Indians prepare additional lands for cultivation, and it promised to deliver the entire Ak Chin water allotment through the Central Arizona Project. The 1985 amendments to the Ak Chin settlement act reflected these changes.

Only time will tell whether the Ak Chin and San Xavier agreements will prove satisfactory alternatives to reserved water rights litigation. Much will depend on how conscientiously the federal government adheres to its promise to deliver water to the reservations. Every tribal government in the Southwest is monitoring the implementation of these settlements. If the reservations get the water they have been promised in these settlements, it will be added encouragement to other southwestern tribes now litigating their water rights to consider negotiations more seriously. Conversely, if the federal commitment to upholding these agreements falters and the affected tribes are forced to sue for money damages instead, other tribes will be stiffened in their resolve—as expressed by one Apache leader—to "never discuss water rights outside the courthouse."[37]

There is also serious doubt as to whether Congress will be able to finance dispute settlement through major reclamation expenditures in the future. If and when it is finally completed, the CAP will be the second largest (and most expensive) single reclamation project ever bankrolled by the federal government—surpassed only by California's Central Valley Project in extent of water conveyed. As discussed in more detail below, it is unlikely that in these deficit-ridden times Congress can or will settle regional water disputes—even those it was ultimately responsible for creating in the first place—through massive new water project appropriations.

ALTERNATIVE FUTURES AND
A MODEST PROPOSAL

Scenario 1: More of the same. This is the likeliest near-term outcome, as the tribes fight to keep their suits in federal court, the states fight to remove them to their own jurisdiction, and the transaction costs involved in litigation continue to mount. There will be a continuing effort to get Congress to legislatively limit the Winters Doctrine, which the civil rights coalition will continue to oppose. Negotiation will enjoy only limited success, as litigants await the outcome of pending major cases to find out which side will obtain the greatest future bargaining power, based on those precedents.

Scenario 2: Legislative solutions—Water rights termination or an Indian/reclamation coalition. As the U.S. population continues to migrate to the Southwest, and western influence in Congress continues to grow, the frustration of development expectations caused by Indian water rights litigation may yet trigger federal legislation terminating or limiting the Winters Doctrine. But in addition to the dubious moral and constitutional validity of such an approach, it would be very expensive as well. Even if Congress decided to terminate Indian water rights, under current proposals it would be obligated to pay the Indians fair market value for those rights, as determined by the U.S. Court of Claims.

The possibility of congressional termination of non-Indian rights to satisfy Indian claims seems a far more remote possibility than its opposite, described above. Non-Indian political power in Congress is growing and is likely to continue to grow much more quickly than is tribal political influence.

Less morally objectionable but no less costly is the approach exemplified by congressional settlement of the Ak Chin and Papago disputes—more water projects. Throughout most of this century the powerful western reclamation lobby and its champions in Congress have almost totally ignored the rights and needs of southwestern Indian reservations in developing major reclamation projects. But now that serious federal project funding has apparently dried up, the reclamation lobby has suddenly discovered the plight of the poor Indian. For example, it has been suggested that an unstated but crucial purpose of the Ak Chin and Papago water rights settlement legislation was to morally obligate Congress to resume appropriations for the Central Arizona Project, which in the late 1970s was languishing unfunded and uncompleted on the Carter administration's water project "hit list."

If this approach is more fully developed, Indian tribes and reclamation lobbyists will formally join forces, and every future western water project proposed to Congress will contain a major Indian reservation component. Members of Congress who oppose these projects will be vulnerable to accusations that they are insensitive to the legitimate water rights claims of an impoverished rural minority group. This strategy will also put the conservationists in an interesting position; fighting reclamation proposals that will benefit Indian reservations will once again open them to charges of elitism and socio-economic indifference. But for this strategy to succeed, project boosters will have to find a way to divert or disguise a lot of federal red ink before they can develop any more southwestern water.

Scenario 3: The negotiation alternative. According to dispute settlement theorists, the rational disputant will choose that settlement method demonstrating the highest probability of yielding a desired outcome at the lowest cost and with the least risk. This explains the Indians' historic preference for litigation. While not cheap, it has been effective; and their odds of winning future disputes have enhanced their present bargaining power. Furthermore, the lessons of history have taught them that negotiation can be risky indeed.

During the nineteenth century, western tribes signed treaties with the federal government wherein they collectively relinquished control over about 200 million acres of land in return for much smaller federal reservations and the promise of continued congressional support in the form of food, shelter, farming implements, and other supplies necessary for becoming economically self-sufficient. But the promises made by one session of Congress were more often than not either incompletely honored or ignored altogether by later ones. Short of suicidal attempts at open warfare, the nineteenth-century tribes had no means of forcing the federal government to keep its word.

Now that the Interior Department is urging the tribes to negotiate their water rights claims as the federally preferred means of dispute settlement,[38] many tribes fear that if they do make such agreements, the same thing will happen to their water in the future as has happened to most of their land in the past. At the same time, though, the tribes have recently been losing their jurisdictional disputes before the Supreme Court; and the prospect of state adjudication of their claims is making the litigation alternative look far riskier and less successful—but no less costly—than it has been previously. If negotiation could be made less risky and more cost-effective, yet produce minimally acceptable outcomes, it could become a much more attractive dispute-settling option.

Enhancing the Negotiation Potential

Because of the diversity of issues, personalities, and geographic circumstances involved in southwestern Indian water rights controversies, no one dispute-settling method will ever be equally attractive to all disputants in all cases. Turnovers in tribal, federal, and state government leadership, decisions in pending court cases, and the future economic health of the American Southwest will all influence to some degree what dispute-settling methods are attempted in the future and how successfully they are employed.

The premise underlying the policy recommendations at the close of this chapter is that it will be to the ultimate benefit of all parties concerned if the range of effective, acceptable dispute-settling options is broadened. To that end, the following recommendations focus on ways to help make the negotiation process more fair and more cost-effective, and the implementation of negotiated agreements less risky for all parties concerned.

The Interior Department is now actively urging southwestern tribes to negotiate rather than litigate their water rights claims, but many tribes are suspicious of any consensus-based proceedings. They see the department as having had a major role in giving away their water to non–Indians in the first place. One way to avoid these conflict-of-interest charges would be to remove negotiation jurisdiction from the Interior Department, and vest it instead in an intergovernmental Indian water rights commission, in which the department would participate but which it would not control.

Sitting on such a commission would be representatives of western state governments, western tribes, both houses of Congress, and the Interior Department. Five possible functions of such a commission would be 1) to foster regional water resources planning between Indian and non–Indian governments; 2) to establish general guidelines and principles for a water rights negotiation process; 3) to draft model agreements for intergovernmental policy coordination in the areas of water resource management and water quality control; 4) to provide a hydrologic data base sufficient to enable intergovernmental planning and negotiation to occur; and 5) to provide a staff of facilitators (either employees or consultants) capable of chairing negotiations. Due the commission's composition, its major decisions on issues such as adoption of guidelines and the appointment of mediators would have to be consensual rather than by majority vote. Likewise, resort to the commission's services would have to be with the consent of all parties to a given dispute, rather than coerced.

A thoughtfully conceived funding mechanism to support the commission's work and implement its agreements could simultaneously make negotiation more cost-effective, decrease the risks of implementation failure, and increase the supply of water necessary to satisfy both Indian and non–Indian demands. At present, a shortage of funds to solve the water rights dilemma through enhancing current water supplies is as much a problem as are conflicting legal claims. Neither side in these disputes is willing to relinquish through negotiation what they consider valid legal claims without receiving something in return, and Congress is now clearly unwilling to undertake massive new water projects. There is also plenty of historical evidence to suggest that even if a current Congress did promise more water, a future Congress might forget to deliver it.

Congressman Udall was all too aware of the vagaries of incremental project funding when he drafted the Papago Settlement Act. To help Congress keep its word, what he did was to call for a one-time appropriation to establish an implementation trust fund, the interest from which would be used to finance water delivery.[39]

A similar mechanism could be used to implement Indian water commission agreements. Rather than trying to get annual appropriations through Congress, federal lawmakers instead could enact legislation attaching a temporary ten-year self-terminating surcharge on the sale of water and power from all federal reclamation projects. The proceeds from the surcharge would go into a trust fund, the interest from which would be used to finance the resolution of Indian water rights conflicts.

In addition to financing the commission's activities, there are at least two ways a surcharge fund could be used to make water available to satisfy legitimate Indian claims. The first is by financing state-of-the-art conservation retrofitting of the water works of existing federal projects and project customers. The Metropolitan Water District (MWD) of Southern California recently proposed such an arrangement to the Imperial Irrigation District (IID) in which MWD will finance the upgrading of IID's irrigation facilities in exchange for the water conveyed.[40] Similarly, the water saved by retrofitting elsewhere in the West could substantially increase available supplies; a little-known study issued in the latter days of the Carter administration estimated that in the lower Colorado River Basin alone, water savings through conservation retrofitting could amount to as much as 25 percent of total current agricultural use.[41]

Another means of satisfying legitimate Indian Winters Doctrine claims would be the use of surcharge trust fund proceeds to buy up water rights from willing sellers. Right now about 85 percent of southwestern water is used for agriculture and range. But as reclamation project delivery contracts are renegotiated to reflect current market values for water, certain kinds of farming in parts of the Southwest are becoming increasingly marginal. Voluntary reassignment of those rights from unprofitable agriculture to satisfy a tribal Winters right—compensating willing sellers through surcharge fund revenues—could facilitate the equitable reallocation of a lot of water. And properly adjusted, the surcharge itself could provide an impetus for conservation by direct and indirect reclamation project customers (agrarian *and* urban).

Politically difficult as even a temporary water and power surcharge on reclamation project proceeds might initially be to establish, it does broadly distribute the costs of satisfying legitimate Winters Doctrine claims among those who have been enjoying the benefits of using (arguably) Indian water over the last eight decades. And it is apparent to all serious students of the Indian water rights dilemma that there is no easy, cost-free solution to the problem that does not transgress on the valid legal claims of one party or another, whether those claims originated under state or federal law.

In the final analysis, disenfranchising either the Indians or prior appropriators isn't a cost-free exercise anyway. The difference is that payment will not be in the form of use-based revenue, but in the denigration of our self-image as a just society.

NOTES

1. Statement of U.S. Senator Arthur Watkins (Republican, Utah), chairman of the Senate Subcommittee on Indian Affairs, 1952; reprinted in Getches *et al., Federal Indian Law* (1979), p. 90.

2. A summary of southwestern Indian water right disputes active as of 1982 is in J. Folk-Williams, *What Indian Water Means to the West: A Sourcebook* (1982), pp. 30–92.

3. Cohen, *The Erosion of Indian Rights, 1950–53*, 62 *Yale Law Journal,* pp. 348, 390 (1953).

4. *U.S. Constitution:* art. I, sec. 8, cl. 3; art. II, sec. 2, cl. 2; and art. VI, cl. 2, respectively.

5. *Cherokee Nation v. Georgia,* 30 U.S. (5 Pet.) 1 (1831).

6. *Johnson v. McIntosh,* 21 U.S. (8 Wheat.) 543 (1823).

7. *Worcester v. Georgia,* 31 U.S. (6 Pet.) 515 (1832).

8. *Waters & Water Rights,* sec. 50 *et seq.* (R. Clark ed., 1967, and Supp., 1978).

9. 207 U.S. 564 (1908).

10. A definitive article on the *Winters* decision within its historical context is Hundley, *The Winters Decision and Indian Water Rights: A Mystery Reexamined,* 13 *Western Historical Quarterly,* 17 (1982).

11. *Skeem v. U.S.,* 273 F. 93 (9th Cir. 1921); *U.S. v. Walker River Irr. Dist.,* 104 F.2d 234 (9th Cir. 1939); *U.S. v. Powers,* 305 U.S. 527 (1939); *U.S. v. Ahtanum Irr. Dist.,* 236 F.2d 321 (9th Cir. 1956).

12. 373 U.S. 546 (1963).

13. In *Federal Power Commission v. Oregon,* 349 U.S. 435, 75 S. Ct. 832, 99 L.Ed. 1215 (1955), the Supreme Court upheld the FPC's authority to reserve federal lands and unappropriated water for nonconsumptive use in a privately owned hydroelectric facility, against Oregon's argument that the state should have exclusive jurisdiction over water rights regulation on nonnavigable streams. However, in this case, the court determined that the FPC's reservation powers were expressly delegated by Congress in the Federal Power Act (75 X. Ct. at 836–7). In contrast, the court in *Arizona v. California* upheld for the first time federal executive branch authority to

reserve unappropriated water for non-Indian uses based solely on the judicially created *Winters* Doctrine.

14. One vocal critic of the "practicably irrigable acreage" criterion established by the Supreme Court in *Arizona v. California* alleges that the decision theoretically entitles Arizona Indians alone to more than the total annual flow of the Colorado River. These calculations are based on the assumption that approximately one third of the 19.4 million acres of Indian lands in Arizona are irrigable (6.4 million acres), and that the annual duty of water per acre will be 4.59 acre-feet. This would result in a hypothetical annual call of 29.38 million acre-feet—about one and a third m.a.f. more than the erroneously high 28 m.a.f. average annual flow rate used in formulating the Colorado River Compact. Shrago, *Emerging Indian Water Rights: An Analysis of Recent Judicial and Legislative Developments*, 26 *Rocky Mtn. Min. Law Inst.*, 1105, 1116 (1980).

15. 426 U.S. 128 (1976).

16. 424 U.S. 800 (1976).

17. Space limitations preclude a discussion of Indian water rights claims based on theories other than the Winters Doctrine. See Merrill, *Aboriginal Water Rights*, 20 *Natural Resources Journal*, 45 (1980).

18. Folk-Williams, *supra*, note 2.

19. 43 USC Sec. 666 (1976).

20. *Arizona v. San Carlos Apaches*, 51 USLW 5095 (U.S. July 1, 1983).

21. The *Akins* decision, *supra*, note 16; *Arizona va. California*, 51 USLW 4325 (U.S. March 30, 1983); *Montana v. U.S.*, 450 U.S. 544 (1981); *Pyramid Lake Paiute v. Truckee Carson Irr. Dist.*, 51 USLW 4974, (U.S. June 24, 1983); and the *San Carlos Apache* decision (*idem*). As noted earlier, the *Akins* decision applied the McCarran Amendment (compulsory water rights adjudication in state courts) to Indian reservations; *San Carlos* reaffirmed *Akins*. The *Pyramid Lake Paiute* decision rejected an attempt by the Paiutes to overturn a decades-old consent decree quantifying their rights at what the Indians considered unreasonably low levels. The *Montana* decision held that states—not Indian tribes—hold title to the beds of navigable rivers flowing through Indian reservations. In its supplemental decree to *Arizona v. California* in 1983, the high court rejected the findings of its own special master, in refusing to amend what the master found to be a mistakenly low original calculation of the practicably irrigable acreage as the basis for quantifying Indian rights. The tribes were not restricted solely to agricultural applications of the water they were awarded. *Arizona v. California*, 439 U.S. 419, 422 (1979).

22. Burness *et al. The "New" Arizona v. California: Practicable Acreage and Economic Feasibility*, 22 *Natural Resources Journal*, 517 (1982).

23. P. Maxfield *et al. Resource Law on American Indian Lands* (1977), at pp. 218–33.

24. 439 U.S. 419 (1979).

25. Pub. L. 97–293, Sec. 306(c) (2), (d) (1982).

26. *Colville Confederated Tribes v. Walton*, 647 F.2d 42 (9th Cir. 1981).

27. 46 Fed. Reg. 944 (1981).

28. *Montana v. U.S., supra,* note 21.

29. *State of Washington v. EPA,* 752 F.2d 1465 (1985).

30. *Inventory of Hazardous Waste Generators and Sites on Selected Indian Reservations,* prepared under contract to the E.P.A. by the Council of Energy Resource Tribes (CERT/TR–851025, Project No. 061–1025), July 1985.

31. Note, *Indian Reserved Water Rights: The Winters of Our Discontent,* 88 *Yale Law Journal,* 1689, 1703–4 (1979).

32. National Water Commission, *Water Policies for the Future* (1973), at 475–83.

33. *U.S. and Papago Indian Tribe v. City of Tucson et al.,* No. CIV 75–39 TUC (Jaw) (1975).

34. Ariz. Rev. Stat. Ann. Sec. 450441 *et seq.* (1980).

35. Pub. L. 97–293, Title III, 97th Cong., 2nd Sess. (1982).

36. Pub. L. 95–238 (1978).

37. Statement of Ronnie Lupe, chairman, White Mountain Apache Tribe, in American Indian Lawyer Training Program, *Indian Water Policy in a Changing Environment* (1982), at 143.

38. "Watt Seeks Negotiated Settlement for Indian Water Claims Suits. . . . " (U.S. Dept. of Interior news release, July 14, 1982).

39. Note 35, *supra,* at Sec. 313.

40. Z. Willey, *Economic Development and Environmental Quality in California's Water System,* University of California, Institute for Governmental Studies (1985).

41. U.S. Dept. of Interior, Dept. of Agriculture, and Environmental Protection Agency, *Irrigation Water Use and Management,* Interagency Task Force Report (June, 1979); discussed in Willey, *idem* at 24–25.

III   Allocation and Management Issues

10 Prospects for Interbasin Water Transfer in the Southwest

Kent W. Olson

The history of large-scale interbasin water transfer is an important part of the history of the Southwest, especially in the desert environments of Arizona and California. There, enormous projects have been completed that transfer water over long distances, often through formidable terrain, to meet the needs of the rapidly expanding population of southern California and central Arizona, and to grow water-intensive crops.

The damming and diversion of the once-mighty Colorado River has been so extensive that hardly a drop now travels the entire length of its natural channel to the Gulf of California. The triumph over nature has not been nearly so complete for the rivers of northern California; many still remain that have not been diverted to the south. However, we have not seen the last of attempts to intercept and reroute water that some contend is wasted when it flows freely to the Pacific Ocean.

Still, the focus of concern in recent years has not been exclusively on this part of the Southwest. Much of it has shifted eastward to the plains of western Oklahoma, west Texas, and eastern New Mexico—principally to the area overlying the Ogallala aquifer.

The Ogallala is a vast groundwater formation that underlies much of the so-called High Plains and supports a thriving agriculture-based economy that stretches from the bottom of the Texas Panhandle to South Dakota (see Figure 1). It is widely believed, however, that rising costs of lifting this water will greatly reduce the acreage now devoted to irrigated farming, and significantly lower regional output, income, employment, and population.

These consequences are expected to be most pronounced for the area overlying the Ogallala in eastern New Mexico and in the Oklahoma and Texas Panhandles. Here, some farmers have already reduced their irrigated acreage, and a recent study projects a net loss of nearly 1.7 million irrigated acres for this region by 2020.[1]

Several types of government action have been proposed as means of reducing or eliminating the adverse impact of this loss. However, the one that most excites the imagination of water planners is large-scale interbasin water transfer to this region. In fact, there is a long-standing interest in such transfers. The Bureau of Reclamation sketched the principal features of a plan for conveying 4.9 million acre-feet of water from eastern Oklahoma to the Oklahoma Panhandle over twenty years ago.[2] Two years later, an even grander scheme was outlined in *The Texas Water Plan*,[3] which proposed construction of a system of canals, pumps, pipelines, and reservoirs capable of transferring 17.3 million acre-feet per year from the Mississippi River to west Texas.

The Texas plan received a crippling blow when state voters turned down a proposed constitutional amendment in 1969 for a $3.5 billion bond issue for water resource development. Interest in the Bureau's plan for Oklahoma diminished greatly following the agency's estimate that benefits from irrigated agriculture would be only one-sixth as large as the costs of building and operating the project.

The dream of transferring water from East to West was not dead in Oklahoma, however, and in 1980 the Oklahoma Water Resources Board rekindled interest in the state by proposing a new, smaller version of the Bureau's project (SWCS in Figure 1).[4] Two years later, water transfer advocates were given additional options with the release of the so-called High Plains Study, in which several technically feasible interstate-interbasin transfer routes were identified by the U.S. Army Corps of Engineers (Routes C and D in Figure 1).[5]

Although the Corps of Engineers reported reconnaissance level cost estimates for these routes, they were instructed by Congress not to do any benefit-cost analysis. The Oklahoma Water Resources Board, on the other hand, contracted with university economists for a complete economic evaluation of their proposal.[6]

The results of that evaluation provide a valuable benchmark for assessing the economic feasibility of large-scale interbasin water

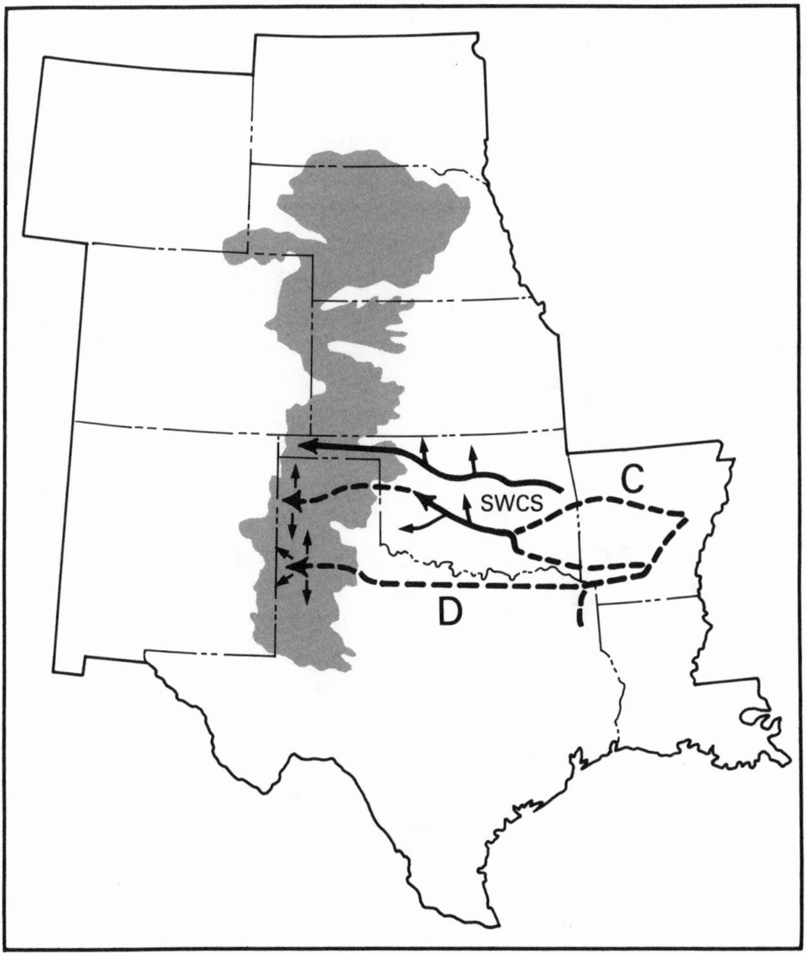

Figure 1.   Proposed Transfer Routes Southern High Plains

transfer in the southern plains region. These results, which will be outlined in the next section, clearly imply that the Oklahoma project would be a bad investment for the state from an economic point of view. Following that, we ask whether the dynamics of distributive water politics are likely, anyway, to favor the adoption in Oklahoma of such a project. Finally, we draw some lessons for Texas from the results of the Oklahoma study, and ask whether there, too, as well as elsewhere in the Southwest, distributive politics are likely to prove stronger than unfavorable comparisons of benefits and costs.

ASSESSMENT OF THE OKLAHOMA PLAN

Oklahoma, like so many western states, is plagued by an uneven distribution of economically useful water resources. Large amounts of rain fall in the eastern half of the state, but the bulk of total water consumption is accounted for by agricultural activity located in the more arid western region. The state's largest metropolitan area (Oklahoma City) lies on the edge of the more humid region, but currently receives much of its water supply from distant sources.

Water resource planners who have assessed the state's resources and needs periodically raise the prospect of future water shortages, most recently in the *Oklahoma Comprehensive Water Plan* (OCWP).[7] The most widely publicized of these shortages is projected to occur in the Oklahoma portion of the High Plains as a result of the overdraft of the Ogallala aquifer. Significant shortages are also projected to occur, however, in the Oklahoma City area, as well as in the southwest portion of the state. These shortages are projected to persist even after groundwater and surface water supplies available within each area are fully developed through conventional means such as wells, dams, and interbasin transfer projects.

To alleviate these shortages, the authors of the OCWP recommend construction of a massive interbasin transfer project, or State-wide Water Conveyance System (SWCS in Figure 1). The northern component of this system would intercept 1.2 million acre-feet of water per year from Lake Eufaula and Robert S. Kerr Reservoir that would normally flow down the Arkansas River, and transfer it to north central and northwest Oklahoma. Although rationalized as a replacement for declining groundwater stocks in the Ogallala aquifer, it would go mostly to meet projected demands for new irrigated acreage on the High Plains. The southern portion of the SWCS would transfer 487,000 acre-feet per year from southeast Oklahoma to the Oklahoma City area, principally for household and industrial use, and 823,000 acre-feet per year from the same sources to southwest Oklahoma where it would be used primarily to meet projected needs for new irrigated acreage. The total undiscounted cost of the entire system is estimated at nearly $18 billion in 1978 dollars.

What follows are the results of a cost-benefit analysis of the SWCS, in which costs and benefits are confined to those paid for or received by residents of Oklahoma. These are based upon a revision of an earlier study financed by the Oklahoma Water Resources

Board.[8] This review contains only a small part of the information generated by that study. Although a description of the basic methodology is provided, it is brief. Emphasis has been placed, instead, on an assessment of the key determinants of economic feasibility.

Project Benefits

The SWCS would deliver water via water wholesalers and/or retailers to households, farms, and business establishments. The monetary value of benefits is the amount of money users would be willing to pay for this water.

Household Benefits. Much of the water targeted for the Oklahoma City area would be sold to household users. To determine the willingness to pay for this water, the area under each annual demand curve corresponding to the extra amount that would be available with the SWCS was estimated. We assumed, as did project planners, the absence of alternative sources of supply. Thus, benefit estimates produced within this scenario clearly constitute the upper bound of the range of possible estimates.

Agricultural Benefits. Given the large proportion of project water intended for irrigated agriculture, and the keen interest shown by western agricultural interests in the SWCS, an extensive analysis of potential water use by farmers was conducted by agricultural economists at Oklahoma State University, using a linear programming model combined with a farm budget generator.[9]

The objective of this analysis was to select the set of farm budgets from among hundreds of enterprises' budgets representative of a wide variety of soil types, crops, farm sizes, and water situations that would maximize net returns to land and management. Two linear programming solutions were obtained: one that corresponds to the maximization of net returns without the SWCS, and one that corresponds to the maximization of net returns with the SWCS. The difference in maximum net returns constitutes the change in farm income attributable to the SWCS, and the maximum amount farmers would pay for project water at the farm headgate.

Industrial Benefits. The smallest proportion of project water is intended for industrial water users. However, Oklahoma water planners believe that water shortages in this sector would have serious economic consequences. To determine the impact on industrial water users, C. K. and C. J. Liew constructed an interregional variable coefficient input-output model of Oklahoma.[10] In this model, project water offsets shortages that would otherwise trigger increases in water prices and changes in technical and trade coefficients. Thus, unlike traditional input-output models, this model determines an optimal response by the industrial sector to exogenous changes in water availability, just as the linear programming model determines the optimal response for the agricultural sector.

Using this model, forecasts were made of value added by industry, both with and without water supplies provided by the SWCS. The changes in value added were then divided into changes in profit-type income, employee compensation, and indirect business taxes.

The change in profit-type income represents the maximum amount owners of business enterprises would be willing to pay for project water. It is the counterpart of the net returns to land and management in agriculture and constitutes the upper bound of project benefits to industrial water users.

Recreation and Flood Control Benefits. The SWCS would also include several new reservoirs. There would undoubtedly be some recreation and flood control benefits produced by these reservoirs; however, they are likely to be quite small. The fact that these reservoirs have not previously been pursued for the purpose of flood control suggests that their value as flood control structures is small. Also, the dams would be built either in areas already rich in water-based recreation opportunities or in areas that are sparsely populated—thus reducing the likelihood that they would service unmet recreational demands.

Estimated Benefits. Each of the relevant benefits was estimated for each year in the assumed project lifetime (1991–2040) using the methodologies described above. Table 10.1 contains the sums of the discounted, or present, values of each of these estimates from the perspective of 1978 (the last year for which consistent data were available at the time of the study).

Three (real) discount rates were used because economists do not agree on the value of the appropriate rate for public projects. If all funds raised to finance the project were to come from private consumption, use of the social rate of discount would be appropriate. For this rate Gramlich's "golden rule" value of 3.5 percent was used.[11] Alternatively, if all funds were drawn from private investment, the appropriate rate would be the before-tax rate of return on normally risky private securities. Following procedures developed by Seagraves,[12] this rate was determined to be approximately 9 percent in

Table 10.1   Oklahoma Statewide Water Conveyance System
Present Value of Project Benefits (*Millions 1978 Dollars*)

Benefit Type	Discount Rate		
	.035	*.065*	*.09*
Industrial	31.0	13.0	7.2
Household	811.1	265.9	98.2
Agricultural	2318.7	982.6	536.8
Total	3160.8	1261.5	642.2

1978. A rate of 6.5 percent was also used, to represent the rate prescribed for federal water project evaluation in 1978 by the Water Resources Council.

Project Costs

Project costs (Table 10.2) were determined from unpublished, field-level data provided by the Oklahoma Water Resources Board. No independent cost estimates were made. However, there is good reason to believe that this estimate is too low.

The cost data provided by the Water Resources Board were based on the average price of electricity in Oklahoma of 3 cents per kWh in 1978. It is doubtful that this is the correct shadow price of electricity, given the nature of public utility price determination, and federal controls on natural gas prices (natural gas is used extensively in Oklahoma to generate electricity). It is also doubtful that the relative real price of electricity would remain at 3 cents over the life of the project.

The SWCS would require 8.8 billion kWh of electricity per year when in full operation, an amount large enough relative to the projected state generating capacity that new capacity would have to be added to meet project demands. Thus, the cost of electricity for the project should at least be approximated by the cost per kWh from new generating plants in 1978.

Most observers identify coal as the most likely fuel for future electricity generation in Oklahoma. According to estimates provided by Schurr,[13] electricity from new coal-fired plants in the Southwest

185

Table 10.2   Oklahoma Statewide Water Conveyance System
             Project Costs (*Millions 1978 Dollars*)

Type of Cost	Undiscounted Cost
Construction	7,804.00
Oper., Main., Energy	9,992.00
Total	17,796.00

Discount Rate	Present Value of Total Cost
.035	6,792.99
.065	3,482.50
.09	2,284.18

Power Pool Region would cost from $.0367 to $.0422 per kWh (in 1978 dollars).

The price of electricity is not the only cost parameter requiring special attention. Virtually no work has been done to date on the environmental impact of the project. This is an omission of first-rate importance, but the effort involved did not seem justified in view of the otherwise large gaps (*see below*) between benefits and costs.

These field-level cost estimates also do not include the cost of conveying water from the terminal storage reservoirs to the farmers' fields. This is a significant omission, amounting to about $2150 per acre. Given the projected rate of water use per acre, the assumed project life, and an assumed interest rate of 6.5 percent, the cost of this project feature alone is over $15 for every acre-foot of water transferred.

There is a fourth problem worth mentioning: no allowance is made for the opportunity cost of the water that would be transferred. The implicit assumption here is that this water would have no value in alternative uses over the operating lifetime of the project. However, the project water may be useful for several other purposes including: navigation, hydroelectric power generation, recreational boating and swimming, municipal and industrial water supply, dilution of water pollutants, maintenance of the water-based ecology of rivers, bays, and estuaries, and fish and wildlife propagation. Water planners may attempt to minimize the opportunity cost of water withdrawals by restricting them to levels that would not interfere

Table 10.3   Oklahoma Statewide Water Conveyance System
Present Value of Benefits and Costs (*Millions 1978
Dollars*)

Discount Rate	Benefits	Costs	Benefits–Costs
.035	3,160.8	6,793.0	−3,632.2
.065	1,261.5	3,482.5	−2,221.0
.090	642.2	2,284.2	−1,642.0

with base flows necessary to maintain these other uses. Typically, however, there are serious disagreements over the adequacy of planned base flows.

The water that would be transferred by the northern component of the SWCS would come mainly from high spring flows of the Arkansas River. This type of scalping operation may interfere little with in-stream uses. However, potential effects on downstream users lie outside the jurisdiction of the sponsoring state, and it follows that this issue has not been adequately addressed.

A fifth reason for an underestimate of costs is the neglect of the real possibility that the agricultural production supported by this project would displace agricultural production elsewhere in the country. There is a social cost associated with this effect if land, labor, and capital in the areas where displacement occurs are rendered idle for extended periods of time.

Economic Feasibility

Would project benefits exceed costs? The comparison of benefits and costs requires the choice of an investment criterion. Table 10.3 illustrates how the elements in the preferred investment criterion, the present value of benefits minus the present value of costs, vary with the discount rate. Note that the value for this criterion is negative for all three discount rates, although less negative the larger the rate. This somewhat unusual relationship occurs because the SWCS has a large share of total costs paid out after operations begin.

Given that the costs included in this comparison are underestimated, and that household benefits are overestimated, the SWCS clearly looks like a losing proposition for the State of Oklahoma. At the very best, the pay-back will be no more than 46 cents on each dollar invested.

The principal problem is the same as the one pointed out previously by critics of the California Water Plan[14] and the Central Arizona Project[15]; namely, too much of the water is intended for irrigated agriculture, where the value of water is relatively low, and too little of the water is intended for household and industrial uses, where the value of water is relatively high.

The Arizona and California experiences show, however, that dismal economic prospects are not always enough to stop the development of water transfer projects. This seems to be especially true where proponents are successful, as they were in these states, in convincing voters that less water means less economic growth.

Many people in Oklahoma also believe that water is the key to economic growth. It is not fashionable in Oklahoma, however, to evoke the image of rapid population in-migration, as was done so successfully in Arizona and California. The argument is made instead that new water supplies will have such a large and widespread indirect impact on the state's economy that faster growth is inevitable. Indeed, this claim has such appeal to so many noneconomists that it requires careful examination.

Indirect (Secondary) Impact

In fact, the SWCS *would* produce a large indirect impact on the Oklahoma economy, as a result of the interindustry effects initiated by 1) purchases of materials, equipment, and services (including on-site labor) by construction firms; 2) changes in household choices in the face of rising water prices; 3) changes in the production of primary agricultural commodities, and 4) changes in industrial production. However, such impacts generate economic growth only to the extent that they produce a net increase in income, in which case the latter can also be included on the benefit side of the project evaluation ledger. The tasks, then, are to estimate the size of this indirect impact and to determine how much of it constitutes a net increase in income.

Indirect impacts were estimated with the aid of the Liew and Liew input-output model[16] and its associated value-added multipliers. Two types of impacts were estimated: those initiated by changes in final demand, and those initiated by changes in supply. The first type is what Howe and Easter[17] refer to as backward linkages only; the second type is an example of forward linkages.

In both cases, type II value-added multipliers were combined with ultimate changes in final demand to determine the indirect change in value added. The latter is an estimate of the indirect impact of the transfer project.

Backward Linkages Only. Changes in final demand for the backward-linkages case were examined for each type of primary impact: construction,[18] agricultural, industrial, and household.

In the industrial and agricultural cases, all production in excess of interindustry requirements was considered an increase in final demand.

In the household case, two possibilities were considered: 1) that households would change their pattern of expenditures on goods and services in the face of rising water prices, and 2) that they would change their place of residence. Impacts of the first relationship proved impossible to determine without more time and resources than were available. However, this impact would probably be quite small, because reductions in household nonwater expenditures would be matched by government expenditure of additional receipts from water sales.

Whether households would change their place of residence in the face of rising water prices is unknown. However, their response probably depends on how much they would have to pay for water relative to their income. Even with a perfectly inelastic supply curve for household water, the typical household water bill would constitute less than 2 percent of average household income by the year 2040. Thus, the location effect is likely to be virtually zero.

Forward Linkages. Impacts initiated by changes in final demand, although significant, are usually smaller than impacts initiated by changes in supply. Supply-induced impacts exist at the state level, however, only if the expansion of an industry would be constrained by a shortage of state-produced inputs.

In this case, study of technical and trade coefficients indicated two *potential* bottlenecks in the absence of the SWCS. The more important of these is the possibility that the region's cattle feedlots could not otherwise obtain feedgrains and alfalfa hay. The less important is the possibility that regional cotton gins and compresses would cease to operate without the water provided by the SWCS.

There is little doubt that such linkages would accompany an increase in crop production. It does not necessarily follow, however, that they can be attributed to interbasin water transfer. For forward linkages to be credited to the SWCS, they must pass the "with-

without" test. That is, they count only if they would be present *with* the project but *not* present *without* the project. One of the two potential forward linkages passes this test; the other probably does not.

There is actually a potential *two-stage* forward linkage for feed-grains: from feedgrains to feedlots, and from feedlots to meat processing. The linkage from feedlots to meat processing may pass the "with-without" test in the sense that meat will not be imported in large quantities for processing in the absence of locally produced fat cattle, nor will fat cattle be shipped very far for processing in an age of packaged beef and refrigeration. However, a forward linkage between feedgrains and feedlots is so uncertain that the feedlot–meat processing linkage cannot be credited to the SWCS.

If there were a decrease in the production of feedgrains on the southern High Plains, it is likely that feedlot output would be very little affected. Although feedgrains are an important input for feedlots, the comparative advantage enjoyed by this region in feedlot operations is only partly due to the availability of local feedgrains. Even more important are the region's advantages in terms of a relatively dry and mild climate, the ready availability of feeder cattle, well-developed financing and marketing institutions, and accessible markets for fed cattle.[19] Also, there is a high likelihood that wheat, which is now largely shipped out of the region, will become a good substitute for grain sorghum and corn—the region's principal feed-grains historically.

These factors suggest that the region's feedlot industry will continue to grow without the expansion of irrigated agriculture. Indeed, the region's locational advantages have by now been so clearly demonstrated that grain sorghum would be imported from the northern High Plains if there were a shortage of it on the southern High Plains. Feedlot operators in the latter region have always imported corn, and would continue to do so in the absence of the SWCS.

In the case of cotton, regional cotton ginning, compressing, and warehousing activity would decline in the same proportion as the decline in cotton production; cotton would not be shipped into the area for basic processing. If cotton production were to increase there would be an increase in ginning and compressing in the same proportion; cotton would not be shipped out of the area for basic processing. Thus, cotton ginning and compressing pass the with-without test for forward linkages. However, these activities add little value to har-

Table 10.4   Oklahoma Statewide Water Conveyance System:
Present Value of Indirect Impact with Forward and
Backward Linkages (*Millions 1978 Dollars*)

Discount Rate	Backward Linkage Only	Forward Linkage Only	Total Indirect Impact
.035	4,428.9	6,536.0	10,964.9
.065	2,197.4	3,242.8	5,440.2
.090	1,337.2	1,973.5	3,310.7

vested cotton (20–25 percent), and the increase in cotton production accounts for only a small part of the benefits attributable to the SWCS. Thus, it is unlikely that a full accounting for this linkage would add much to the indirect impact of the project.

Still, it is instructive to estimate the indirect impact associated with both types of linkages as a means of illustrating what is at stake for evaluators. These impacts were estimated using techniques developed by Howe and Easter.[20] The results are listed in Table 10.4.

It is easy to see from this table why the relevance of forward linkages is such a critical issue, and why the indirect impact argument is so attractive to project proponents.

A comparison of the estimates in Table 10.4 with those in Table 10.3 shows that the sum of total indirect impacts and project benefits would exceed project costs. The sum of project benefits and indirect impacts from backward linkages, alone, exceeds project costs at a discount rate of 3.5 percent, and virtually equals project costs at a discount rate of 6.5 percent.

Indirect impacts can be added to benefits and compared with project costs, however, only insofar as they are estimates of a *net* increase in income. In a fully employed economy where resources have alternative uses, incomes associated with indirect impacts will be virtually offset by income that would have been created anyway by the indirect impacts associated with alternative resource uses. Thus, those who claim an impact on economic growth from the SWCS can do so only if the project serves as a means of generating jobs for the otherwise unemployed.

How high would unemployment rates have to be to make benefits as large as costs? High enough that the gap between benefits and costs would be offset by the net increase in income attributable to indirect impacts. The required unemployment rates were calculated using a labor supply response function developed by Haveman and Krutilla, which associates rates of unemployment with probabilities of using otherwise unemployed labor.[21] These calculations indicate that if backward linkages only are relevant, long-run unemployment rates would have to range from 16 to 25 percent (for discount rates of 3.5 and 6.5 percent). If forward linkages also count, the required unemployment rates range from 9 to 14 percent (for discount rates of 3.5 to 9.0 percent).

None of these unemployment scenarios seems likely, and it is difficult to escape the conclusion that the SWCS would not usher in an era of economic growth for Oklahoma.[22] Indeed, its construction and operation would be more likely to impoverish the economy; *i.e.*, consign it to a lower growth path than one it could achieve in the absence of the project.

Of course, the failure of the SWCS to pass a benefit-cost test is no guarantee that project proponents will be dissuaded from their quest for support. There was ample evidence before they were built that the California Aqueduct and the Central Arizona Project would fail the same test. When all is said and done, a benefit-cost analysis is only one among many inputs in the political process—and not necessarily a very effective one in the face of powerful vested interests.

Thus, the determination of whether there will be large-scale water transfer in the Southwest's future involves more than economics. One must venture into the realm of distributive water politics. The Oklahoma experience again is illustrative.

WATER TRANSFER POLITICS IN OKLAHOMA

Oklahoma as well as most southwestern states has been quite successful in attracting resources for water resource development through the political process, especially at the federal level. There is reason to believe that future decisions will be made this way as well. However, several factors suggest that large-scale water transfer is unlikely to be an outcome of this process, at least in the foreseeable future, and in most cases, these factors are present in the water politics of other states in the Southwest.

Basin-of-Origin Opposition. There is evidence of considerable opposition to east-west water transfer in eastern Oklahoma. To western Oklahomans water is a requirement to preserve farming, to maintain the region's economic base; in other words, water transfer is this region's salvation. To eastern Oklahomans, water is required to spur recreation and industrial development in a region marked by poverty and high unemployment; water transfer is this region's affirmation of the adage that the rich get richer and the poor get poorer.

Water planners pose the issue as one of transferring surplus water. Eastern Oklahomans pose the issue as a transfer of basic wealth. One needs little imagination to guess their reaction to the study results reported above, which imply that they would have to subsidize such a transfer with their tax dollars as well.

It is this last point that may serve as the focus of the strongest opposition. Eastern Oklahoma's water resource infrastructure falls far short of meeting projected needs,[23] and it is not uncommon for communities in this region to suffer water shortages during droughts. This will probably trigger a movement in future legislatures to "keep the tax dollars at home" for use in solving the region's own problems—a movement likely to succeed, moreover, given the historical strength of eastern Oklahoma in the state legislature. Regional rivalries are also a part of the water politics of California, Texas, and other southwestern states.

Out-of-State Opposition. Although the SWCS is a state project, its physical effects would spill over into adjoining states. The northern portion of the project would intercept flood waters that would otherwise flow down the Arkansas and Mississippi Rivers to the Gulf of Mexico. The southern portion would intercept water that would normally flow down the Red River on its way, also, to the Mississippi delta.

It would be a surprise, indeed, if there were no downstream interests adversely affected by these diversions. What is "surplus" water to Oklahoma is less likely to be "surplus" to downstream beneficiaries of these flows. Individuals, communities, and industries outside Oklahoma currently use water from the affected streams for a variety of purposes, and some of this water also contributes to the maintenance of a rich natural environment.

The potential for interstate conflict is probably not as great in this case as it was for the Central Arizona Project, given the greater margin here between appropriable and appropriated flow. However, several states' interests are involved, and environmental groups are much better organized now than they were two decades ago. Moreover, Oklahoma has yet to take any meaningful steps to engage in a serious dialogue with its neighbors on these matters.

Prospects for Federal Assistance. Federal dollars have played a vital role in the development of Oklahoma's water resources. With their aid, for example, Oklahoma has gained an inland seaport (the Port of Catoosa, just outside Tulsa), and created more inland lake shoreline than all but three other states. It is unlikely, however, that federal money will be available for the financing of the SWCS.

We mentioned above that the Bureau of Reclamation bowed out as a potential project sponsor nearly two decades ago as a result of its own benefit-cost calculations. The results of the SWCS study will surely reinforce its perception of the wisdom of that decision.

The Corps of Engineers, on the other hand, has a full agenda of other projects in Oklahoma, including a large-scale effort well under way to remove the natural chlorides from the Red River. There are signs, moreover, that their future efforts—encouraged by key members of Oklahoma's congressional delegation—will be focused largely on helping eastern Oklahoma to realize its potential from development of its own water resources.

Furthermore, as we have seen in Chapter 6 and elsewhere in this book, most analysts feel the days of federal generosity in funding new water projects have passed.

Desire to Diversify. Oklahoma's economy, like that of other states in the Southwest, has traditionally been heavily dependent on agriculture, oil, and natural gas. The state has suffered greatly from this dependence in recent years, and there is almost universal acknowledgment of the need to diversify, to develop sectors whose fortunes are likely to rise steadily in the economy of the future.

The other side of this coin is the waning support for the development of the traditional sectors, such as agriculture. Even if this sector were to experience a remarkable resurgence, the lessons of the last decade are going to be long remembered and will dampen the electorate's enthusiasm for large-scale development of irrigated agriculture.

Ability to Finance. The plans for the SWCS were undoubtedly spurred by the tremendous growth in state government revenues that Oklahoma experienced in the 1970s as a result of the OPEC-inspired boom in oil and gas prices. It was possible then to imagine that the state could someday afford to make up the difference between what users could pay and the project costs, either out of annual tax revenues or from a trust fund financed out of earmarked severance taxes on oil and gas.

However, the energy-price bust of the 1980s initiated a large decline in state revenues, and created a backlog of unmet needs in all areas of government spending. These events clearly exposed the inherent instability of the state's severance taxes, and strengthened the hand of advocates for other types of state expenditures, such as education and highways. It is probably going to be some time before very many people would argue that Oklahoma taxpayers could finance something like the SWCS.

Diminished Sense of Urgency. One of the primary products of waiting to build the SWCS has been the provision over time of better information about the nature of the problem and peoples' ability to cope with it. We have to understand, for one thing, that depletion of the Ogallala will be quite gradual, allowing a long lead time for adjustment on the part of farmers, business owners, and families. More importantly, however, we have learned that there is great potential for water conservation in irrigated agriculture, and that farmers will adopt new technologies and practices when it is in their economic interest to do so.[24]

Knowledge of these facts is not yet widespread outside the immediately affected areas. However, there is no reason to believe they will remain unknown when the effort is made once more to revive interest in something like the Oklahoma Statewide Water Conveyance System.

OTHER DISTRIBUTION SYSTEMS
PROPOSED FOR THE SOUTHWEST

As indicated above, proposals for large-scale, east-west water transfers have also been made to replace declining groundwater stocks in the Texas and New Mexico portions of the Ogallala aquifer. The most recent of these are the two routes identified by the Corps of Engineers, depicted as C and D in Figure 1. Although these routes have not been subjected to a benefit-cost analysis it is possible to make some inferences about the likely outcome of such analyses from the results reported above for the SWCS.

Both routes would be similar to the SWCS in that they would require long-distance transmission of large quantities of water, gen-

Table 10.5   Comparison of Transfer Project Costs (*1978 Dollars*)

Route	Annual Yield (Thousand Acre Feet)	Cost per Acre Foot
SWCS	2,510	222
C	1,850–6,040	434–597[a,b]
D	1,550–8,700	308–370[a]

Sources: SWCS—Oklahoma Comprehensive Water Plan (1980)
C and D—High Plains Associates (1982)
a: Smaller cost corresponds to larger yield.
b: Costs for route C–3, the lowest cost alternative.

erally in an uphill direction. To achieve this, each project would require a series of large pumping plants using enormous amounts of electricity.

The Corps of Engineers has not estimated the benefits of these projects, but the Corps has produced an estimate of project costs, expressed per acre-foot of water transferred. These costs are displayed in Table 10.5, along with the per-acre equivalent of the costs reported for the SWCS. Column Three shows that there are economies of scale in water transfer, a factor not considered by the planners of the SWCS.

Water provided by routes C and D would greatly increase the region's crop production. Irrigated acreage would expand by 11–24 percent between 1978 and 2020, and net returns to farmers would rise by 8–14 percent over this same period from annual application of the first 1,250,000 acre-feet. Additional, but undetermined, increases in irrigated acreage and net returns would accompany larger amounts transferred.

The analysis of the SWCS indicated benefits to farmers from that project of $73 per acre-foot of water (at a discount rate of 6.5 percent). Similar benefits would be realized from water transferred via Route C, which would provide water to areas in Texas and New Mexico with crop-growing potential similar to that in the areas receiving water from the SWCS.

Benefits from water delivered to farmers have not been estimated for Route D. However, the High Plains Study contains estimates of benefits per acre for water transferred to the entire High Plains, arranged by amount and acreage, from which an estimate can be deduced.[25]

It is well documented that benefits from irrigation generally increase as one moves south from the Oklahoma Panhandle toward the fertile cotton lands of Texas—*i.e.*, toward the land likely to be served by Route D. Thus, as a first, but high approximation, Route D is assumed to provide water to the farmers who could realize the highest net returns, or benefits, on the High Plains. Calculations based on data provided in the High Plains Study indicate that these benefits would average from $150 to $175 per acre-foot.

Given these estimates, the economic feasibility of Routes C and D appears to depend on the relevance and size of indirect impacts, just as it did for the SWCS. As in that case, the impacts would undoubtedly be large, but the increase generated in net income would be only a small portion of the impact.

The Texas Panhandle is a major locus of feedlot activity, so there are potential forward linkages from feedgrain production to feedlots to meat processing. As in Oklahoma, however, these linkages would not require that water be transferred to the region; the Texas Panhandle also has locational advantages for feedlots that outweigh the region's advantage in producing feedgrains.

A forward linkage from cotton harvesting to initial processing can be attributed to Route D, and backward linkages are relevant for both projects. Given the wide margin between costs and benefits per acre-foot reported above, however, project feasibility could probably be assured only by unrealistically high unemployment rates, as in the Oklahoma case.

This is about as far as one can go in applying the economic prospects for the SWCS to these other routes. It is far enough to suggest that transfer proponents may have to sell these projects on the basis of noneconomic considerations, but of course a more definite analysis is needed to determine this for sure.

However, this may be imputing too much, once again, to the power of economic analysis as a tool of political persuasion. The fate of water transfers anywhere in the Southwest in the future will undoubtedly depend on their political prospects, independent of their inherent economic desirability.

NOTES

1. High Plains Associates, *Six-State High Plains Ogallala Aquifer Regional Resources Study*, Austin, Texas, July 1982, chap. 6.

2. U.S. Department of the Interior, Bureau of Reclamation, *Water: The Key to Oklahoma's Future*, Oklahoma City, October 1966.

3. Texas Water Development Board, *The Texas Water Plan*, Austin, Texas, 1968.

4. Oklahoma Water Resources Board, *Oklahoma Comprehensive Water Plan*, Oklahoma City, Oklahoma, 1980.

5. U.S. Army Corps of Engineers, Southwestern Division, *Six–State High Plains Ogallala Aquifer Regional Resources Study, Water Transfer Elements* (Appendixes A–E), Dallas, Texas, September 1982.

6. The final results of this evaluation are reported in Kent W. Olson, *Statewide Water Conveyance System—Net Benefit Analysis*, Oklahoma State University, Office of Business and Economic Research, 1980. These results are based on the findings of two companion studies: Chong K. Liew and Chung J. Liew, *The Economic Effects of a Projected Water Shortage on Oklahoma's Future*, University of Oklahoma, Center for Economic and Management Research, 1980; and D. Kletke, J. Warren, D. Ray, H. Mapp, and C. Wang, *Effects of a Cross–State Water Transfer on Irrigated Agriculture in Oklahoma*, Oklahoma State University, Department of Agricultural Economics, 1980.

7. Oklahoma Water Resources Board, *op. cit.*

8. Olson, *op. cit.*

9. Kletke, *et al., op. cit.*

10. Liew and Liew, *op. cit.*

11. Edward M. Gramlich, *Benefit–Cost Analysis of Government Programs*, Englewood Cliffs, N.J.: Prentice-Hall, Inc., 1981, pp. 101–7.

12. James A. Seagraves, "More on the Social Rate of Discount," *Quarterly Journal of Economics*, 84(30), 1970, pp. 430–50.

13. Sam H. Schurr, *Energy in America's Future*, Baltimore: Johns Hopkins University Press, 1979, p. 275.

14. Joe S. Bain, Richard E. Caves, and Julius Margolis, *Northern California's Water Industry*, Baltimore: Johns Hopkins University Press, 1966; Jack Hirschleifer, James C. DeHaven, and Jerome W. Milliman, *Water Supply: Economics, Technology, and Policy*, Chicago: University of Chicago Press, 1969.

15. William E. Martin, "Economic Magnitudes and Economic Alternatives in Lower Basin Use of Colorado River Water," *Natural Resources Journal*, 15, 1975.

16. Liew and Liew, *op. cit.*

17. Charles W. Howe, and K. William Easter, *Interbasin Transfers of Water*, Baltimore: Johns Hopkins University Press, 1971.

18. The techniques used to allocate construction expenditures are from Robert H. Haveman, and John V. Krutilla, *Unemployment, Idle Capacity,*

and the Evaluation of Public Expenditures, Baltimore: Johns Hopkins University Press, 1968.

19. C. B. Thompson, "The Future of Cattle Feeding," in G. B. Thompson and C. C. O'Mary, *The Feedlot,* 3d Ed., Philadelphia: Lea and Febiger, 1983, pp. 285–96.

20. Howe and Easter, *op. cit.*

21. Haveman and Krutilla, *op. cit.*

22. The required unemployment rates are those high enough to ensure that the project will use just enough resources with a shadow price of zero. Since it is likely that the true, but unknown shadow price exceeds zero, the rates reported here are an underestimate of the true required rates.

23. This point is clearly documented in the *Oklahoma Comprehensive Water Plan,* Oklahoma Water Resources Board, *op. cit.,* chap. 7.

24. "Aquifer Depletion Rate Levels," *The Cross Section,* 31(3), 1985, pp. 1, 3.

25. High Plains Associates, *op. cit.,* 6–88, 6–89.

11 The Federal Interest in Flexible Interstate Water Allocation in the Southwest

John Merrifield

Budget-cutting pressure, high construction costs, and the small number of remaining potential reservoir sites[1] are forcing water resource managers to shift from structural approaches to increase supplies,[2] to demand management and the redistribution of existing supplies. Current institutional arrangements in the Southwest may be incapable of meeting that challenge. Much has been written about the institutional (legal) barriers to the transfer of water rights within particular states (see, for example, Chapters 1 and 2 of this volume.) However, very little has been written about barriers to interstate water transfers and their economic cost. The purpose of this chapter is to shed some light on the future cost of such barriers and the implications of those barriers to efficient water management in the future of the Southwest. There are many social goods other than economic efficiency, but efficiency losses that result from the pursuit of other goals ought to be known.

The major river basin of the Southwest, the watershed of the Colorado River, includes Arizona, California, Nevada (lower basin), Colorado, New Mexico, Utah, and Wyoming (upper basin). The analysis in this chapter is limited to the laws,[3] starting with the Colorado River Compact of 1922, that assign each state a share of the river's annual flow. According to former Utah Senator Frank Moss, "the compact allotted each basin a share for all time to come."[4] Perhaps each state's share was also intended to be "for all time to come"? It's not surprising to hear "[I]t is a widespread belief that insurmountable legal impediments prevent states from selling their water."[5] Hirshleifer *et al.* admit " . . . there is at least the theoretical possibility of interstate or even international purchase of water rights . . . "; but suggest "a higher-order political rigidity makes it commonly impossible for one water jurisdiction to sell title or rights to another."[6]

Another reason for failure to question the method of determining the interstate distribution of water is that " . . . the consideration of efficient interregional allocation of resources and output, from the standpoint of national welfare, has few spokespersons."[7] Indeed, only the president has anything like a national constituency, and even he is elected by carrying individual states. Therefore, it's likely that water allocations never did reflect national economic efficiency concerns, and the allocations are certainly not efficient once they are decades old. Now that full appropriation of the river is at hand, the cost of ignoring economic efficiency concerns will become more evident. National income would be higher if market-based reallocations were feasible. If it becomes apparent that the barriers to interstate transfers are costly, existing policies should be reviewed.

Another cost of barriers to interstate water transfers is the construction of economically unwise water projects (*i.e.*, when benefits are less than costs). According to Keith *et al.*, "the desire of states to claim their full share has led to several reclamation projects that might not have been justified on either economic or egalitarian grounds. The feeling is that Utah must claim 'her water' at any cost."[8] Hirshleifer *et al.* agree that barriers provide "an incentive to rush into construction to nail down the supplies involved." That issue will receive no further attention here. Also, the unresolved federal reserved water rights issue is largely ignored (see Burton, Chapter 9, and McCool, Chapter 7, of this volume for a discussion). Quantification of those rights could impose another constraint on water transfers.

In the next section current allocations of Colorado River water and their legal foundations are defined. In the following section, some data are presented. These support the assertion of Gardner that the value of water varies significantly among the Colorado Basin states.[9] Therefore, market-based interstate water reallocations would increase national income. The section concludes with a brief discussion of how market mechanisms could be implemented to facilitate such reallocations. Water value measurement difficulties are discussed in the next section. Trends that could change the cost of tolerating transfer barriers are then discussed. A summary and conclusions are presented in the last section.

THE INSTITUTIONAL FRAMEWORK

The Colorado River Compact of 1922, the nation's first interstate stream compact, split the basin's estimated annual flow between the lower and upper basin states. The compact provided that the lower basin states receive 75 million acre-feet of water at Lee Ferry, Arizona, during every ten-year period.[10] Actually, the lower basin has received 7.5 million acre-feet (maf) each year, plus 0.75 maf for the upper basin share of Mexico's annual allotment of 1.5 maf.[11] During compact negotiations, it was believed that the upper basin states would also divide up 7.5 maf annually, but estimated average flows have since been revised downward.[12] The Bureau of Reclamation estimates that flows available to the upper basin range from 5.8 to 6.5 maf.[13] Cummings and McFarland suggest an even smaller lower bound; an annual *average* of 5.25 maf (4.75 maf with evaporation losses), with the upper basin share ranging from 1.85 to 8.65 maf per year 68 percent of the time.[14]

After sending 0.05 maf to the upper basin slice of Arizona, the upper basin states share the available flow according to the following negotiated percentages. Colorado, New Mexico, Utah, and Wyoming are entitled to consume 51.75 percent, 11.25 percent, 23 percent, and 14 percent, respectively.[15] Upper basin water is about 1 maf from full appropriation[16] and should reach full appropriation in the early 1990s.[17]

Nearly all lower basin water is in use. California, Arizona, and Nevada are entitled to 4.4, 2.8, and 0.3 maf, but completion of the Central Arizona Project (CAP) will cut available water to 4.0, 2.5, and 0.29 maf, respectively.[18] The shares are still a matter of some dispute among the lower basin states.[19] Generally, the Colorado River is 120 percent committed and 85 percent used.[20]

SOME PRELIMINARY EVIDENCE

Unfortunately a reliable estimate or forecast of the national income loss due to the rigidity of the interstate allocations would require that demand for Colorado River water by irrigated agriculture (the lowest valued and dominant water consumer) be estimated in each basin state. Water is not allocated by markets, however, so water prices and marginal value are not directly observable. Furthermore, the data that would be needed to estimate value aren't readily available, so a reliable estimate is beyond the scope of this paper. Some of the problems that would be encountered in the course of an estimation effort are discussed in the next section.

Irrigated agriculture is the dominant consumer and marginal (lowest value) user of Colorado River water in every state except Nevada.[21] Therefore, national income losses depend only on interstate differences in the marginal value (adjusted for transportation costs) of water for irrigation. If transfer barriers were removed, marginal values (and prices), adjusted for transportation costs and return flow considerations, would eventually converge to a single value for all basin states. With effectively equal prices in each basin state, higher value water users (mines, industries, and municipalities, for example) would motivate interstate transfers only when their increased demand for water meant that irrigators in their own states could profitably buy water from irrigators in other basin states.

The data in Table 11.1 suggest, but don't prove, that the marginal value of water differs significantly among basin states. Care must be taken in interpreting the data. There are several reasons why crop value per acre-foot numbers (Table 1, column 4, dollars per acre-foot, $/af) don't represent water's value. Water is but one of many inputs that contribute to crop value. Furthermore, the numbers are an indication of the average crop value per acre-foot, rather than marginal value. A competitive market price for water would reflect the addition to or subtraction (marginal change) from crop value that could be expected to follow a change in water available of one unit.

Despite the data limitations, significant patterns are evident. With the possible exception of Utah, irrigation water is more valuable in the lower basin states of Arizona and California than in the upper basin states. According to Welsh, a considerable amount of potentially irrigable land is available in the lower basin, much of it quite close to the river.[23] Utah's $/af numbers appear to be inflated relative to the other states because a bigger share of Utah's Colorado River water is used to supplement irrigation water from other sources. Curtailment of some deliveries in 1983 and 1984, combined with unusually heavy precipitation, seems to have further inflated Utah's 1983 and 1984 $/af numbers. Loss of supplemental water in

Table 11.1   Value of Crops Irrigated by Colorado River Water by State

		Crop Value	Value/ Irrig Acre	Allocated (af)	$/af
Arizona	1982	$380,395,669	$1,239.91	1,614,234	$235.65
	1983	$334,771,133	$1,235.08	1,556,270	$215.11
	1984	$376,310,736	$1,284.81	1,585,486	$237.34
California	1982	$568,268,900	$1,005.45	2,649,928	$214.45
	1983	$815,211,244	$1,537.38	2,525,372	$322.81
	1984	$912,445,247	$1,747.75	2,733,535	$333.80
Colorado	1982	$49,190,444	$226.85	669,848	$73.44
	1983	$63,542,777	$294.10	616,145	$103.13
	1984	$58,460,092	$335.90	673,974	$86.74
New Mexico	1982	$991,818	$293.35	18,365	$54.01
	1983	$870,415	$253.40	15,893	$54.77
	1984	$1,085,526	$351.19	16,570	$65.51
Utah	1982	$120,822,011	$335.27	422,892	$285.70
	1983	$147,763,076	$395.08	224,267	$658.87
	1984	$140,547,285	$366.32	223,099	$629.97
Wyoming	1982	$3,687,000	$67.74	67,948	$54.26
	1983	$3,833,053	$70.37	60,774	$63.07
	1984	$4,294,369	$79.12	63,850	$67.26

Note: Nevada is omitted because its small water allocation will soon be committed to non-agricultural uses.

Source: U.S. Bureau of Reclamation, 1982, 1983, and 1984. Summary Statistics (Volume 1): Water, Land, and Related Data. Department of the Interior, Denver.

wet years will have only a minor impact on crop value (column 1 in Table 1) or value per acre (column 2 in Table 1).

Generally, smaller upper basin crop values (per acre and per maf) are consistent with its smaller share of irrigated acreage in cropland and the lower basin's richer soil and longer growing seasons.[24] Cropland accounts for 79.5 percent, 82.2 percent, 68.0 percent, and 71.7 percent of the irrigated acreage in Colorado, New Mexico, Wyoming, and Utah, respectively.[25] The cropland percentages are smaller in the parts of those states served from the Colorado River Basin. Noncropland irrigated acreage is virtually all pastureland. A small fraction of each state's acreage is labeled "other." In California and Arizona, cropland accounts for 91.7 percent and 89.6 percent of irrigated acreage, respectively. Smaller upper basin water values are also consistent with the availability of some unclaimed upper basin water.

Even though precise water value data are not revealed by Table 1, differences between upper and lower basin values appear to be large. Indeed, the gaps appear to be large enough to survive some downward adjustment for transportation costs, in-transit evaporation losses, the sunk capital costs of large water projects, and the higher percentage of return flows (allowing water reuse) from upper basin water deliveries. Since the amount of water irrigators want to purchase is believed to be very price sensitive (elastic), even small differences in water value among basin states would motivate very large market-based or federal government-mandated interstate transfers.[26]

Markets and decentralized decision-making would be preferable to further government intervention in water allocation decision-making. Such a change in water management institutions would not occur quickly or without considerable political trauma (see De Young and Jenkins-Smith, Chapter 12, for the details), especially in light of the considerable misinformation surrounding the expanded use of markets. The consequences of not doing so would be even more traumatic. For without market price data, it is difficult and expensive to maintain current information on the value of water. Therefore, even the most politically independent, well-meaning and well-informed officials will make errors. Their ability to make (and periodically reconsider) the appropriate trade-offs between often conflicting goals such as equity, stability, and economic efficiency would be greatly impaired. Government-mandated reallocations will involve involuntary exchange and will create conflict whenever water is taken from someone who doesn't agree with the government's definition of "just compensation." Also, the current situation demonstrates that many of the government's outdated institutional arrangements continue to survive and even grow, including some that were never appropriate. Thus new forms of government intervention and the resulting reallocations might ultimately be no better than the old.

Anderson has explained in detail the changes that would have to precede a successful larger role for market mechanisms in water reallocation decisions.[27] Transfers must be truly voluntary—that is, on a willing buyer and seller basis. Rights to appropriate water must be divisible, owned outright separate from land, and should be defined in terms of consumptive use. The much-reduced government role would include collecting hydrologic data, pollution control, processing third-party impairment claims, and perhaps the purchase of some water rights for public-good functions of water. Defining rights in terms of consumptive use would by itself eliminate many third-party impairment claims. Beneficial use tests and use-it-or-lose-it requirements should be eliminated. They would reduce the rights of ownership and thereby distort market prices, and they would no longer perform any useful function. If water rights are transferable, owners will sell whatever is worth more on the market than it is to them.

VALUE MEASUREMENT PROBLEMS

In the absence of market prices (usually the case), the most acceptable method of water valuation is residual imputation.[28] The cost of all resource inputs except water is subtracted from total crop value. What's left is the imputed value of water. The marginal and average value of a unit of water is determined by dividing the imputed value by the quantity used. Accuracy of the value estimates depends on the degree to which the price of other resource inputs reflects their marginal value (the change in total value of output is achieved by using the last unit of a resource input), market distortions in the valuation of output (like crop price supports), and the assumption that water's average value is the same as its marginal value.

Several sources of measurement error are implied in the preceding sentence. Because of return flows, some diverted water is used more than once. Many relevant crop prices are artificially high because of price support programs. One resource input, entrepreneurial skills and farm labor supplied by landowners, is often not explicitly assigned a price, and if one is assigned, it may not reflect its marginal value. There is no assurance that water's marginal value is equal to its average value. For several reasons, including the doctrine of prior appropriation, the marginal value of water is likely to be lower.

During low flow periods under prior appropriation, only the most senior rights can be exercised. Senior rights holders receive their entire entitlement before remaining appropriators receive anything. The last acre-foot received by the senior use contributes less to total output than would an extra acre-foot for users at the end of the list, who receive little or no water. Since junior rights holders are less certain of deliveries occurring each year, they tend to build smaller diversion facilities and so use less water than their identical neighbors (marginal values are then different) even when water is plentiful.[29]

Another source of uncertainty—and therefore another distortion of water diversion and use decisions and value calculations—is that in some basin states (Arizona, for example), water rights do not represent fee simple ownership. Instead they are rights to use that can be regulated or taken. Because of the uncertain nature of ownership benefits, the price an irrigator would be willing to pay for a right to divert water would not fully reflect its marginal value.

Alternate supply cost pricing is sometimes used to measure the marginal value of water. The cost of replacing an existing water supply with water from the next best source is the assigned marginal value of the existing supply. For instance, Welsh suggested that Arizona abandon the CAP, and instead sell the water to California.[30] The large sum assumed to be generated by such a sale was based on the assertion that water from an expansion of California's state water project would be replaced. California may prove to be willing to pay hundreds of dollars per acre-foot to import more water instead of paying a fraction of that amount to buy water from local irrigators, but, generally speaking, it would be unwise to base value measurements on economic irrationality. The usually erroneous assumption underlying alternate supply cost pricing is that irrigators would still buy the same amount of water at the higher price of the alternate supply source. The immense subsidization of irrigation water supplies throughout the West has discredited that assumption.

TRENDS AFFECTING INTERSTATE
DIFFERENCES IN WATER VALUE

This section would have been much easier to write prior to 1987. If written then it would have stated that development of the fossil fuel resources of the upper basin would more than likely shrink, if not erase, the gap between upper and lower basin water values. By buying some irrigation water rights, energy developers would have driven up the marginal value of remaining irrigation water. However, the crash in oil prices early in 1986 has at least postponed, and perhaps completely averted, that outcome.

The future course of fossil fuel prices will be an important determinant of the relative value of water in Colorado River Basin states (see Castberg, Chapter 13, for a more in-depth discussion). Previous large errors in energy price forecasts have shown that making such prognostications is a risky business. The future course of energy prices is uncertain, with oil prices again likely to lead the way. The raw data on worldwide oil reserves suggest that the increased consumption that followed the recent plunge in prices is likely to concentrate half of the remaining reserves in the hands of Persian Gulf OPEC members by the end of the century.[31] Given the political instability common to the Middle East, it seems safe to say that energy prices will rise again. However, all-important price stability at higher levels is less certain. Instead, prices may rise and fall as periods of calm alternate with political upheavals.

Without fairly stable higher energy prices, the upper basin's population growth, even in percentage terms, is unlikely to keep up with the lower basin. The combination of a warmer climate and an aging population suggest continued brisk population growth in the lower basin states. In this scenario, water value differences between the upper and lower basin states grow larger.

Crop price changes will be major determinants of water value levels. To the degree that different states specialize in different crops, crop price changes will influence interstate differences in the marginal value of water. If President Reagan's successor could be assumed to share his wish to phase out crop price subsidy programs, a reduction in the price of many directly supported crops and their closer substitutes would be anticipated, at least until stockpiles are cut. Persistent budget-cutting pressures on any new administration would at least suggest that crop subsidy programs will, at most, be maintained at current levels.

Still unquantified federal reserved water rights are not evenly distributed among the basin states (see Burton, Chapter 9, for a discussion of the status of American Indian claims). Once quantified, if they are not readily transferable at least within states, differences among basin states in the value of remaining, nonfederal reserve water rights could be greatly affected. Barriers to water transfers within states have received much more analytic scrutiny than interstate transfer barriers, but that has not made the intrastate barriers any less formidable.

SUMMARY AND CONCLUSIONS

The purpose of this chapter has been to suggest, and offer support for, the premise that national income would be higher in the absence of existing barriers to interstate water transfers. Barriers come in the form of interstate compacts negotiated by basin states, ratified by the Congress, and interpreted by the courts. Discussion has been limited to the compact, subsequent legislation, and court interpretations that govern the allocations to states of Colorado River water. Compacts are costly barriers because original negotiators and ratifiers and subsequent court interpreters gave little or no weight to national economic efficiency considerations, nor is there a periodic review process to take account of such considerations.

On the basis of physical factors (land quality, length of growing season), demographic trends (retirees moving to the Sunbelt), a temporary setback in fossil fuel developments in the upper basin, and some data on crop production on irrigated acreage, it appears that the marginal value of water is higher in the lower basin states of Arizona, California, and Nevada than in the upper basin states, and will remain so into the foreseeable future. The widespread belief that the amount of water irrigators will seek to purchase is very sensitive to its price suggests that even small differences among states in the marginal value of water would motivate large transfers of water.[32] Policymakers should be convinced to set up a system of water allocations that is flexible and responsive to market forces. Resistance to wider use of market mechanisms now could lead in the future to costly government intervention to establish new and perhaps rigid allocations of water in the Southwest.[33]

NOTES

1. G. Weatherford and H. Ingram, "Legal–Institutional Limitations on Water Use," in E. A. Engelbert and A. F. Scheuring (eds.), *Water Scarcity: Impacts on Western Agriculture* (Berkeley: University of California Press, 1984).

2. Some analysts have suggested that in the Colorado River Basin additional storage capacity will cost the basin more in evaporative losses than could be gained by the added capacity.

3. Subsequent and related litigation: Boulder Canyon Project Act of 1928, Arizona v. California (1963), Colorado River Basin Project Act of 1968, Mexican Water Treaty of 1944, and the Upper Colorado River Basin Compact of 1948. See M. B. Holburt, "Colorado River Water Allocation," *Water Supply and Management* 6 (Spring 1982), pp. 63–73.

4. F. E. Moss, *The Water Crisis*, (New York: Praeger, 1967), p. 80.

5. F. Welsh, *How to Create a Water Crisis* (Colorado: Johnson Publishing, 1985), p. 122.

6. J. Hirshleifer, J. C. DeHaven, and J. W. Milliman, *Water Supply: Economics, Technology and Policy* (Chicago: University of Chicago Press, 1970), pp. 333 and 369.

7. F. Giarratani and E. M. Hoover, *An Introduction to Regional Economics* (3rd ed.), (New York: Knopf, 1984), p. 355.

8. J. E. Keith *et al.*, "Western Economic Development and Water Planning: Bureau of Reclamation," *Journal of the Water Resources Planning and Management Division*, March 1979, pp. 161–70.

9. B. D. Gardner, "Institutional Impediments to Efficient Water Allocation," *Policy Studies Review* 5 (November 1985), pp. 353–63.

10. Holburt.

11. R. G. Cummings and J. W. McFarland, "Reservoir Management and the Water Scarcity Issue in the Upper Colorado River Basin," *Natural Resources Journal* 17 (January 1977), pp. 81–95.

12. H. S. Burness and J. P. Quirk, "Water Law, Water Transfers and Economic Efficiency: The Colorado River," *Journal of Law and Economics* 23 (April 1980), pp. 111–34.

13. J. C. Anderson and J. E. Keith, "Energy and the Colorado River," *National Resources Journal* 17 (April 1977), p. 157–68.

14. Cummings and McFarland.

15. Anderson and Keith.

16. Burness and Quirk.

17. Holburt.

18. Burness and Quirk.

19. *Ibid.* and Holburt.

20. L. P. Pringle, *Water: The Next Great Resource Battle* (New York: Macmillan, 1982).

21. M. M. Kelso, W. E. Martin, and L. E. Mack, *Water Supplies and Economic Growth in an Arid Environment: An Arizona Case Study* (Tucson: University of Arizona Press, 1973). Most of Nevada's small entitlement of less than 0.3 million acre-feet goes to municipal users. With continued urban growth, the marginal value of Colorado River water may soon be much

higher there than in any of the other basin states. Nevada is omitted from discussion of differences in the marginal value of water in irrigation.

22. U.S. Bureau of Reclamation, 1982, 1983, and 1984. Summary Statistics (vol. 1): Water, Land, and Related Data. Department of the Interior, Denver.

23. Welsh.

24. Burness and Quirk.

25. U.S. Census of Agriculture, 1978.

26. See Anderson and Keith; Kelso, Martin, and Mack.

27. T. L. Anderson, *Water Crisis: Ending the Policy Drought* (Maryland: Johns Hopkins University Press, 1983).

28. S. L. Gray and R. A. Young, "Economic Issues in Resolving Conflicts in Water Use," Colorado State University, Colorado Water Resources Research Institute, 1983.

29. Burness and Quirk.

30. Welsh.

31. C. Flavin, "World Oil: Coping with the Dangers of Success," Worldwatch Institute Paper No. 66 (1985).

32. Because the available data are but poor proxies for the appropriate data to back the preceding sentences, the conclusions reached can be readily disputed. An effort should be made to address the issues raised in the section concerning Value Measurement Problems and to generate better quality data.

33. I should like to acknowledge here the help I have received from various sources. Several University of Hawaii librarians (from both the Hilo and Manoa campuses) spent considerable time helping me locate relevant materials. Jay Anderson (Utah State University), Bruce Billings (University of Arizona), Ronald Cummings (University of New Mexico), Clynn Phillips (University of Wyoming), and Walt Eifert (University of Wyoming) all provided helpful suggestions, words of encouragement, and indispensable reference materials. However, the opinions expressed and the errors that may be present are the sole responsibility of the author.

12 Privatizing Water Management: The Hollow Promises of Private Markets

Tim De Young and
Hank Jenkins-Smith

Privatization has become a magic word in some circles. Its mere utterance can transform a hopelessly inefficient bureaucratic program into a golden opportunity for demonstrating the virtues of private ownership and free market exchange.[1] Water resources management in particular has been a popular target for privatization advocates, especially in the Southwest where costly public programs have heavily subsidized irrigated agriculture. For example, in the previous chapter John Merrifield argues, in part, for increased marketability and privatization. As the costs of developing additional supplies become unacceptable throughout the region and support for reclamation projects wanes, demands for the reallocation or transfer of water have grown. A persistent and increasingly popular reallocation approach is offered by an identifiable group of "new resource economists" whose vision of the future is predicated on the establishment of private markets. Such markets would be characterized by individual ownership of water rights, voluntary exchange by numerous buyers and sellers, and a government role limited to specification of water rights and enforcement of contracts.[2]

In our view, significant privatization of water allocation in the Southwest in the future seems improbable, if not undesirable. Water is a fugitive resource that often defies simple monetary valuation, a necessary prerequisite to market exchange. Moreover, opposition to private water market transactions can be expected from opponents who often have considerable political and legal resources at their disposal. In a sense, opposition to a private approach is reflected by the complex web of public institutions that control water throughout the Southwest and West. At the same time, increasing demands for relatively finite supplies of water highlight the need for policies that will both improve the efficiency of use and allow reallocation of water from lower to higher valued uses. It is our judgment that market-oriented policies will best fulfill these objectives, but it is not clear that either extensive private ownership of water rights or a negligible public sector role is necessary or even probable. The increasing popularity of the market-oriented approach among influential constituencies nonetheless suggests that market-style voluntary transactions will play an increasing role in water allocation in the Southwest.

Total privatization of water allocation thus appears to be an exaggerated but not entirely inaccurate vision of the future. In the following sections, we try to bring this vision into focus by looking more closely at the privatization scenario and the potential sources of opposition to the private market approach. We conclude with our own prediction of how the debate over privatization will be resolved in the future.

PRIVATIZING WATER ALLOCATION

According to Terry Anderson, one of the leading new resource economists, creating private markets for water would promote more efficient allocation, eliminate prospects of shortage, and limit conflict in distribution.[3] A similar theme is struck by Del Gardner, who offers three choices for the future: 1) the hopelessly inefficient performance of existing institutions, 2) centralized allocation decisions by administrative boards that "will be no better and may be much worse than the present institutions," or 3) water markets for rights in which "exchanges can be freely made . . . whether or not new water is developed."[4] Given the choice between freedom under market mechanisms or the conflict and inefficiency engendered by the faceless bureaucracy, the market solution is made to seem quite appealing.

The private market argument generally finds its roots in individualistic utilitarianism.[5] Following Bentham, utility theorists have held that the basis of social value resides in the individual, rather than in collectivities.[6] Social well-being is best determined by the summation of individual utilities because individuals are best able to discover their own subjective valuation of goods and services. Further, when key assumptions of the competitive market model are met, markets are efficient mechanisms for allocations of valued things in that exchange occurs only when it is mutually beneficial to trading partners. Under appropriate conditions, it is held, markets will generate allocations of valued things from which no further improvement in the well-being of any individual is possible without a concomitant reduction in the well-being of some other individual.

Some market proponents rely more heavily on a libertarian (or Lockean) argument that free markets provide the best bulwark against infringements on individual liberty.[7] The institutions of private property and voluntary market transactions permit the pursuit of individual values with a minimum of governmental interference. Less government involvement, in turn, reduces opportunity for infringement of individual liberty. The appeal of the private market argument is based on two assumptions. First, markets are perceived to be efficient mechanisms for allocation of valued things. Second, markets perform on the basis of voluntary exchange among individuals, obviating the need for costly and authoritarian bureaucratic manipulation.

Applied to water markets, the realization of the benefits of private market allocation requires that water be viewed by potential market participants as a commodity—and thus be subject to meaningful relative valuation. Further, the benefits and costs of various uses of water must accrue to the individual water holder, lest serious externalities result to the detriment of the broader community. Additional requirements include the generation of sufficient information about water exchange for participants to make well-informed choices, clearly defined and exchangeable water rights, and a relatively costless forum for exchange of such rights.

How is privatization to be accomplished? First and foremost, existing water allocation systems must be fundamentally transformed. The doctrine of riparian rights, which treats water as a common property subject to state regulation for which users may have rights (but not ownership), must be replaced by a system analogous to the doctrine of prior appropriation (which does confer ownership). In the same fashion, "project water"—water supplied and collectively owned by federal and state water supply systems—must be allocated to individual project recipients. Wahl, for example, recommends assigning farmers water rights equivalent to customary deliveries for irrigation.[8]

Water users may oppose private markets to the extent that their investments are dependent upon established systems of water law. But advocates of the private market reason that farmers who directly or indirectly own most of the rights to water would benefit as the rights to water are clarified, transfer restrictions relaxed, and the value of water increases. Nonagricultural users would also benefit because they would be able to purchase rights to established supplies formerly locked up in lower-valued uses. Local water agencies would have to shed their traditional role as allocators of water, and would assume new roles, primarily as brokers of water rights for constituents and as arbiters of disputes between private rights owners. At present the variable definitions of water rights and—more importantly—the limitations on water trade across political jurisdictions constitute serious inhibitions to the functioning of the water market. Privatization and deregulation will be required to remove such institutional "impediments."

The preferred scenario of the water market advocates thus entails change on many fronts; legal institutions, regional and local use patterns and values, the roles played by local water agencies, and political jurisdictions must be substantially reformed to allow for widespread adoption of private markets as institutions for allocation of water resources. Recent institutional changes in methods of water allocation have incorporated a number of market principles, and some rudimentary private water markets have appeared.[9] Although no comprehensive evaluation is available, preliminary assessments are quite positive.[10] However, much stands in the way of widespread application of the free-market approach to water allocation.

SOURCES OF OPPOSITION TO THE
PRIVATE MARKET APPROACH

Opposition to privatization stems in part from the fear that allowing water to "flow uphill to money" via unfettered private transactions may threaten both environmental quality and the rights of nonurban constituencies by ignoring the noneconomic values associated with traditional water use.[11] Markets are seen by others as "nothing less than a program for the redistribution of control over western water resources toward those parties most able to purchase scarce water rights."[12] The move toward water markets could result in increased conflict—especially played out in the courts—as groups with limited economic resources pursue litigation against relatively rich cities, downstream states, and energy companies as a means of protecting their interests.[13] Thus, in contrast to the promarket view, privatization may become a *source* of conflict over the control of resources, instead of offering an acceptable conflict resolution mechanism.

Underlying the resistance to privatization is a set of arguments that water transfers in particular cannot conform to the requirements for optimal allocation by private market mechanisms. One of the most significant categories of market failures concerns market externalities—costs or benefits of the production and consumption of water that are not captured in the price that consumers pay (and producers receive). When costs of a particular kind of water consumption and use are not included in its price to consumers, water is likely to be overconsumed or put to uses that would not be economically feasible if the user were paying the true cost of water, thus creating waste.

Most of the concern expressed about water market failure turns on the expectation that significant negative externalities would result from water transactions. Attention has been particularly focused on the negative externalities of water exchange: pollution, soil erosion, downstream effects, loss of instream uses.[14] In this view, markets would produce too much water for some uses, at the expense of other uses that preserve values not accounted for in the market price of water.

Negative externalities exist to some extent because water possesses many of the characteristics of a public good. Clean water like clean air is often a nonmarketable resource in the sense that consumption is nonexclusionary. Due to its public good characteristics, certain uses of water may be undervalued. Where there are no trusted mechanisms to assign values to certain uses, such as natural habitat protection, water transactions will be opposed by those who value these uses. Some view rural agricultural communities in the same manner. Using water for agriculture produces perceived benefits that are extremely hard to quantify. Water is valued as the cement that bonds social relationships, preserves the community, and provides a foundation for respecting tradition. It is therefore not surprising to find opposition to commodity valuation of water from both environmentalists and from small-scale rural agricultural communities. Rural Hispanics and Indians are two groups with significant claims to water who exemplify this resistance.

Opposition to water markets may also arise when "efficient" allocation results in individual losses. In practice, the perception of efficiency depends upon one's accounting perspective; i.e., the level at which costs and benefits are aggregated. For an individual farmer in a water district, it may be rational to oppose a transfer of district water if such a transfer threatens the quality or availability of his water entitlement. The premise here is that policy preferences primarily are determined by individual-level calculations of utility. We can expect vigorous opposition to market transfers of water to the extent that personal investment in water-dependent activities is threatened. In a recent survey of water policy preferences in New Mexico, a state where market transfers are encountered by a relatively lenient regulatory structure, opposition to markets was found to be directly related to personal investment factors, including ownership of water rights and the use of water for irrigation. In contrast, support for a commodity view of water was strongest among those with low personal investment, i.e., urban residents who did not use water for agriculture or own water rights.[15] These findings suggest that, for those with the highest stakes in water use and those most likely to wade into the political battle over water policy, security and control over water resources are more important than efficiency per se. Such a conclusion does not bode well for widespread adoption of private markets in the future.

Yet another important "market failure" believed to apply to water exchange stems from the observation that the supply of water is characterized by decreasing average costs—larger water projects can deliver water at a smaller cost per cubic foot than smaller water projects. If that is true, a competitive market in water would give way to control by one or only a few suppliers of water, who would then be in a position to extract monopoly rents from consumers.[16] Market signals could thus lead to misallocation of resources—and a transfer of wealth from water consumers to water suppliers.

Judicial and Legislative Obstacles
to Private Markets

In a number of recent decisions, the courts seem to be providing increasing support for commodity valuations of water and removal of jurisdictional restrictions on interstate market transactions. As we have seen in earlier chapters, the U.S. Supreme Court in *Sporhase v. Nebraska* (1982) held that water is a commodity subject to interstate commerce clause scrutiny. Following *Sporhase,* lower courts invalidated a New Mexico statutory ban on interstate transfers of groundwater in *The City of El Paso v. S. E. Reynolds* (1983). (See Chapters 2 and 5 for a detailed discussion of the cases.) Taken together, these decisions may signify support for market allocations and pave the way for the emergence of an interstate market for water rights. Moreover, intrastate restrictions on water transfers may also be relaxed to the extent that lower courts follow federal directives.

Nevertheless, emergence of an interstate market in the future in the Southwest is unlikely given the considerable variation in laws governing water use between states. While *Sporhase* indicates that such variations may be struck down as infringements on interstate trade, Trelease argues that *Sporhase* is not applicable to future water management because it interferes with the sovereign power of states to manage natural resources.[17] Moreover, states may respond to court action to retain control over water. For example, a number of states, including New Mexico and Nebraska, are currently contemplating state appropriation of all unappropriated groundwater as a means to guarantee adequate supplies for future use.[18]

To the free-marketeer, governmental restrictions on water rights transfers are deemed "impediments" or "obstacles." While it is true that restrictions may impede or obstruct, many—if not most—of these limits on market transfers serve to protect the interests of established users or others who may be adversely affected. While most of the appropriative rights are transferable, the general rule is that transfers shall not impair the rights of others. Since many users are dependent on return flows, upstream users in most states may only transfer the consumptive use portion of the right. Where riparian rights are recognized (*e.g.*, Texas and California), off-site use of the rights is also prohibited.[19] Another expression of the same concern for rights of third parties is the area-of-origin statutes. Unlike other natural resources, transfers of water generally are not subject to severance taxes, which theoretically compensate the area of origin.

Instead, many states have enacted legislation that prohibits or severely restricts interbasin water transfers. MacDonnel and Howe provide an excellent review of the forms these restrictions may take.[20] Area-of-origin restrictions do not necessarily prevent the evolution of interbasin markets, but significant transaction costs are added.

A related class of state restrictions is public interest provisions in state constitutions and water codes. In a number of recent decisions, state courts have expanded the right of state water officials to prohibit a water transfer on the grounds that the transfer would violate the public welfare or general welfare of the state. Such interests vary by state and court, but may include the protection of fish and wildlife habitat, recreation opportunities, water quality, public access, navigation, and even the maintenance of traditional communities. Moreover, transfers can be prohibited if they are considered to be unnecessarily wasteful or inconsistent with the promotion of conservation.[21]

A related restriction is the public trust doctrine, a judicially created policy that acts to prevent transfers that would adversely affect the people's common heritage of streams, lakes, marshlands, and tidelands. A recent California Supreme Court decision, *National Audubon Society v. Superior Court* (1983), is a case in point. In that case the Court ruled that a transfer of water from Mono Lake to meet the water needs of Los Angeles would violate the public trust of preserving the Mono Lake ecosystem. The state, as public trustee, has a continuing obligation to protect the public's common heritage of natural streams and lakes, the Court said. Because the city of Los Angeles owned perfected rights in Mono Lake waters, the Court did not block a transfer of rights *per se*. However, the implication is clear; voluntary transfers (*i.e.*, sales) between willing participants may be blocked by the courts or by designated administrative bodies in the protection of the public trust.

Finally, interstate markets seem unlikely where interstate and international treaties, compacts, and equitable apportionment decisions allocate specific quantities of surface waters to upstream and downstream jurisdictions. For example, the Colorado River Compact creates extreme difficulties for transfer of water from an upper to lower basin state despite the fact that the water might be worth ten times as much in the lower basin.[22] (See also Merrifield, Chapter 11 in this volume). Along the same lines, both inter- and intrastate transfers are inhibited in a number of states where area-of-origin statutes have been enacted.[23] Market transfers in such situations involve significant transaction costs in the form of litigation or amendment of existing agreements. It is unlikely that individual market participants will be able or willing to pay the transaction costs associated with challenging existing provisions for the reallocation of water across jurisdictions.

Special Water District Restrictions
on Private Water Markets

An extremely complex intergovernmental arena continues to define the evolution of state water policy. In the western states generally, administrative agencies have been given authority to regulate more than 75 percent of the water that is supplied to residential, agricultural, and commercial users.[24] A closer look at the ways in which market transfers are inhibited by special water district statutory provisions and practices is warranted because these quasi-governments not only supply about one half the water used in the West, but also control most of the water used for irrigated agriculture as well.[25]

Water districts effectively inhibit market transfers between willing participants, especially in situations where water will move outside the district's jurisdiction. Transfering water out of a district is complicated because in many states water rights are held in trust by the district. Moreover, transfers occasionally must be approved by a majority of landowners within the district. Districts or states may also impose appurtenancy requirements where water and land rights cannot be severed. Transfers of individual water rights both between and within districts may be possible but often can be appealed by qualified third parties. Under Arizona law, for example, irrigation districts, agricultural improvement districts, and water user associations may veto water transfers both within their jurisdictions and within the drainage basin of operation.[26] While water districts are not the only eligible appellants, a significant proportion of water transfer appeals are filed by districts or their members. Gardner notes that appeals are usually successful (*i.e.,* transfers are prevented) because compensation mechanisms for affected third parties do not exist and because the concern for economic efficiency is often compromised by concern for equity and environmental protection.[27]

Traditionally, water has been priced artificially low in federal reclamation and analogous state projects as a form of agricultural subsidy. As Lee notes, district taxation powers often allow water users the opportunity to realize benefits by imposing costs on the general population.[28] Levy assessments, usually related to land-ownership, are generally used to repay long-term capital expenditures whereas water charges are used to cover the variable costs of providing services. Reliance upon levy assessments allows for costs to be distributed over the entire population, giving agricultural users a substantial subsidy. In consequence, the price of water in these situations is reflective of district financial obligations and/or political preferences rather than the economic value of the resource. Allowing special districts to sell their water rights, presumably at prevailing market rates, may be opposed to the extent that such sales are generally perceived to be a second subsidy. In effect, the district or its constituents would profit from the sale of water that originally was made available only through the largess of the public coffers. Such critiques will surface in direct proportion to market participation of special districts.

To recapitulate, we have sought to depict the foundations and premises of the initiative for a private market policy in water, then to indicate the full range of obstacles that confront that initiative. Based on this review, what are the prospects for the emergence of private markets for southwestern water in the future?

OF GOVERNMENTS AND WATER MARKETS IN THE FUTURE SOUTHWEST

Prospects for unfettered private water markets are grim. Despite compelling theoretical arguments for efficient allocation through markets, the collective ownership of water rights by state political subdivisions, jurisdictional boundary limitations, interstate compacts, and state statutory restrictions are all among the impressive list of institutional restrictions that will inhibit the privatization of water rights transactions. The restrictions are more than perplexing problems for free market economists; they reflect a recognition of the complex and unique role that water plays in society. And yet the impetus for reform continues. The perpetuation of inefficient water uses, the emergence of willing buyers and sellers, unsatisfied Indian claims for water, and environmental degradation are but a few of the factors that will provoke policy reform.

Advocates of water markets respond in several ways to their critics. Some, notably Terry Anderson, argue that careful construction of water rights and market institutions would minimize failure.[29] Others point out that the market failure is only half the story: regulation of water allocation in lieu of markets does not guarantee correction of market failure. Indeed, some would argue that "government failure"—*i.e.*, inefficient allocation of economic resources resulting from political incentives—overshadows the potential market failure.[30]

Proponents of private water markets can also point to significant changes already under way in water use. The marginal value of agriculture in many parts of the Southwest and the dismal economic conditions faced in many agricultural regions have led to increasing economic pressures for farmers and communities to diversify. Reallocation of water to higher-valued uses such as recreation and industry could allow the revitalization of local economies without government subsidies or other forms of public assistance. The higher value of water derived from urban and industrial uses will make agricultural demands for a heavily subsidized and disproportionate share of water increasingly anomalous. The emergence of rudimentary markets in some locales and the more widespread adoption of pricing reforms indicate that voluntary allocations of water through some type of market mechanism often offer the least costly solution.

Despite these changes, it remains highly unlikely that private water markets will dominate water allocation mechanisms in the future. Because anticipated outcomes may not be acceptable either to the general public or to specific constituencies, it is likely that there will be an increasing demand for policy responses that protect collective interests. For example, Weatherford and Ingram contend that state governments will increasingly play an active role in order to "cushion the impact of reallocation upon agriculture in the name of perpetuating the agricultural economy and preserving the rural lifestyle."[31] The free market solution also raises the specter of increased judicial control because the courts typically resolve disputes related to property ownership and third party effects of private transactions. It is unlikely that either the legislative or executive branches of government will welcome increased litigation and increased judicial policymaking, particularly in water resources. The judicial system has proved itself unable to resolve water controversies quickly and efficiently, and the prospects for prevention of future controversies via the courts appears grim. Therefore, barring the establishment of alternative dispute resolution forums, states and their political subdivisions will resist privatization both as an unduly litigious solution and, more importantly, because it may lead to a diminution of their discretionary authority to manage water in the public interest.

The most likely direction for future reform therefore will be a mixture of market transactions and heavy governmental involvement. "Market oriented" solutions defined by statute or contractual agreements and closely regulated by administrative agencies will be the norm. Water will continue to be reallocated among individuals within jurisdictions and there will be some relaxation of jurisdictional restrictions, but such reforms will not be universal and are in themselves a far cry from privatization. Price incentives increasingly will be employed within water jurisdictions because they represent incremental or relatively minor adjustments that produce considerable benefits. Four more dramatic types of market-oriented reforms are likely in the future in the Southwest: 1) increased statewide regulatory control by administrative agencies, 2) contractual agreements between governments, 3) dominance of market transactions by public entities, and 4) the adoption of contract carriage provisions for water transactions. A brief overview of each type of reform provides a glimpse of the future.

Increased Statewide Control

In a number of states, the trend is for state water resource agencies to integrate water management functions into a large multi-faceted agency and at the same time to centralize water management authority at the state level.[32] Priorities for water allocation increasingly are restricted and channeled through extensive public planning processes or by statutory prescription, not by the invisible hand of market transactions.[33] However, state agencies can and have instituted programs that enable the formation of markets within a particular jurisdiction. For example, several recent California legislative enactments are designed to encourage voluntary transfers of state water projects entitlement.[34] Similarly, plans are under way for creation of a water bank in California's Kern County where excess water would be stored in groundwater recharge basins for sale during periods of water shortage. California also has allowed the formation of a formal "exchange pool" market in Los Angeles County's central basin. Groundwater pumpers can buy and sell the right to pump water, but rates are determined by a court-decreed formula based on operating costs, local water assessments, and the current price of water imported into the basin.[35] In each case, the buyers and sellers are public agencies, not private water traders.

In 1980, Arizona enacted a groundwater reform act that provides a statewide regulatory structure for the reduction of agricultural consumption as well as incentives for reallocation of water from agriculture to municipal land industrial users (see Chapter 2). The act is significant for a number of reasons. Implementation of the act has required creation of an extensive water resources bureaucracy including a newly created Department of Water Resources and a number of groundwater management agencies. Moreover, the state has abandoned its traditional *laissez faire* posture toward groundwater in favor of a public resource management approach. While restrictions on water rights trading have been eased, control over water rights remains primarily in public—rather than private—hands.

The emergence of strictly regulated markets and statewide control thus does not necessarily mean that market transactions will not take place. It only suggests that willing buyers and sellers must continue to shoulder the transaction costs that result from institutional restrictions. For most individuals, this means conducting business within relatively confined geographical regions, states, or water districts, according to fairly restrictive rule and procedures. One is reminded of the mercantile economy of colonial days in which buying and selling across jurisdictions was strictly regulated. Although it may be an outdated economic system for most commodities, there seems to be considerable support for "neo-mercantilism" in water management. For example, in New Mexico some respondents to a recent survey noted, "We want to be able to buy and sell water rights, as long as the water stays in the state."[36]

Voluntary Transactions Between Governments

There is a class of consumers that is generally able to pay or even avoid the transaction costs associated with transfers across jurisdictions. Public agencies at the state and local level increasingly have negotiated a wide range of contracts with other agencies to share, sell, or lease water. Cooperative agreements between units of government have a long and varied tradition in water management. Most water districts, for example, contract with state and federal resource agencies for water supplies, operations and maintenance assistance, and other water-related functions. Recent proposals suggest that co-operative agreements will provide increasing opportunities for sharing, leasing or purchasing of water resources between governments.

The most provocative example of such intergovernmental transactions is a proposed agreement between two water districts in California—the Imperial Irrigation District (IID) and the Metropolitan Water District (MWD)—in which the MWD will receive 10,0000 acre-feet of IID's Colorado River entitlement in exchange for financing water conservation facilities in IID's service area. An interesting aspect of this deal is the fact that IID contemplates no net loss of water; the water sold to MWD will be derived from improvements in operating efficiencies that result from ditch lining and reducing return flows. The solution therefore conforms to our definition of a market-oriented reform and appears to be Pareto efficient. Mutual benefit is derived by increasing the efficiency of use. Nevertheless, the agreement has required considerable negotiation and, as of this writing, third-party effects—in this case the environmental costs associated with reducing return flows to the Salton Sea—remain unresolved.[37]

Voluntary transactions between water agencies that own water and organizations that are willing to pay for the use of surplus supplies—or even the temporary use of surplus supplies—offer one of the most promising short-term solutions to increasing demand for finite resources. Such solutions are limited by the amount of available surplus water as well as by the extent to which negative externalities generate opposition by third parties. Ironically, collective ownership of water is a prerequisite for many intergovernmental agreements, so it may be that over time states and their political subdivisions will acquire through appropriation, purchase, or condemnation most if not all of the water rights in watersheds in order to reallocate water through government-to-government transactions. As noted earlier, harbingers of this approach can be seen in state plans to appropriate unappropriated groundwater.

The Tilted Playing Field in Water Markets

Private individuals and groups will in many instances continue to be at a competitive disadvantage with regard to public water agencies in water market exchanges. Public agencies typically have deeper pockets because they can often increase revenues (*i.e.*, increase water fees) as costs rise, whereas the revenues of private traders tend to be more limited. Public agencies also have presumed longevity (and solvency) whereas private firms can and do go out of business. Because public agencies can shoulder greater costs with greater assurance of having the necessary funds available for future payment, they will appear to be a better risk than will private market participants. These advantages will serve to maintain the predominance of public actors in water market exchanges in the future.

Where, then, will private actors play a significant role in water transfers? Private water rights interests have been most successful in jurisdictions where institutional barriers to water transfers are minimal. For example, Western Water Rights Management, Inc., is compiling a portfolio of Colorado water rights for investors in a $35 million water management fund.[38] It is noteworthy that the company limits its acquisitions to Colorado, where rights can be transferred with relative ease. This is indicative of a trend in which private actors play the role of entrepreneurial middlemen by acquiring privately held irrigation rights for eventual sale to thirsty cities and industry. We would expect that in the future private actors will play a major role only in localized areas, and specifically only in those jurisdictions that have limited transfer restrictions.

Contract Carriage as a Partial
Solution to Natural Monopoly

As we noted earlier, one objection to private markets for water stems from the natural monopolistic qualities of large water delivery systems: large capital costs relative to operating costs lead to declining average costs, forestalling market competition. In view of this, there is a strong impetus for state governments to pass "contract carriage" provisions for major water systems, requiring them to deliver water at a fixed fee (to cover capital and operating costs) when a private deal has been struck between a buyer and seller of water.[39] The primary virtue of contract carriage is that water exchanges are allowed in spite of the natural monopolistic features of large water delivery systems.

Contract carriage will not prove to be a panacea for all water users, however, As has been true in the natural gas industry, contract carriage will prove beneficial primarily to large volume consumers. Large volume transactions are generally required to generate significant economies via direct contract trades. The result—as has been seen in natural gas pricing—is for the delivery system to reduce prices markedly for large volume users to avoid losing them as customers, while passing an increasing share of the system's capital costs on to those consumers least likely to leave the system— primarily small volume consumers. This dynamic has led to extensive efforts by some natural gas consumer groups to limit the shifting of costs from large to small volume users.[40] A similar move can be expected with respect to water transfers, which is likely to lead to extensive public restrictions on contract carriage provisions for water trades.

SUMMARY

We have outlined numerous obstacles to the development of a restricted private market for southwestern water. While we do anticipate the growth of market-style reallocations to higher economically valued uses, exchanges will continue to be closely regulated as well as limited to specific jurisdictions. "Interference" by public agencies will continue and in many cases is sure to increase. Thus, to those captivated by the free marketeers' vision of an unfettered private market for water, the future may indeed appear quite dismal. In our view, however, recent adoption of innovations based on market principles by public water agencies suggests that prospects for more efficient water use in the Southwest are *not* so bleak after all.

NOTES

1. E. S. Savas, *Privatizating the Public Sector: How to Shrink Government* (Chatham, N.J.: Chatham House, 1982); and George Downs and Patrick Larkey, *The Search for Government Efficiency: From Hubris to Helplessness* (New York, N.Y.: Random House, 1986).

2. For purposes of clarity and consistency, we will refer to water markets so defined as "private water markets." These are distinct from "market oriented" systems of water exchange that seek more modestly to increase water exchanges among public entities and to loosen constraints on private exchange within political jurisdictions.

3. T. Anderson, *Water Crisis: Ending the Policy Drought* (Baltimore, Md.: Johns Hopkins University Press, 1983).

4. Delworth Gardner, "Institutional Impediments to Efficient Water Allocation," *Policy Studies Review,* Vol. 5, No. 2, (1985), pp. 353–63.

5. George Stigler, "The Development of Utility Theory," in Stigler, *Es-*

says in the History of Economics (Chicago, Ill.: University of Chicago Press, 1965).

6. Otto Ekstein, "A Survey of Public Expenditure Criteria," in *Public Finances: Needs, Sources, Utilization.* Universities National Bureau for Economic Research (Princeton, N.J.: Princeton University Press, 1961).

7. F. A. Hayek, *The Constitution of Liberty* (Chicago, Ill.: University of Chicago Press, 1960); and R. Nozick, *Anarchy, State and Utopia* (New York, N.Y.: Basic Books, 1974).

8. R. Wahl, "Cleaning Up Kesterson," *Resources,* No. 83 (Spring 1986).

9. Bonnie Saliba, "Market Transactions and the Pricing of Water Rights in the West," in Steve Shupe (ed.), *Water Marketing: Opportunities and Challenges of a New Era* (Denver, Colo.: University of Denver College of Law and Watershed West, 1986).

10. See, *e.g.,* L. MacDonnell and C. W. Howe, "Area of Origin Protection in Transbasin Water Diversions: An Evaluation of Alternative Approaches," in Steve Shupe (ed.), *Water Marketing: Opportunities and Challenges of a New Era* (Denver, Colo.: University of Denver College of Law and Watershed West, 1986).

11. F. Lee Brown and Helen Ingram, *Water and Poverty in the Southwest* (Tucson, Ariz.: University of Arizona Press, 1986).

12. Steven Mumme and Helen Ingram, "Community Values in Southwest Water Management," *Policy Studies Review,* Vol. 5, No. 2, (1985), pp. 365–81.

13. John Folk-Williams, S. Frye, and L. Hilgendorf, *Western Water Flows to the Cities* (Santa Fe, N. Mex.: Western Network, 1985).

14. K. Boulding, *Western Water Resources: Coming Problems and the Policy Alternatives* (Boulder, Colo.: Westview Press, 1980).

15. Tim De Young, *Preferences for Managing New Mexican Water* (Las Cruces, N. Mex.: New Mexico Water Resources Research Institute. Technical Completion Report No. 184, 1984).

16. G. William Shepherd, *The Economics of Industrial Organization* (Englewood Cliffs, N.J.: Prentice-Hall, 1979), Chap. 3.

17. J. Frank Trelease, "Discussion," in Ernest A. Englebert (ed.), *Water Scarcity: Impacts on Western Agriculture* (Berkeley, Calif.: University of California Press, 1984).

18. *Water Market Update,* March 1987, Volume 1, Number 3; and DuMars *et al., State Appropriation of Unappropriated Groundwater: A Strategy for Insuring New Mexico a Water Future* (Las Cruces, N. Mex.: New Mexico Resources Research Institute, Report No. 200, January 1986).

19. Gary Weatherford and Steven Shupe, "Reallocation Water in the Arid West," in Steve Shupe (ed.), *Water Marketing: Opportunities and Challenges of a New Era* (Denver: University of Denver College of Law and Watershed West, 1986).

20. MacDonnel and Howe. See note 10.

21. Charles F. Wilkinson, "Public Interest Constraints on Water Transfers," in Steven Shupe (ed.), *Water Marketing: Opportunities and Challenges for a New Era* (Denver: University of Denver College of Law and Watershed West, 1986).

22. Gardner, 1983.

23. L. MacDonnel *et al., Guidelines for Developing Area-of-Origin Compensation,* Technical Completion Report (Ft. Collins, Colo.: Colorado Water Resources Research Institute, 1986).

24. E. P. La Veen and R. N. Stavins, "Institutional Impediments for More Efficient Use and Allocation of Irrigation Water in the West." *Report* (Berkeley, Calif.: The Rural America Task Force, The Ford Foundation, September 1981, p. 31).

25. John Leshy, "Irrigation Districts in a Changing West—An Overview," *Arizona State Law Journal,* Vol. 2, (1982), pp. 345–76.

26. MacDonnel and Howe, 1987.

27. Gardner, 1985.

28. D. Lee, "Political Provision of Water: An Economic/Social Choice Perspective," in Jay Corbridge (ed.), *Special Water Districts: Challenge for the Future* (Boulder, Colo.: University of Colorado Natural Resources Law Center, 1983).

29. T. Anderson, "Conflict or Cooperation: The Case for Water Markets." Working Paper, Political Economy Research Center, Montana State University, 1983.

30. Lee, See note 28.

31. Gary Weatherford and Helen Ingram, "Legal–Institutional Limitations on Water Use," in Ernest A. Engelbert (ed.), *Water Scarcity: Impacts on Western Agriculture* (Berkeley: Calif.: University of California Press, 1984).

32. See Zachary A. Smith, "Centralized Decision-making in the Administration of Groundwater Rights," *Natural Resources Journal* 24 (July 1984), p. 24, for a division of centralized administrative arrangements.

33. Terry Edgmon and Tim De Young, "Categorizing State Models of Water Management," in J. G. Frances and R. Ganzel (eds.), *Western Public Lands* (Totowa, N.J.: Rowmand and Allanheld, 1984), pp. 232–47.

34. James T. Markle, "Facilitating Voluntary Water Transfers in California," in Steve Shupe (ed.), *Water Marketing: Opportunities and Challenges of a New Era* (Denver, Colo.: University of Denver College of Law and Watershed West, 1986).

35. *Water Market Update.*

36. De Young, *Preferences for Managing New Mexican Water.*

37. Dennis B. Underwood, "A Case Study: Imperial Valley, California," in *Proceedings, Western Water: Expanding Uses, Finite Supplies* (Boulder,

Colo.: University of Colorado School of Law, Natural Resources Law Center, June 2–4, 1986).

38. Sharon Gross, "The Galloway Project and the Colorado River Compact: Will the Compacts Bar Transbasin Water Diversions?" in Steve Shupe (ed.), *Water Marketing: Opportunities and Challenges of a New Era* (Denver: University of Denver College of Law and Watershed West, 1986).

39. This has been the direction taken by the Federal Energy Regulatory Commission regarding natural gas regulation.

40. Jon Wellinghoff, "What do '436,' '436-A,' '451,' '311,' '7(c),' Mean to the Residential Gas Consumer?" in Hank Jenkins-Smith (ed.), *Natural Gas in the Western U.S.: Regulation in the Next Decade.* Special issue, *Natural Resources Journal, forthcoming* Vol. 27 No. 4 (Fall 1987) pp. 829–840.

13 Water and the Future of Energy Development in the Southwest

A. Didrick Castberg

It is becoming more and more difficult to remember the long lines of cars waiting for gasoline, the gas quotas, and other aspects of the gasoline shortage we experienced several years ago. In the late 1980s there is a seeming abundance of gasoline, the Organization of Petroleum Exporting Countries (OPEC) is in disarray, coal is experiencing a rebirth as a fuel, and the development of and research into alternative forms of energy is lagging. Despite the political crises in the Middle East there seems to be no shortage of oil. One fact, however, remains constant, and that is fossil fuel resources are finite. The supply is limited, increased exploration and the current means of extraction will result in little additional supplies, and therefore we will eventually run out of such fuels.

Water, on the other hand, is already in short supply, especially in the American Southwest. As population migration brings more people and industry, and the demand for food and services increases, the limited supply of water becomes more acute and more tangible. Although blessed with abundant sunshine, that part of the country has little water, the latter being largely a consequence of the former. And as population and industry increase in the Southwest, so does the demand not only for water but also for power.

WATER AND ENERGY PRODUCTION

Water and energy are inextricably linked. The development and production of electrical power from most available sources requires water. Thus the demand for power has an impact on the supply of water. The most direct relationship between water and power, of course, is hydroelectric power. Hoover Dam is probably the best-known source of such energy in the Southwest. The fact is, however, that new water sources in the Southwest capable of generating sufficient hydroelectric energy to be cost-effective are virtually nonexistent. Water is also necessary in the production of geothermal energy, the development and production of synthetic fuels, the production of nuclear energy, as well as conventional combustion of oil and the extraction and transportation of coal. About the only energy sources that do not directly require water are solar and wind, and even those energy sources require relatively small amounts of water to produce the solar cells and wind generation equipment. Unfortunately these sources are not, as yet, economically viable for widespread application.

The Southwest is not energy-resource poor to the extent that it is water poor. The Four Corners area, for example, is particularly rich in fossil fuels (primarily coal and oil from shale) and nuclear fuels, with some potential for geothermal resources. In addition, sunshine provides the potential for energy associated with solar power. Approximately 60 percent of the nation's uranium reserves are found in the Southwest, as are 45 percent of the nation's underground coal reserve base and 75 percent of the strippable reserve base.[1] Coal, in addition to being a source of energy through direct combustion, is also a source of synthetic fuels (through coal gasification and liquefaction), so the coal reserves are especially important, though nonrenewable, sources of energy. Oil shale resources are also found in the region; the Green River Formation in Colorado, Utah, and Wyoming contains between 1.4 and 3 trillion barrels of shale oil, with about 80 percent of this located in Colorado.[2] Tapping these resources, however, is another matter.

The primary and largest source of water and energy development potential in the region exists in the Upper Colorado River Basin. This area contains one twelfth of the land area of the forty-eight states and includes most of the energy resources discussed above.[3] Although it is difficult to accurately predict demand for and availability of water in this area, Kneese and Brown have attempted to predict water losses in the Upper Colorado Basin based on projections that assume the construction of oil shale, coal gasification, and fossil fuel electric plants in the region (an assumption that it seems, at least for the time being, will not be realized). Their projection is that the total water loss will increase from 3.8 billion acre-feet per year in 1974 to between 6.2 and 6.5 billion acre-feet in the year 2000. The supply flow was assumed to be 5.8 billion acre-feet per year.[4] Thus, it can be seen that should these plants be constructed the water use would increase substantially. The accuracy of these projections is clouded, of course, by such factors as changing weather patterns, migration patterns, effects of conservation, unpredictable technological breakthroughs, and world and national politics. Nevertheless, it may be best to assume a worst-case scenario when planning for the energy future of the Southwest.

A primary potential source of energy in the Southwest is oil from oil shale. The Green River Formation in Colorado, Utah, and Wyoming, for example, may contain more oil than is presently available in all known conventional reserves.[5] But the exploitation of those resources would require the investment of vast sums of money and huge amounts of water. The water required for extraction of petroleum from oil shale varies depending on the method used for extraction. In-situ and modified in-situ processes use the least water (estimated at from 71 to 278 gallons of water per barrel of oil), and surface retorting uses from 207 to 224 gallons per barrel[6] or between 5,000 and 13,000 acre-feet per year for a 50,000 barrel-per-day plant.[7] Water for an oil shale facility is used for a variety of purposes, including mining and crushing, retorting, shale disposal, power plant cooling towers, revegetation, and human uses, with shale disposal being by far the greatest user, approximately 43 percent of the total.[8]

Coal is also found in great abundance in the Southwest, much of it of the low sulfur variety (less than one percent sulfur, and therefore cleaner burning and less polluting). Although Wyoming contains the largest amount of coal in the western United States, Colorado, New Mexico, and Utah contain significant amounts, with estimates going as high as 23 billion tons.[9] Because most of the coal-burning electrical plants are located in the East, transportation is a major obstacle to the economical development and use of coal. Thus many are looking at coal gasification and liquefaction as a more cost-effective method of transporting energy resources. Similarly, coal slurry pipelines (where coal is crushed and mixed with water for transportation through pipelines) are an available option, but an option not without significant problems, including pipeline easements and adequate water supplies.[10] Water requirements for gasification or liquefaction are estimated to vary between 4,000 and 15,000 acre-feet per year for a plant processing 250 million cubic feet per day, with the lower figures for high–Btu plants and the higher for low–Btu plants.[11] Water requirements for coal slurry pipelines depend on the amount of coal to be transported and the distance. For example, a pipeline to move between 30 and 40 million tons per year from Wyoming to Louisiana would require up to 20,000 acre-feet per year.[12]

Nuclear power seems by some to be all but forgotten as a future source of energy. Problems with the development of nuclear power seem to have been largely political, although there are some technological obstacles that may need to be overcome. These issues will be discussed below, but it is appropriate here to discuss briefly water requirements for nuclear power plants. Nuclear plants obtain their heat for generating steam from nuclear fuel through controlled chain reactions. Light water reactors, the most commonly used type of reactor in the United States, use large quantities of water for their cooling condensers—a 1,000 megawatt plant typically requires approximately 5 million cubic meters (over 1 billion gallons) of cooling water per day.[13] Most of the water used is returned to its source (at a higher temperature, of course), but some is lost to evaporation. This means, then, that nuclear plants must be located in close proximity to a substantial source of water and that thermal pollution must have a minimal impact on the local ecosystem. While water for nuclear plants may not be widely available, the fuel is.

Colorado, New Mexico, and Utah contain an estimated 80,500,000 short tons of uranium ore, or 182,000 short tons of U_3O_8 (uranium oxide).[14] The uranium oxide, or yellowcake, must be enriched before it is suitable as a nuclear fuel. A typical nuclear power plant will require 110 tons of enriched uranium oxide fuel pellets, with about 33 percent of this fuel being replaced each year.[15] Thus, it can be seen that the nuclear fuel resources of the Southwest are substantial. However, a safe method for disposing of more than 35 tons of used fuel pellets per year must be found. The mining of uranium ore is not particularly dangerous, at least from a radiation point of view, but the usual dangers associated with mining apply to uranium, and there is also the possibility of excessive ingestion of radon gas, found in high concentrations in uranium mines.[16] As is the case with mining activities generally, fairly substantial quantities of water are required.

Geothermal resources are also found in the Southwest, with the largest known geothermal fields being in California. There has been relatively little exploration for or exploitation of these resources in other parts of the Southwest, although Arizona, New Mexico, and Utah have several proven geothermal reserves and many suspected reserves.[17] Even if geothermal energy were being aggressively pursued, however—which it is not—these sources would supply only a fraction of the total energy needs of the area. Most of the water requirement for a geothermal power plant is for the cooling towers that function to remove waste heat from the plants. As much as 600,000 acre-feet per year may be required for an 8,000–MW plant, although the requirements vary considerably depending upon the type of plant.[18] While some of the water can be recycled, there are considerable losses due to evaporation. Geothermal power plants use more water per kilowatt hour than virtually any other energy production process, approximately 6.8 liters per kwh compared to nuclear plants at 3 liters/kwh, fossil-fueled electric at about 2 liters/kwh, and coal gasification at between .3 and 2 liters/kwh.[19] Where the plants are in close proximity to each other and to a reliable and sufficient source of water, such as "The Geysers" in northern California, significant amounts of energy can be produced with little impact on other water users.

Table 13.1 provides a breakdown of water requirements for various types of energy production. As can be seen, the requirements vary considerably, but all types require significant amounts of water.

SOURCES OF WATER FOR ENERGY

The major source of water for energy development in the Southwest is surface water, primarily in the Upper Colorado Basin. Groundwater in proximity to major energy resources is largely confined to the Piceance Basin, with quantities largely unknown and unexploited.[20] Mine drainage water could be a valuable source of on-site water for some projects, but the amount available and its quality varies considerably.[22] Clearly the major source for most power plants and processing facilities will be the Upper Colorado River Basin, and it is on this source that we must focus our attention. Estimates of the amount of water available in the Upper Colorado River Basin vary, and in any event there are serious questions about the availability of this water for southwestern energy development.[23] (See Utton, Chapter 4, for a further discussion). Water resources exist, of course,

Table 13.1   Water Requirements for Various Types of Energy
Production.[21]

Energy Activity	Water Requirement
Geothermal	54.54 AF/yr/MW
Strip coal mining	204 AF/106 tons
Oil shale—surface extraction	13,400–20,100 AF/yr
Oil shale—underground extraction	6,800–10,600 AF/yr (50,000 bpd)
Oil shale—in situ retorting	3,000–5,700 AF/yr
Oil shale—modified in situ	5,000–8,000 AF/yr
Coal gasification—lurgi process	5,600–9,000 AF/yr
Coal gasification—synthane process	6,694–10,500 AF/yr (250 mmcfd)
Coal gasification—synthoil process	9,655–13,000 AF/yr
Coal-fired electric generation	
—wet tower cooling	9.0491–12.200 AF/yr/MW
—40% wet tower cooling	3.6179–4.4063 AF/yr/MW
—10% wet tower cooling	0.9023–1.1038 AF/yr/MW
—dry tower cooling	0 AF/yr/MW
Nuclear power electric generation	
—wet tower cooling	17.0123–19.3946 AF/yr/MW
—40% wet tower cooling	6.1457–7.4022 AF/yr/MW
—10% wet tower cooling	1.4900–1.8571 AF/yr/MW
—dry tower cooling	0 AF/yr/MW

elsewhere in the Southwest. Most, if not all, of the surface water in
the area has long been appropriated, so those seeking new sources
must either look to groundwater sources or to the purchase of appropriated water.[24] The area suffers from various degrees of groundwater
overdrafting and ground and surface water pollution as well.[25] While
water may be available for energy uses, it is not always where it is
needed for energy development.

THE ISSUES

Supply

It seems clear that given projected demand and assuming somewhat stable prices the Colorado River will not be capable of supplying sufficient water for all projected needs in the future. Even the
most optimistic scenarios use guarded language: for example, " . . . it
seems apparent that with wise management and development of the

water resources in the Upper Basin, a moderate level of oil shale development probably could be sustained."[26] Other scenarios are more pessimistic: " . . . projected depletions for energy through 2000 are about equal to those projected for agriculture, and together account for most of the remaining allocation of water to Upper River basin states"[27] or " . . . the Upper Colorado River Basin states are fast approaching a situation in which the surface waters to which they are entitled under the Colorado River Compact will be fully appropriated and consumed if growth in use continues."[28] There would be a severe problem without the energy development variable; with it, the problem becomes acute. And yet the demand for energy is going to increase at the same time the demand for water increases. It is questionable whether the necessary capital will be invested in oil shale, coal, and geothermal energy projects, let alone nuclear power, without guarantees of sufficient water, even if the price of oil increases substantially. Competition for water is keen, with the primary competition to energy users coming from agriculture, which historically and legally has had an upper hand. (See Chapter 1 for a discussion.) Although agricultural uses are not likely to increase markedly, their users' legal claims to water may cause problems for energy producers.

The Law

The legal aspects of surface water allocation are not nearly as complicated as those of groundwater, but they are perplexing nonetheless.[29] This is further complicated by the fact that "in much of the rural West, water is held almost in reverence. Water rights are heirlooms to be treasured beyond their intrinsic value. There is real resistance to the notion that water is an article of commerce, a subject for trading in the market-place."[30] As we have seen in Chapter 2, water usually must be put to a beneficial use with what is "beneficial" to be determined by the state.[31] The state, in turn, may condemn water rights for preferred uses.[32] Water for use in oil shale development, coal gasification, uranium ore mining, geothermal cooling, or coal slurry pipelines has historically not been seen as a beneficial use. In some states, energy producers have been able to purchase water rights.[33] Such purchases, however, are often subject to numerous restrictions or are not permitted at all in some states. (See Wehmhoefer, Chapter 2, this volume, for a more detailed discussion.)

At first glance, it would seem that there is a steady, albeit slow, development of water markets, and that the energy industry is in a position to benefit from this development. That industry, after all, has the economic resources necessary to obtain water through outright purchase where possible and through legislation resulting from industry lobbying and/or court decisions obtained through the industry's vast legal resources where the law needs to be changed. Thus, in the long run, agricultural and other prior appropriation users will lose out to the superior resources of the energy industry. This first-glance scenario, however, is not necessarily an accurate prediction of the future as regards water for energy in the Southwest. Environmental concerns may change this picture considerably, as would federal assertion of long dormant reserved water rights.[34] Water law is presently in flux, and for development to take place in alternative energy requiring large amounts of water there must be stability and predictability, as well as flexibility.[35] The demand for stability, predictability, and flexibility will very likely result in a much expanded federal role in water management (see Chapter 5, this volume), and ultimately it is likely that energy users will prevail. This, however, is a long-term scenario, as flux will continue to characterize the area in the short term. Given the long lead time necessary to develop alternative sources of energy and the water necessary to that development, it is not unlikely that another energy crisis will occur before a comprehensive federal policy has been adopted and industry has acted in response to that policy.

Indian water rights present a further complication of the future water and energy situation in the Southwest. As we have seen in Chapter 9, Indian water rights is a potential political and economic thicket, and the sooner the issues are resolved the better it will be for energy development and all concerned in it.

Finally, the legal problems associated with geothermal resources are particularly complex, as there seems to be no consistency between the states in their definition or classification of geothermal resources. Is it groundwater, or gas, or mineral? This is further complicated by the fact that some geothermal energy plants use geothermal steam and some use hot water to produce electricity.[36] These legal problems do not directly affect the use of groundwater or surface water for geothermal cooling towers, but they do affect the development of geothermal resources in general and therefore indirectly affect the cooling water quantity question.

Quality

Water quality is just as much a problem as water quantity, both in terms of the quality of water needed for various types of energy development and the quality of water discharged from energy resource development and production facilities. As Flug *et al.*, have stated:

> Colorado River water use for meeting the increasing energy needs of the United States is concerned primarily with the mining and processing of large quantities of coal, oil shale, and uranium and for waste heat disposal from thermal electric and synthetic fuel conversion plants. Abundant water supplies to develop these resources, however, are not readily available nor is the capacity of the Colorado River to assimilate the salinity that might be contributed by expanded energy developments.[37]

There are multiple sources of pollution. Oil shale production is particularly polluting, resulting in waste water contaminated with such compounds as ammonia, chlorine, sulfates, mercury, selenium, arsenic, phenols, carboxylic acids, silt, and salt.[38]

Coal, which in the West is largely obtained by strip mining, requires a considerable amount of water (see Table 1) and results in heavily polluted wastewater, primarily in the form of acids. Polluted water also results from the mining of uranium ore. Geothermal energy use of water for cooling towers is generally nonpolluting, but the large quantities needed may result in zero discharge and therefore virtually zero replenishment. The geothermal effluents (spent geothermal fluids) contain some pollutants, but preliminary research indicates that these effluents could be used for beneficial purposes.[39] The primary pollutant in nuclear wastewater is thermal, as water discharged from the plants may be ten to fifteen degrees Fahrenheit hotter than that entering. This may have detrimental effects on river or lake ecosystems, although there are methods of cooling or using the heated water for other purposes before discharge that could ameliorate this problem. The major problem of radioactive waste disposal is beyond the scope of this paper, but it is a primary reason for the present moratorium on nuclear power plant construction.

Wastewater can be treated so that its quality is as good or better than new after it is used in energy development and production. The question is not one of technology but of cost. Many developers have concluded that the cost of adequately treating water for discharge is just as expensive as or more expensive than treating it for recycling. This is especially true in the oil shale industry, but applies as well to strip mining of coal.[40] Water polluted from uranium mining and processing is particularly difficult to treat adequately, so zero discharge is the norm here too. Zero discharge seems like the answer to the pollution problem, but it really is not. Zero discharge of water does not mean that the water somehow disappears, but that it is not discharged into its original source. It may be discharged into holding ponds, where evaporation eliminates the fluids but not the solid contaminants. The polluted water may seep into the ground and thereby pollute the groundwater, or the solid wastes may not be disposed of properly. Zero discharge, then, eliminates some problems but creates others. In the end, it means higher costs.

CONCLUSIONS

This chapter has been based upon certain assumptions. Primary among them is the assumption that the demand for energy in the Southwest will continue to increase while the amount of water available for all uses will remain relatively static. A second assumption is that the supply of fossil fuel, particularly oil, is finite. There is a tendency to confuse cost with supply, and inasmuch as the cost of oil is currently low little thought has been given to what will happen when the supply starts to dwindle, due either to natural or to political causes. A third assumption is that there is presently little incentive for the energy industry to invest the large sums necessary to develop alternative sources of energy. At present there is no crisis, nor is one foreseen for some time to come. Finally, it is assumed that there will be substantial conflict among users and potential users of water in the Southwest, and that ultimately the energy users will prevail.

There are many possible solutions to the problems that will result if the assumptions above are correct. And while some of the solutions may be technological in nature, all solutions require a political commitment. Some have called for a "water ethic" that would serve as the basis for future water policy.[41] This would very likely lead to significant federal intervention in what has previously been primarily a state function; it would also likely lead to higher energy costs and higher food costs. Federal incentives to stimulate alternative energy development would seem out of the question in this period of huge federal deficits, although there could be mandatory energy and water conservation programs that would cost little; these would have the greatest impact on agricultural users.[42] Resumption of development of nuclear power plants might prove technologically feasible, but the political obstacles are enormous. A free water market, resulting from, among other things, increased transferability of water rights, might well bring about greater efficiency in water usage, but also might result in significantly increased costs, considerable litigation, and fundamental unfairness to certain users.[43] There simply are no easy solutions.

The coming conflict over water and energy in the Southwest will very likely result in more uniform water policies among the states involved, either through interstate compacts, adoption of model codes, or federal intervention. This is clearly the first (and perhaps most difficult) step necessary for the ultimate resolution of the problem. It must be followed, however, by a comprehensive water use policy, enforcement machinery, and impartial adjudication. Neither energy users nor agriculture should prevail in this conflict, but for a compromise to take place it will be necessary to develop institutional barriers to the overwhelming resources of the energy industry. This runs counter to interest group politics, but has proven possible in the past with regard to environmental concerns. It should at this point be mentioned that the environmental movement may play a significant role in this struggle through litigation to restrict or prohibit certain uses of water—or all uses from certain sources.[44] Just how this struggle will take place, when it will peak, and what the eventual outcome will be is difficult to predict. What is certain, however, is that conflict is inevitable, that it will be long and costly, and that the outcome will have profound effects on the future of the American Southwest.

NOTES

1. Allen V. Kneese, and F. Lee Brown, *The Southwest Under Stress* (Baltimore and London: The Johns Hopkins University Press, 1981), p. 16.

2. J. P. Fox, *Water–Related Impacts of In–Situ or Shale Processing* (Berkeley: Lawrence Berkeley Laboratory, U.C., 1980), p. 4; and Michael R. Stansbury, and Joseph E. Patten, "Will Synfuel Development Drain the West Dry?" *Consulting Engineer* 57 (Sept. 1981), pp. 91–96.

3. Kneese and Brown, p. 44.

4. *Ibid.*, p. 53.

5. Fox, p. 4.

6. *Ibid.*, p. 10.

7. Stansbury and Patten, p. 92.

8. *Ibid.*

9. Kneese and Brown, p. 17, and Stansbury and Patten, p. 93.

10. Charles L. Neff, (Recent Development) "Interstate Transfers of Water: South Dakota's Decision to Market for Coal Slurry Operations," *Tulsa Law Journal* 18 (1983), pp. 515–27; and Stansbury and Patten, p. 93.

11. Stansbury and Patten, p. 94.

12. Fox, p. 95.

13. G. Tyler Miller, Jr., *Energy and Environment*, 2nd ed. (Belmont, Calif.: Wadsworth Publishing Company, 1980), pp. 96–97 and 142–43.

14. Kneese and Brown, p. 17.

15. Miller, p. 96.

16. Arell Schurgin, and Thomas C. Hollocher, "Radiation-Induced Lung Cancers among Uranium Miners," in Union of Concerned Scientists, *The Nuclear Fuel Cycle*, Cambridge and London, MIT Press, 1975, pp. 9–40.

17. Miller, p. 125.

18. Edgar W. Butler, and James B. Pick, *Geothermal Energy Development* (New York & London: Plenum Press), 1982, p. 70.

19. G. H. Davis, and F. A. Kilpatrick, "Water Supply as a Limiting Factor in Western Energy Development." *Water Resources Bulletin* 17 (February 1981), pp. 29–35.

20. William M. Alley, "Ground Water for Oil–Shale Development, Piceance Basin, Colorado," *Ground Water* 21 (July–August 1983), pp. 456–64; and Charlotte Robinson and Mary E. Walta (*Note*), "Water for Oil Shale: Framework for the Legal Issues," *Denver Law Journal* 58 (1981), pp. 703–14.

21. Taken from Butler and Pick *op. cit.*; and Rangesan Narayanan and Douglas R. Franklin, "An Evaluation of Water Conservation Techniques in the Upper Colorado River Basin," *Water Resources Planning Series UWRL/ P–82/07* (Logan: Utah State University), 1982.

22. Energy and Resources Consultants, Inc. *Water Use and Reuse Opportunities and Costs at Oil Shale Plants* (Boulder, 1983). Report No. RU 81/11, prepared for Bureau of Reclamation, Department of the Interior.

23. Kneese and Brown, p. 44.

24. Zachary A. Smith, *Interest Group Interaction and Groundwater Policy Formation in the Southwest* (Lanham, Md.: University Press of America, 1985).

25. *Ibid.*

26. Stansbury and Patten, p. 92.

27. Davis and Kilpatrick, p. 31.

28. Kneese and Brown, pp. 58–59.

29. Robert E. Clark, "Ground Water Law: Problem Areas," *Natural Resources Lawyer* 8 (1975), pp. 377–90; and Frank J. Trelease, "The Changing Water Market for Energy Production," *Journal of Contemporary Law* 5 (Winter 1978), pp. 83–93.

30. Trelease, p. 86.

31. See Chapter 2, this volume; and George Vranesh and Eugene Riordan, "Water for Synfuels Development: Problems in Acquisition and Development," *Natural Resources Lawyer* 16 (1983), pp. 439–68.

32. *Ibid.;* see also Chapter 5, this volume.

33. See Vranesh and Riordan, p. 444, for example.

34. On the environmental issues, see Richard Ausness, "Water Rights, the Public Trust Doctrine, and the Protection of Instream Uses," 1986, *University of Illinois Law Review,* pp. 407–37; on federal assertion of rights, see Robert H. Abrams, "Water in the Western Wilderness: The Duty to Assert Reserved Water Rights," 1986, *University of Illinois Law Review,* pp. 387–405.

35. Stability, predictability, and flexibility may well be mutually inconsistent. See Lynda L. Butler, "Defining a Water Ethic through Comprehensive Reform: A Suggested Framework for Analysis," 1986, *University of Illinois Law Review,* pp. 439–80.

36. See generally: Ruth Musgrave Silver and Stephen P. Comeau (Comment), "Geothermal Energy: Problems and Shortcomings of Classification of a Unique Resource—A Look at Problems with Water Law, with Particular Emphasis on New Mexico," *Natural Resources Journal* 19 (April 1979), pp. 445–549; and Owen Olpin and Dan Tarlock, "Water That Is Not Water," *Land and Water Law Review* 13 (1978), pp. 391–440; and Owen Olpin and Barton H. Thompson, "Water Law and the Development of Geothermal Resources," *Natural Resources Lawyer* 14 (1982), pp. 635–55.

37. Marshall Flug *et al.*, "Impact of Energy Development upon Water and Salinity in the Upper Colorado River Basin," *Water Supply & Management* 6 (1982), pp. 199–220; at 207.

38. Robinson and Walta, p. 712; see also Energy Resources Consultants; Kneese and Brown pp. 62–64; and *Ibid.*

39. V. W. Kaczynski *et al.*, "Utilization of Geothermal Effluents to Create Waterfowl Wetlands," *Transactions* (Geothermal Resources Council) 5 (October 1981), pp. 603–6.

40. Energy Resources Consultants, p. 7.

41. See Butler, *op. cit.*, pp. 440–1.

42. Trelease, *op. cit.*, p. 83, has said: "The use of water in the energy industry is on the whole a more efficient, more productive use than the

growing of hay, fodder and feed for the meat and dairy industry." Thus, allocations based on efficiency would clearly benefit energy users.

43. See Freyfogle, *op. cit.*, pp. 510–14.

44. See the discussion of *United Plainsmen* and *National Audubon Society* cases in Ausness, *op. cit.*, pp. 421–28.

14   Adjusting to Groundwater Depletion: The Case of Texas and Lessons for the Future of the Southwest

Otis W. Templer

The Southwest is heavily dependent on groundwater.[1] Given this dependence, water policy analysts and policymakers are constantly seeking ways to improve groundwater management to prevent waste and assure a dependable long-term supply. Texas, both by virtue of its groundwater laws and its development of groundwater resources, exemplifies the problems associated with the management of groundwater resources. Hence the Texas experience will provide lessons for the future of the entire Southwest.

In this chapter we examine: 1) the slow-paced evolution of groundwater management institutions in Texas; 2) the efforts of local districts and water users to adjust to the progressive depletion of underground water, a common problem in much of West Texas; 3) obstacles that continue to impede significant groundwater management and conservation reforms, as well as the prospective effect of new groundwater legislation; and 4) implications of the Texas situation for the broader southwestern region.

In Texas, groundwater is an especially important resource because about 60 percent of water use is supplied by underground reserves. A very large part (approximately 75 percent) of the water applied to the state's 8 million acres of irrigated cropland is pumped from a number of widely dispersed major and minor aquifers. Only a few years ago dependence on groundwater was even greater, but new surface water development, rising fuel costs, and the gradual depletion of some groundwater reserves have somewhat lessened this reliance. In many areas of water-short West Texas groundwater is the only available source of supply, and pumpage for irrigation and municipal-industrial purposes continues at high levels.

In contrast to this, the legal-political framework for the effective management and conservation of underground water has developed very slowly, and Texas underground water law is distinctly different from that of the other western and southwestern states. In Texas, the absolute ownership, or strict common law, rule pertains to percolating groundwater, and the courts and legislature have failed to modify this doctrine to any significant degree. It would appear that there is no particular impetus or public mandate to change this deeply entrenched system, except in a few areas with particularly pressing groundwater problems. Thus, any valid prediction or speculation concerning the future development of Texas groundwater law can only find credence in relation to its past evolution.

TEXAS GROUNDWATER LAW[2]

In general, Texas courts divide subsurface water into two disparate legal classes: 1) water flowing in well-defined underground streams, and 2) percolating groundwater.[3] However, Texas courts apply a legal presumption that *all* groundwater is percolating.[4]

Many western states once applied the absolute ownership, or "English," rule, and saw little reason to alter the rule. (See Chapter 2 for a further discussion.) Improved technology, more accurate scientific and hydrologic knowledge, and rapidly increasing use caused this attitude to change.[5] Except for Texas, the western states now apply the prior appropriation doctrine or variations of the common law doctrine of reasonable use or correlative rights to percolating groundwater.[6]

One legal scholar recently observed that Texas groundwater law is striking in its "paucity," when compared to surface water law, and in its relative "uniqueness" when compared to other western states, because only Texas and some eastern states still retain the strict common law rule.[7] Shortly after the turn of this century, the rule was firmly established by the Texas Supreme Court in *Houston and T. C. Ry. Co. v. East* (1904).[8] Under this doctrine, the overlying landowner may, except for malice or wanton conduct, pump and put to use the water beneath his land, irrespective of the impact in depriving adjoining or more distant landowners and water users of underground or related surface water.[9]

In the landmark *East* case the defendant railroad company drilled a large-capacity well on its property in Denison on the Red River in humid northeastern Texas. The company pumped about 25,000 gallons per day (gpd) to supply its locomotives and shops—a minuscule amount by today's standards—and as a result the plaintiff's shallow domestic well on adjacent land went dry and he sued. In deciding the case in favor of the railroad company, the court relied on *Acton v. Blundell*, an 1843 English case, and *Frazier v. Brown*, an 1861 Ohio case, which was quoted with approval in the *East* case as follows:

> . . . as between proprietors of adjoining land, the law recognizes no correlative right in respect to underground water percolating, oozing, or filtrating through the earth; and this mainly from considerations of public policy: 1) because the existence, origin, movement, and course of such waters . . . are so secret, occult, and concealed that any attempt to administer any set of legal rules in respect to them would be involved in hopeless uncertainty, and would therefore, be practicably impossible.

The court concluded in the *East* case that:

> . . . the owner of the land is the absolute owner of the soil and percolating water, which is a part of and not different from the land.

Since then the rule has not been significantly modified, though it has been elaborated and clarified in a few subsequent court decisions[10] so it is now established that: 1) landowners can sell their groundwater rights, 2) underground water can be used either on the land from which it is produced or elsewhere, and 3) there remains the firm presumption that all groundwater is percolating unless there is proof it flows in an underground stream, a contention that has never been sustained in Texas cases.

A half century after the *East* decision, the Texas Supreme Court considered another important groundwater case, *Corpus Christi v. Pleasanton* (1955).[11] The court again upheld the long-standing common law rule.[12]

Much more recently, the Texas Supreme Court had another occasion to examine the common law rule in *Friendswood Development Company v. Smith–Southwest Industries, Inc.* (1978).[13] This decision again reaffirmed the basic doctrine of the *East* case, but the court recognized in the opinion that "some aspects of the English or common law rule are harsh and outmoded." This suit involved a claim for damages by landowners who alleged that defendants' extraction of groundwater for industrial purposes had caused surface subsidence of their lands. The court did decide, however, that in future cases of land subsidence caused by excessive groundwater withdrawals liability would be imposed for damages resulting from negligent pumping.[14] In the *Friendswood* case, the court took great care to limit its decision to cases of damage resulting from surface subsidence, a significant problem only along portions of the Texas Gulf Coast.[15] In sum, groundwater law as developed by Texas courts has undergone only minor modification, remaining nearly static for over eight decades.

Underground Water Conservation Districts

In Texas, it has long been realized that some form of groundwater management is desirable, and as early as 1913 the newly created Board of Water Engineers pointed out the necessity for regulation. Not until the 1930s, however, when irrigation with groundwater was rapidly expanding did this need become widely recognized. Demands for regulation to prevent overdevelopment and groundwater waste were made repeatedly, and unsuccessful legislation that might have accomplished these objectives was introduced at least four times in the 1930s and 1940s.[16] Finally, in 1949, a statute passed providing for the voluntary establishment of local underground water conservation districts (UWCD's).[17] This law was passed in the face of stiff opposition and caused much political controversy.[18] Thus, local UWCD's exercise about the only control over landowners' rights to groundwater, though the validity of private groundwater rights is always specifically acknowledged in groundwater statutes. In addition to districts formed under this general law, groundwater districts may also be formed by special legislation, and their powers and responsibilities are often quite different from those of general law UWCD's.[19]

In the almost four decades since its passage only a few districts have been created under the general law or by special legislation, though the pace is quickening. Through 1984, 11 UWCD's had been established and Figure 2 illustrates their geographic location over at least some of the intensively irrigated portions of most major aqui-

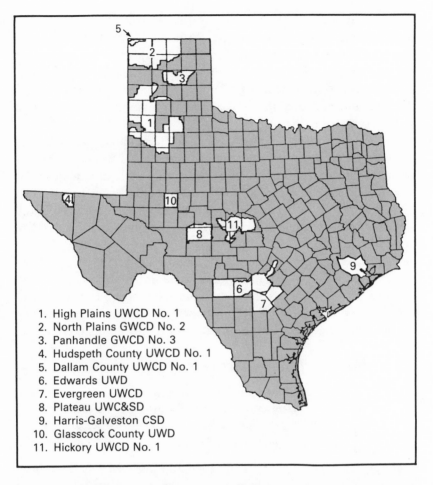

Figure 2. Underground Water Conservation Districts of Texas

fers. As might be expected, most are located in water-short West Texas, where dependence on groundwater is so heavy. Table 14.1 provides more detailed information about the formation, status, and extent of each district. Since 1984, eleven more UWCD's have been formed, including one general law and ten special law districts. All of these more recent districts are comparatively small, extending over a single county, or less, in area. Collectively, the 22 UWCD's encompass all or parts of 54 Texas counties and have a total area of approximately 45,000 square miles.

It is evident that there are still many areas that rely heavily on groundwater and some overlying major aquifers that are not included within a district. In addition, some listed UWCD's are relatively inactive. An example is the tiny Dallam County UWCD No. 1, formed in 1959 in the northwestern Panhandle. The district covers only one precinct, is too small to provide an adequate tax base, and is considered by some people to be defunct.[20] However, the Texas Water Commission considers any UWCD providing it with a current list of directors as still being active.

Several factors have hampered the establishment and operation of local UWCD's. Because landowners of particular sections of the designated underground reservoir may elect not to be included in the proposed district, in theory a patchwork of regulated and unregulated areas may result. This has not proven to be as much of a problem as was originally anticipated, but precincts in several counties did vote not to be included in High Plains UWCD No. 1, the first district formed.[21] Several areas where the Ogallala aquifer on the High Plains is subjected to heavy pumping have voted down district formation entirely. In 1973, voters in seven southern High Plains counties overlying an intensively developed portion of the aquifer for the second time rejected creation of proposed South Plains UWCD No. 4.[22]

One district manager described a major problem as being:

> ... the district's limited income and nearly unlimited responsibilities. The voting public determined the extent of their funding. It has not been uncommon for the voters to elect to participate in a district, but refuse to tax themselves to provide such service.[23]

Finally, procedures for creating general law districts have been very complex and time-consuming, normally requiring at least twelve to eighteen months. For this reason, and because special law districts can be given broader powers or more specific functions, most recently formed districts have been created by the legislature.[24]

GROUNDWATER MANAGEMENT AND CONSERVATION ACTIVITIES

The widely variable physical and hydrologic environments of Texas inevitably result in equally diverse groundwater management and conservation problems, as shown by these examples. Land surface subsidence and salt water intrusion problems are largely confined to the extensive Gulf Coast aquifer, especially in the Houston–

Galveston area. Here, heavy withdrawals of groundwater by municipal-industrial users made it necessary to limit pumpage to equal recharge to the dewatered aquifer and served to encourage users to switch to readily available surface water resources.[25] The Houston–Galveston Coastal Subsidence District (CSD) was formed in 1975 by special legislation. The powers of the district are broader than those of most other groundwater districts, and include authorization to regulate spacing of wells and production from wells through the use of permit fees based on the quantity of groundwater pumped.[26] This practice was upheld by the Texas Supreme Court in *Beckendorff v. Harris–Galveston CSD* (1978).[27] In its specialized role, the Harris–Galveston CSD has proved to be the most successful of all districts in actually regulating groundwater exploitation.[28]

The Edwards Limestone aquifer of the Balcones Fault Zone along the southern margins of the Edwards Plateau is unique. Streams crossing the outcrop area lost large quantities of water to the very porous limestone. Water movement through the aquifer resembles a surface stream in many respects, and the aquifer is capable of rapid recharge and discharge. Pumpage of the western part of the aquifer can result in reduced springflow and stream base flow in the eastern part.[29] The Edwards aquifer provides all the public water supply for seventeen towns and cities with a population of over one million, including the city of San Antonio, and the federal government has designated the Edwards as a "sole source" aquifer, with the attendant possibility of eventual federal intervention in the aquifer's management. Here another special law district, the Edwards Underground Water District, was formed in 1959 for the purpose of recharging the aquifer and preventing waste and pollution.[30] However, it was given no control over well spacing or water production. Area landowners have resisted all attempts at more stringent regulation.

The gradual depletion of nonrenewable groundwater resources is the major problem confronting the extensive Ogallala aquifer of the High Plains and most other small aquifers in basin deposits in largely agricultural arid and semi-arid West Texas.[31] The depletion problems common to this region have for the most part generated much less public concern than the previously discussed groundwater problems in the more urbanized and humid portions of the state.

General law districts, such as most of those in West Texas, have rather broad statutory powers to make and enforce rules for "conserving, protecting, recharging, and preventing waste" of groundwater.[32]

Table 14.1 Underground Water Conservation Districts of Texas

Name and Headquarters	Date Created	General or Special Law	Counties	Area (sq. mi.)
1. High Plains Underground Water Conservation District No 1. Lubbock, Texas	1951	General	Parmer, Lubbock and parts of Deaf Smith, Randall, Potter, Armstrong, Castro, Bailey, Lamb, Hale, Floyd, Cochran, Hockley, Lynn, Crosby	10,649
2. North Plains Ground Water Conservation District No. 2 Dumas, Texas	1955	General	Sherman, Hansford, Ochiltree, Lipscomb and part of Hartley, Moore, Hutchinson	8,056
3. Panhandle Ground Water Conservation District No. 3 White Deer, Texas	1956	General	Parts of Potter, Carson, Gray	1,760
4. Hudspeth County Underground Water Conservation District No. 1 Dell City, Texas	1957	General	Part of Hudspeth	440
5. Dallam County Underground Water Conservation District No. 1 Texline, Texas	1959	General	Part of Dallam	278

6. Edwards Underground Water District, San Antonio, Texas	1959	Special (Acts 1959, Chap. 99)*	Uvalde and parts of Medina, Bexar, Comal and Hays	4,258
7. Evergreen Underground Water Conservation District, Pleasanton, Texas	1965	Special (Acts 1965, Chap. 197)*	Atascosa, Wilson	2,021
8. Plateau Underground Water Conservation and Supply District, Eldorado, Texas	1965	Special (Acts 1965, Chap. 517)*	Schleicher and parts of Irion, Tom Green, Concho, Menard, Sutton	1,875
9. Harris-Galveston Coastal Subsidence District, Friendswood, Texas	1975	Special (Acts 1975, Chap. 284)*	Harris, Galveston	2,111
10. Glasscock County Underground Water District, Garden City, Texas	1981	Special (Acts 1981, Chap. 489)*	Glasscock	898
11. Hickory Underground Water Conservation District No. 1 n.a.	1982	General	Parts of Concho, McCulloch, San Saba, Llano, Mason, Kimble, Menard	2,301

*General and Special Laws of the State of Texas

Source: Data supplied by Texas Department of Water Resources.

However, the most significant conservation rules enforced by the UWCD's are those controlling well spacing through a permit system, and controlling off-farm waste of groundwater.[33] High Plains UWCD No. 1 considers the latter problem to be of such importance that it devotes a major part of its research, demonstration, and public education programs and most of its enforcement activities to combating off-farm waste.[34] None of the UWCD's on the High Plains have attempted to control on-farm waste, nor have any attempted groundwater production control.[35]

Though the UWCD's of West Texas are hesitant to invoke more stringent regulation of groundwater use and production, they do perform some significant functions in encouraging voluntary groundwater conservation,[36] as evidenced by the activities of High Plains UWCD No. 1, headquartered in Lubbock and the oldest and largest of the districts:

1. The district encourages local farmers to adopt water-conserving water and land use practices.
2. High Plains UWCD No. 1 provides services to area farmers directed toward improving water use efficiency and measuring the rate of groundwater depletion.
3. The district is engaged in cooperative research with state agencies and universities on methods of increasing local water supplies and improving water use efficiency.
4. High Plains UWCD No. 1 devotes considerable effort to educating irrigators, the general public, and area schoolchildren on the problems of groundwater depletion and the need for water conservation.

The extent to which UWCD's are responsible for the adoption of water conservation practices and for slowing the decline of the aquifers they overlie is difficult to measure.[37] Proponents of the local district approach to groundwater management report that in 1951 High Plains farmers applied about two acre-feet of irrigation per acre, and they take credit for the fact that this rate has declined to approximately one acre-foot per acre in 1983, a reduction of about 50 percent.[38]

OBSTACLES TO REFORM

Critics point out a number of perceived inadequacies in Texas groundwater law that impede more effective management and conservation. Johnson contends that Texas landowners lack effective groundwater rights, notwithstanding recognition of their "absolute ownership," because each landowner has the right to pump at will.[39] The English rule is said to encourage a race for the available groundwater supply, and to promote rapid and sometimes wasteful utilization of a dwindling resource. According to Clawson such a system "almost forces each landowner to use whatever water he can get before someone else uses it."[40] Thomas had this caustic assessment of the rule as applied in Texas:

> A landlord is clearly lord of his land, and he cannot be denied the right to drill a well in it and extract water therefrom. If he stops the flow of a neighbor's spring or dries up his well, the neighbor has no recourse; if his neighbor gets the jump on him, he is the loser. In the world of absolute rights it is not easy to protect private interests from themselves or for themselves.[41]

The extent to which Texas groundwater law encourages competing landowners to develop a common groundwater supply cannot be measured with absolute certainty, and the few court cases involving groundwater disputes would seem to indicate little competition. However, because Texas courts have generally adopted a "hands off" policy in such litigation both landowners and attorneys realize the improbability of obtaining relief for damages. Among other often mentioned inadequacies of Texas law are: 1) lack of coordinated management of surface and groundwater rights, the former subject to state regulation and the latter largely unregulated, thus severely limiting opportunities for conjunctive management of interconnected water resources; and 2) lack of policies for determining desirable pumping rates from renewable aquifers and optimal rates of depletion of nonrenewable aquifers.[42]

A voluminous literature contains countless proposals for revising and reforming Texas groundwater law.[43] Such proposals have ranged in scope from recommending a comprehensive statewide groundwater management system to quantifying groundwater rights through adjudication, as is currently being done with surface water rights, to more stringent local regulation in areas with critical groundwater problems.[44] A number of constitutional, statutory, or case law precedents are said to support the proposed reforms. However, most authors readily admit the improbability of achieving sweeping changes.

Whether proposed regulation should be statewide, broadly re-gional, or local in extent is a major item of controversy. Proponents of continuing the local district approach[45] proclaim the success of UWCD's in conserving groundwater and point to surveys of public opinion that show a marked public preference for local control.[46] High Plains farmers show even stronger sentiment for the view that if there must be groundwater regulation, it should be local.[47] The issue of *who* should regulate groundwater and the obvious preference for unrestricted private or limited local control make the question of *what* would be the most effective approach largely academic.[48] Re-form of Texas groundwater law by the courts or legislature faces formidable obstacles.

Attempts to persuade the courts to alter the common law rule have been singularly unsuccessful. It has long been argued that the legal basis for the *East* case, that groundwater is moving beneath the surface in a secret and unkown manner, is no longer true.[49] Today, there is voluminous data on the extent of major and minor aquifers, the quantity of water in storage, recharge and discharge rates, and rates of depletion, and the performance of some aquifers under vari-ous rates of pumpage can be modeled. The recognition and adoption of current scientific knowledge concerning groundwater continues to be thwarted by the legal precedent system.

In the *Corpus Christi* decision, it was indicated that the legisla-ture is the appropriate body to change the common law rule, and this attitude still prevails.[50] In the more recent *Friendswood* case (1978), the opinion stated:

> Providing policy and regulatory procedure in this field is a legisla-tive function. It is well that the legislature has assumed its proper role, because our courts are not equipped to regulate groundwater use and subsidence on a suit-by-suit basis.[51]

The legislature appears little more likely than the courts to make sweeping reforms. According to the Texas Department of Water Re-sources, "Decisions about the time and quantity of use of groundwa-ter reside with a large number of individuals whose actions are difficult to predict."[52] The political power wielded by the vast num-ber of landowners with private, and largely unregulated, groundwa-ter rights is obvious and constitutes a major obstacle to legislative change of the system.[53]

New Groundwater Legislation

In 1985, state legislative leaders sponsored and passed a "comprehensive water package" that addressed a number of water resources development and management problems and will allow implementation of the revised state water plan. Later, Texas voters resoundingly approved two amendments to the state constitution that validated this legislation.[54] At first, it appeared that rather significant changes might be made in groundwater management institutions.[55] However, the eventual result has been termed "the lengthiest, but least meaningful part of the 1985 water package," and the new provisions apply only to general law UWCD's.[56]

Among the new provisions are the following:

1. The 1985 water package authorizes the state to designate areas "with critical groundwater problems," the most limited of the proposals discussed previously. The state can establish a regional advisory committee, prepare a report on regional groundwater problems, recommend creation of a UWCD, hold local hearings, and eventually order an election in which local voters decide whether or not to establish a UWCD.

2. It expands the powers of general law UWCD's, which are now authorized to sell and distribute surface or groundwater and to exercise the power of eminent domain; and expands jurisdiction to smaller wells, including those capable of producing 25,000 gpd or more.

3. Also, the boundaries of UWCD's may follow political or other boundaries, and no longer must conform to the boundaries of an aquifer or subdivision of an aquifer.

This legislation is viewed as having only a limited potential for solving groundwater problems in most areas of the state.[57] There are many exemptions of different kinds of wells from these provisions, and any new UWCD's created must issue permits to existing wells within their jurisdiction, "automatically grandfathering existing overpumpage and depletion problems."[58] New UWCD's may or may not be created, and there is no assurance that they will operate effectively if created. The major leverage the state has to ensure creation of districts is a provision that prohibits any political subdivision where voters have rejected district formation from receiving state financial assistance for water projects. The Texas Water Commission has just designated seventeen critical groundwater areas, including most of the Panhandle–South Plains overlying the Ogallala and the Midland–Odessa region. Thus, in all likelihood, other local UWCD's will soon join those already in existence in West Texas and will operate in much the same fashion.

One possible outcome of Texas's relative lack of attention to groundwater management may be to encourage federal intervention into water management matters that have traditionally been left to the states.[59] Texas, with little federal land and presence, has been much less concerned with this issue than most other western states. Often federal regulations involving seemingly unrelated issues such as water quality or designation of critical habitats for endangered species may be used to control groundwater development in some areas of the state. The author has documented a number of instances of "indirect regulation" in Texas.[60] One West Texas legislator, noting that "if we don't do something [about groundwater management] the federal government is going to do something for us," has introduced two bills in the current legislative session designed to cure some perceived weaknesses of the 1985 legislation. One bill would establish minimum criteria for groundwater regulation by local UWCD's; the other would allow the Texas Water Commission to step in and regulate groundwater use in critical groundwater areas where voters reject UWCD formation.

This chapter has not dealt with the water supply problems of El Paso in far West Texas. (For a detailed examination of the El Paso situation, see Barilleaux and Bath, Chapter 5.) No UWCD's exist in the El Paso Valley, where Texas and the Republic of Mexico share a common aquifer. To meet its future water needs, the city of El Paso is attempting to obtain groundwater from basins in adjacent New Mexico. After El Paso's initial success in the federal courts, the extent to which these efforts will succeed under New Mexico's new "public welfare" standard remains to be determined.[61] If this water transfer is developed, it will be controlled by New Mexico groundwater law, and thus will not bear on the future course of Texas law and its relationship to groundwater depletion problems.

CONCLUSIONS

This chapter has demonstrated the slow-paced evolution of Texas groundwater law and concludes that the common law rule has undergone very little change over more than eight decades. The doctrine is now so deeply entrenched that sweeping reform seems unrealistic.

The courts have refused to significantly alter the rule and the legislature, as evidenced by the groundwater management provisions in the 1985 Texas water package, seems little inclined to act. Still, a groundwater system based on humid-land legal doctrines and developed at a time when groundwater use and hydrologic knowledge were minimal appears to be ill suited to solving the groundwater depletion problems of arid, semi-arid, and sub-humid West Texas.

Though the new legislation may spur the formation of still more local, general law UWCD's, it appears that the solution to most critical groundwater problems in the state will be achieved through special legislation designed to meet very specific local problems such as land surface subsidence on the Texas Gulf Coast or protection of the unique Edwards aquifer. Less eminent or apparent problems such as groundwater depletion in sparsely populated West Texas have evoked little public reaction. Such a piecemeal approach on an emergency basis may come too late for effective measures.[62]

The gradual depletion of nonrenewable aquifers such as the Ogallala aquifer of the Texas High Plains is an insidious problem. Groundwater depletion is usually slow to manifest itself and does not affect all users or areas equally or at the same time. Some areas where the Ogallala is nearly exhausted have already been forced to revert to dryland farming and agricultural income, affecting all segments of the local economy, has declined. Elsewhere improved technology, such as center-pivot irrigation of sandy lands, has permitted greater exploitation of the Ogallala in the past two decades. With or without more intensive regulation and management, the agricultural economy of those areas of West Texas subject to groundwater depletion should not suffer a precipitous decline as some have predicted. Previously discussed water conservation techniques and new research methods, such as secondary recovery of capillary water from dewatered aquifers and recharge with local surface water, hold some promise of extending the life of the Ogallala aquifer for many decades beyond its predicted exhaustion. Despite the long-term decline of local water resources, irrigated and dryland agriculture will remain central to the region's economy for the foreseeable future.

Looking to the future, Texas groundwater management institutions certainly cannot be recommended as a model for other southwestern jurisdictions. The Texas experience is instructive, however, for what it tells us to avoid in groundwater management. Although following different legal doctrines, actual management of groundwater is similar in other southwestern states.[63] In situations where there are no restrictions on groundwater pumping there is little incentive to conserve or manage groundwater for long-term use if the failure to pump only means the resource will be lost to neighbors' pumps. One major impetus for more comprehensive state action may be the threat of indirect regulation of groundwater by federal authorities. Almost half a century ago, Whittlesey had this pertinent admonition: "Laws flagrantly unsuited to regions where they operate ultimately destroy the source which they govern."[64] Can this be what the future holds?

NOTES

1. Arizona, California, New Mexico, Oklahoma, and Texas all receive close to or more than half their water from the ground.

2. This chapter deals with the constraints imposed by Texas law on the management and conservation of underground water resources, a topic addressed by the author in recent years in a number of published and unpublished papers (see below, Templer, 1976, 1978b, 1980, 1982, 1983, 1985, 1986). Though the focus here is on the problems of depletion of nonrenewable aquifers, which generally pertain to arid, semi-arid, and sub-humid West Texas, those portions dealing with general aspects of the evolution and operation of Texas groundwater law and the conservation activities of High Plains local underground water districts are summarized and of necessity sometimes paraphrased or repeated. All material has been updated and revised where possible.

3. Wells A. Hutchins, "The Texas Law of Water Rights," Texas Board of Water Engineers, Austin, Texas (1961), 673 pp., and Wells A. Hutchins, *Water Rights Laws in the Nineteen Western States*, vol. II., Miscellaneous Publication No. 1206. Natural Resource Economics Division, Economic Research Service, U.S. Department of Agriculture, Washington, D.C., (1974), 756 pp.

4. Otis W. Templer, "The Llano Estacado: A Geographic Overview." In: *Land of the Underground Rain, Proceedings of a Water Symposium*, Donald W. Whisenhunt (ed.). Eastern New Mexico University, Portales, New Mexico (1974), pp. 12–22. Otis W. Templer, *Institutional Constraints and Conjunctive Management of Water Resources in West Texas*. WRC–76–1. Water Resources Center, Texas Tech University, Lubbock, Texas (1976), 119 pp. Otis W. Templer, "Texas Groundwater Law: Inflexible Institutions and Resource Realities." *Ecumene* 10(1) (1978): pp. 6–15. Otis W. Templer, "Groundwater Management Institutions in Texas." In: *Regional and State Water Resources Planning and Management, Proceedings of a Symposium,*

Randall J. Charbeneau (ed.). American Water Resources Association, Washington, D.C. (1983), pp. 43–52. Otis W. Templer, "Water Conservation in a Semi–Arid Agricultural Region: The Texas High Plains." In: *Forum of the Association for Arid Lands Studies, Proceedings of the Fort Worth, Texas, meeting,* April 24–27, 1985, Otis W. Templer (ed.). International Center for Arid and Semi–Arid Land Studies, Texas Tech University, Lubbock, Texas, pp. 31–38.

5. Dean E. Mann, "Political and Social Institutions in Arid Regions." In: *Aridity and Man,* Carle Hodge and Peter C. Duisberg (eds.). Publication No. 74. American Association for the Advancement of Science, Washington, D.C. (1963), pp. 397–428.

6. See Chapter 2 in this volume for a discussion of these legal doctrines. For a summary of the application of these doctrines to all western states, see Zachary A. Smith, "Centralized Decisionmaking in the Administration of Groundwater Rights: The Experience of Arizona, California and New Mexico and Suggestions for the Future." *Natural Resources Journal* 24(3) (1984): 641–88.

7. Corwin W. Johnson, Reform of Texas Groundwater Law. In: *Proceedings,* 1982 Water for Texas Conference, Water Issues for Today, for Tomorrow. Texas Water Resources Institute, Texas A & M University, College Station, Texas (1982), pp. 71–77.

8. 98 Tex 146, 81 SW 279, Tex. Sup. Ct.

9. Otis W. Templer, "An Analysis of Playa Lake Water Utilization on the Texas High Plains." *Water Resources Bulletin* 14(2) (1978): pp. 454–65. See also Templer 1976, 1983, and 1985, *supra,* note 4.

10. Texas Water Development Board, "Laws and Programs Pertaining to Texas Land and Water Resources." Report No. 89. Texas Water Development Board, Texas, (1968), 34 pp.

11. 276 SW2d 798, Tex. Sup. Ct.

12. See Templer 1976, 1978, 1983, *supra,* note 4.

13. 576 SW2d 21, Tex. Sup. Ct. (1978).

14. Corwin W. Johnson, "Texas Groundwater Law: A Survey and Some Proposals." *Natural Resources Journal* 22(4) (1982): pp. 1017–30. Terry F. Kenyon, "*Friendswood Development Company v. Smith–Southwest Industries, Inc.,:* There May Be Hope for Sinking Landowners," *Baylor Law Review* 31(1) (1979): pp. 108–20.

15. Don Graf, "Groundwater Management under Current Texas Laws." In: *Environmental Law: Texas Water Resources, 1982,* State Bar of Texas, Austin, Texas (1982), pp. E1–E20.

16. Templer, 1976, 1983, *supra,* note 4.

17. Texas Water Code, Chapter 52, 1976, 1981, 1983.

18. Donald E. Green, *Land of the Underground Rain: Irrigation on the Texas High Plains, 1910–1970.* University of Texas Press, Austin, Texas,

1973, 295 pp. Frank A. Rayner and Leslie G. McMillion, *Underground Water Conservation Districts in Texas,* Texas Board of Water Engineers, Austin, Texas, 1960, 55 pp.

19. Templer, 1978, 1983, 1985, *supra,* note 4.

20. Graf, *supra,* note 15.

21. Templer, 1978, 1983, 1985, *supra,* note 4.

22. Templer, *supra,* note 4.

23. "The Local Institution for Ground Water Basin Management," *The Cross–Section* 22(10) (1971): p. 3.

24. Graf, *supra,* note 15.

25. R. K. Gabrysch and C. W. Bonnet, "Land Surface Subsidence in the Houston–Galveston Region, Texas," Report No. 188 (1976), Texas Water Development Board, Austin, Texas, 19 pp. "Race Against Subsidence," *Texas Water Resources* 1(3) (1975): pp. 1–4. John P. Warren *et al.,* Costs of Land Subsidence due to Groundwater Withdrawal. Technical Report No. 57 (1974), Texas Water Resources Institute, Texas A & M University, College Station, Texas, 79 pp.

26. William J. Brah and Lonnie L. Jones, Institutional Arrangements for Effective Groundwater Management to Halt Land Subsidence, Technical Report No. 95. (1978), Texas Water Resources Institute, Texas A & M University, College Station, Texas, 195 pp. Rick Callaway, Harris–Galveston Coastal Subsidence District—A Report on Its Creation, Powers, Limitations of Powers, and Progress. In: *Issues in Groundwater Management,* Ernest T. Smerdon and Wayne R. Jordan (eds.). Water Resources Symposium No. 12, 1985, Center for Research in Water Resources, University of Texas, Austin, Texas, pp. 225–35.

27. 536 SW2d 239, Texas Supreme Court (1978).

28. Templer 1983, *supra,* note 4.

29. Weldon W. Hammond, Jr., Regional Hydrology of the Edwards Aquifer, South Central Texas. In: *Issues in Groundwater Management,* Ernest T. Smerdon and Wayne R. Jordan (eds.). Water Resources Symposium No. 12, Center for Research in Water Resources, University of Texas, Austin, Texas, 1985, pp. 53–68. See also Templer, 1983, *supra,* note 4, and Otis W. Templer, "Conjunctive Management of Water Resources in the Context of Texas Water Law." *Water Resources Bulletin* 16(2) (1980): pp. 305–11.

30. Mary Q. Kelly, "The Edwards Underground Water District." In: *Issues in Groundwater Management,* Ernest T. Smerdon and Wayne R. Jordan (eds.). Water Resources Symposium No. 12 (1985), Center for Research in Water Resources, University of Texas, Austin, Texas, pp. 237–41; see also Templer, *supra,* note 4.

31. Tommy Knowles, The Ogallala Aquifer—Facts and Fallacies. In: *Issues in Groundwater Management,* Ernest T. Smerdon and Wayne R. Jordan (eds.). Water Resources Symposium No. 12 (1985), Center for Research in

Water Resources, University of Texas, Austin, Texas, pp. 23–31; see also Templer, 1974, 1985, *supra*, note 4.

32. "Districts Make a Difference," *Texas Water Resources* 4(8) (1978): pp. 1–4.

33. Templer, 1985, 1985, *supra*, note 4.

34. Clifford Thompson, "Chronic Tailwater Waste Violators Warned," *The Cross–Section* 29(6) (1983): pp. 1–2.

35. Templer, 1985, *supra*, note 4.

36. Templer, 1985, *supra*, note 4.

37. Templer, 1985, *supra*, note 4.

38. Don Graf, "The Case for Local Regulation." *The Cross–Section* 28(12) (1982): pp. 1–4. Don Graf, Legal Aspects of Groundwater Management in the Ogallala Area. In: *Proceedings of the Ogallala Aquifer Symposium II*, George A. Whetstone (ed.). Water Resources Center, Texas Tech University, Lubbock, Texas, 1984, pp. 465–80. Wayne A. Wyatt, Institutional Aspects of Groundwater Management. In: *Proceedings, 1982 Water for Texas Conference, Water Issues for Today, for Tomorrow.* Texas Water Resources Institute, Texas A & M University, College Station, Texas, 1982, pp. 67–69.

39. Corwin W. Johnson, "The Continuing Voids in Texas Groundwater Law: Are Concepts and Terminology to Blame?" Conference on Water Law, October 3–4, 1985, University of Texas School of Law, Paper No. 5, 15 pp. Corwin W. Johnson, "The Continuing Voids in Texas Groundwater Law: Are Concepts and Terminology to Blame?" *St. Mary's Law Journal* 17(4) (1986): pp. 1281–95. Johnson, 1982, *supra*, note 7.

40. Marion Clawson, "Critical Review of Man's History in Arid Regions." In: *Aridity and Man*, Carle Hodge and Peter C. Duisberg (eds.). Publication No. 74, (1963), American Association for the Advancement of Science, Washington, D.C., pp. 429–59.

41. H. E. Thomas, "Water-Management Problems Related to Groundwater Rights in the Southwest." *Water Resources Bulletin* 8(1) (1972): pp. 110–17.

42. Johnson, *supra*, note 7 and 43; Templer, *supra*, note 4.

43. See, *e.g.*, Brah and Jones, *supra*, note 26; Johnson, *supra*, notes 43 and 7. See also Frank R. Booth, "Alternative Ground Water Laws for Texas." In: *Proceedings, 1974 Water for Texas Conference, Ground Water Management—Current Issues.* Texas Water Resources Institute, Texas A & M University, College Station, Texas, pp. 29–60. George D. Cisneros, "Texas Underground Water Law: The Need for Conservation and Protection of Limited Resource." *Texas Tech Law Review* 11(3) (1980), pp. 637–53. James N. Castleberry, Jr., "A Proposal for Adoption of a Legal Doctrine of Ground Water Interrelationship in Texas." *St. Mary's Law Journal* 7(3) (1975): pp. 503–14. Kirk Patterson, "Legislative Alternatives for Groundwater Management in Texas." In: *Environmental Law: Texas Water Resources, 1982.* State Bar of

Texas, Austin, Texas, 1982, pp. D1–D20. Lt. Gov. William P. Hobby, "Ground Water Issues Facing Texas." In: *Proceedings of the 1974 Water for Texas Conference, Groundwater Management—Current Issues.* Texas Water Resources Institute, Texas A & M University, College Station, Texas (1974), pp. 11–13. Frank F. Skillern, "Emerging Legal Challenges for Groundwater Management. In: *Issues in Groundwater Management,* Ernest T. Smerdon and Wayne R. Jordan (eds.). Water Resources Symposium No. 12, Center for Research in Water Resources, University of Texas, Austin, Texas (1985), pp. 137–63.

44. Templer, 1983, 1985, *supra,* note 4.

45. Graf, *supra,* note 15 and 42.

46. *Texas 2000 Commission Report and Recommendations,* Office of the Governor, Austin, Texas, 1982, 51 pp.

47. Fred M. Shelley, "Groundwater Supply Depletion Problems and Options in West Texas: The Farmer's Perspective." Paper presented at the annual meeting of the Mid–Continent Regional Science Association, Oklahoma City, Okla., 1983, 20 pp.

48. Bill J. Waddle, "Approaches to Ground Water Management." In: *Proceedings, 1974 Water for Texas Conference, Groundwater Management— Current Issues.* Texas Water Resources Institute, Texas A & M University, College Station, Texas (1974), pp. 23–26.

49. See, *e.g.,* J. R. Barnes, "Hydrologic Aspects of Ground Water Control." In: *Proceedings, Water Law Conference, 1956.* University of Texas School of Law, Austin, Texas, 1956, pp. 134–45. W. L. Broadhurst, "Ground Water Hydrology." In: *Proceedings, Water Law Conferences, 1952–1954,* University of Texas School of Law, Austin, Texas (1954), pp. 5–10. Joe R. Greenhill and Thomas G. Gee, "Ownership of Ground Water in Texas: The *East* Case Reconsidered." *Texas Law Review* 33(5) (1955): pp. 620–30. William F. Guyton, "Technological Limitations to Groundwater Management." In: *Proceedings, 1974 Water for Texas Conference, Groundwater Management— Current Issues.* Texas Water Resources Institute, Texas A & M University, College Station, Texas (1974), pp. 113–20.

50. *Corpus Christi v. Pleasanton,* 276 SW2d 798 (1955). *Supra,* note 11.

51. *Supra,* note 13.

52. Texas Department of Water Resources, *Water for Texas, Planning for the Future* (draft). Texas Department of Water Resources, Austin, Texas, 1983, v.p.

53. Templer, 1983, 1985, *supra,* note 4.

54. F. Andrew Schoolmaster, "The Changing Fortunes of Water Development Funding in Texas: A Comparison of the 1981 and 1985 Referenda." *The Environmental Professional* 8(2) (1986): pp. 120–126.

55. Don Graf, "Additional Legislative Powers Needed by Underground Water Conservation Districts in the Ogallala Area." In: *Issues in Groundwa-*

ter Management, Ernest T. Smerdon and Wayne R. Jordan (eds.). Water Resources Symposium No. 12 (1985), Center for Research in Water Resources, University of Texas, Austin, Texas, pp. 243–46. Steve Stagner, "A Legislative Perspective on Texas Groundwater—Constraints and Possibilities." In: *Issues in Groundwater Management*, Ernest T. Smerdon and Wayne R. Jordan (eds.) Water Resources Symposium No. 12, Center for Research in Water Resources, University of Texas, Austin, Texas, pp. 219–224.

56. Kenneth W. Kramer, "The Texas Water Package: The Beginning of a New Era or Business as Usual?" State Bar of Texas, *Environmental Law Journal* 16(3) (1986): pp. 57–63.

57. *Idem*, and Johnson, *supra*, note 43.

58. Kramer, *supra*, note 56.

59. For an examination of these issues, see Zachary A. Smith, "Interstate and International Competition for Water Resources,: *Water Resources Bulletin* 23, No. 5 (October 1987): pp. 873–877; Zachary A. Smith, "Competition for Water Resources: Issues in Federalism," *Journal of Land Use and Environmental Law* 2, No. 2 (Spring, 1987): pp. 177–193. Zachary A. Smith, "Stability amid Change in Federal–State Water Relations," *Capital University Law Review* 15, No. 3 (Spring, 1986): pp. 479–491; and Zachary A. Smith, "Federal Intervention in the Management of Groundwater Resources," *Publius: The Journal of Federalism* 15, No. 1, p. 145 (Winter, 1985): pp. 145–159.

60. Otis W. Templer, "Indirect Regulation of Water Resources in Texas: The Edwards Limestone Aquifer." Paper presented at the 17th American Water Resources Association Conference, San Francisco, California (Oct. 13, 1982), 15 pp.

61. Wyatt L. Brooks and Valerie M. Fogelman, "New Mexico Continues to Study Water Embargo Measures: A Reply to the State Water Law Study Committee." *Texas Tech Law Review* 16(4) (1985): pp. 939–62. Pete Schenkkan and Lee Wilson, "Some Issues in Interstate Water Transfer—The El Paso Case." In: *Issues in Groundwater Management*, Ernest T. Smerdon and Wayne R. Jordan (eds.), Water Resources Symposium No. 12 (1985), Center for Research in Water Resources, University of Texas, Austin, Texas, pp. 93–109. Pete Schenkkan, "The El Paso Case: Interstate Issues in State Groundwater Regulation," Conference on Water Law, October 3–4, 1985, University of Texas School of Law, Paper No. 7 (1985), 29 pp.

62. Jean O. Williams, "Ground Water Management Potentials," *Water for Texas* 2(6) (1972): pp. 4–6. Jean O. Williams, "Some Challenges and Opportunities in Groundwater Management." In: *Issues in Groundwater Management*, Ernest T. Smerdon and Wayne R. Jordan (eds.). Water Resources Symposium No. 12 (1985), Center for Research in Water Resources, University of Texas, Austin, Texas, pp. 127–34.

63. For a discussion of the experience in several states see Zachary A.

Smith, *Interest Group Interaction and Groundwater Policy Formation in the Southwest* (Maryland: University Press of America, 1985); and Zachary A. Smith, "Rewriting California Groundwater Law: Past Attempts and Prerequisites to Reform," *California Western Law Review* 20, No. 2, p. 223 (1984).

64. Derwent Whittlesey, *The Earth and the State*, Henry Holt and Company, New York, 1938, 618 pp.

15   Results and Conclusions

Zachary A. Smith

The editor of an anthology always hopes that the papers selected will contribute to the major theme of the book and will not, as many anthologies do, run off in many different directions. I think that, in varying degree, we have been successful in providing that unity. The major themes and issues that run through the book will undoubtedly have an impact on the water problems and the future of the Southwest.

As we saw in Chapters 2 and 14, water laws in the Southwest were developed to aid growth and development and have not always adapted well to conditions of scarcity.[1] This is particularly true of groundwater law in California and Texas. Since both surface and groundwater are largely appropriated and put to beneficial use in the Southwest, conflicts will necessarily be involved in any change of use between established users and new users. For example, the cities of Tucson, Santa Fe, and Denver were recently involved in conflicts over extending water to new users and the price of such new services.[2]

The fact that most water has been appropriated and that many parts of the Southwest either are now or will be experiencing shortages in the foreseeable future[3] has led many policymakers and scholars, including several contributors to this book, to question existing systems for transferring or selling water rights. As we have seen, in many states transfers of water rights are restricted (*i.e.*, only allowed under certain conditions) or limited (*e.g.*, attached to land or prohibited where water will be removed from a groundwater basin or watershed). Chapters 10, 11, and 13 all suggest that the transfer of water rights promises to be a volatile political issue in the Southwest in the future. Proponents of the transferability of water rights argue that transferability will enable water to seek its market price and therefore be put to its highest and best use. Opponents of transfers and sales of water rights argue that transferability would work to the disadvantage of established uses and lead to greatly increased cost of water. These increased costs, the opponents to transferability argue, would be easy for municipal, manufacturing, and extractive industries to pay and would be difficult if not impossible for agricultural interests to pay.

Related to the transferability issue is the issue of severability of water rights from the land. If water rights are not severable, any entity wishing to acquire rights would be required to purchase the land to which the water rights were attached. This is currently the practice in many parts of the Southwest. Agricultural interests, the primary holders of water rights, would generally prefer that water rights not be severable from the land and that those wishing to acquire rights also be required to acquire land.

As Chapter 13 illustrates, energy development in the Southwest will play an important part in future battles over water use in the region. Water is necessary for many aspects of energy production and development, including mining, processing, transportation, refining, and conversion to other forms of energy. A major portion of U.S. coal reserves and shale oil resources are found in the arid Southwest, and since the early 1970s various steps have been taken by the federal government to encourage production of these resources.[4]

Shale oil development, using optimistic figures, consumes an average of 14,000 acre-feet of water a year for the production of 100,000 barrels of oil per day. While coal slurry pipe lines (thought by many to be more economical in the long run than rail transport for the movement of coal) need approximately equal amounts of water and coal to operate. In addition, power plants using water for the steam generation of electricity are estimated to use between 3,000 and 15,000 acre-feet per year per 1,000 megawatt capacity.[5]

Given the interest of the federal government in developing domestic energy resources and the vast quantities of water necessary for many types of energy development, it seems inevitable that the future of the Southwest will involve conflict over water resources between energy companies and the current holders of water rights.

As we have seen, pollution of both groundwater and surface water promises to be a problem in the near future for southwestern water policymaking. Several contributors to this volume have discussed pollution problems, notably along the border areas and in conjunction with energy development. In various parts of the Southwest pollution from toxic wastes, mineralization, and nonpoint surface runoff threatens water supplies. For example, in 1979 the Arizona Department of Health Services, Division of Environmental Services, Bureau of Sanitation, working under an EPA grant, identified 1,540 impoundments of liquid wastes in the state. These wastes were from a number of sources including municipal, industrial, mining, and agricultural discharges. The study summarized what it termed "average" surface impoundments in Arizona and concluded that they had a strong potential to contaminate water supplies. The average surface impoundment was described as "unlined and its purpose is to dispose of an unknown quantity of waste which is more hazardous to health than untreated sewage . . . the impoundment has no artificial barrier to prevent infiltration . . . has been in existence for 10 years . . . " and is within one mile of water used for drinking purposes.[6] The situation is alarmingly similar in many other parts of the Southwest.

As Chapter 5 demonstrated, the extent of federal involvement over water management is another issue that promises to play a role in future southwestern water policymaking. Federal-state relations involving water use and management have undergone a number of changes since World War II. Federal lands—be they reserved for aesthetic, recreational, or military purposes—and the management of waters on or originating on those lands promises to be a controversial issue in the future of the Southwest. The federal government has for the most part taken the lead in developing surface water supplies. This is not surprising, given the superior resources available to the federal government for building expensive surface water storage and delivery systems.[7] As we have seen most expect this trend to end (if it has not already) and there is some question about the ability of state governments to fill this void.

In groundwater management, however, there are a number of reasons why the federal government may be motivated to intervene in state groundwater management in the future. Perhaps the most important of these has to do with the fact that groundwater basins that cross state or international borders are often poorly managed. As we have seen, competition for groundwater resources has led to inefficient management. Without controls over groundwater extractions the groundwater pumpers who save water run the risk that some other extractor will take that water.

In a recent survey conducted by the author of individuals responsible for water planning in state governments, competition for groundwater resources was found to exist in various parts of the Southwest, including all along the Mexican border, the borders between Nevada and California, in the El Paso region between New Mexico and Texas, Oklahoma, Kansas, and Colorado, as well as in other places.[8]

To the extent that state water policymakers are unable to control the exploitation of groundwater basins shared with other states there may be increased pressure for federal intervention to improve management and the likelihood of economic long-term utilization of the groundwater basins involved. Given the political orientation in many parts of the Southwest toward individual freedom and against federal interference in state or individual prerogatives, it is possible that the future of southwestern water policymaking will also see conflict between state governments and the federal government over the management of water resources on private, as well as federal lands.

Somewhat related to the federal involvement and transferability issues are questions of regional competition or conflict for water resources. Regional conflict over water resources is not new to the Southwest. Competition between northern and southern (and central) California for water resources originating in the north has been a part of the water politics of that state for most of the twentieth century. We have seen examples of this competition in Chapter 5, in conflicts between New Mexico and El Paso, Texas, for water in eastern New Mexico. And in Chapter 10 questions of conflict and the desirability of transporting water from eastern Oklahoma to the Oklahoma and Texas panhandles were addressed. We anticipate that these and other regional conflicts could intensify in the future. As growth continues there will undoubtedly be those in the Lower Colorado Basin, for example, increasing their demands for water that originates in the Upper Colorado Basin. Also, states in the Great Lakes region have, in the past, feared efforts would be made to transfer water from that area to the Southwest.

The role of agriculture and ranching in the future of the Southwest is at the heart of many of the issues facing policymakers. Public opinion surveys have, in the past, shown that the public supports agriculture in the Southwest and favors existing or increased allocations of water for agricultural use.[9] However, local and state governments actively pursue industries and growth that put pressure on agricultural users of water. Urban growth in the Southwest has been steady since World War II and will probably continue to be so. To the extent that there is conflict between agriculture and the new municipal and industrial interests, trade-offs inevitably will be made. For example, during the battle over a new groundwater code in Arizona major participants were agricultural interests, mining companies and municipalities. The fact that agriculture held rights to over 85 percent of the water necessarily meant there had to be trade-offs made between the interests of agriculture and other users. As it turned out, agricultural interests were not happy with the resulting 1980 Arizona Groundwater Management Act. The *Arizona Republic* commented after a three-day meeting of representatives from agriculture, mining, and municipal interests in Castle Hot Springs that "agriculture's representatives on the state's groundwater management study commission enjoyed Castle Hot Springs and its warm water pool last week, but not much else. They came away feeling like they've been cooked."[10]

It is likely that in future battles in the Southwest between agriculture and other users for agriculture's water supply the farmers more often than not will lose out. Agriculture won't be lost in the area, but clearly there will be pressures for conservation (*e.g.* drip irrigation, laser leveling) and there will necessarily be pressure to switch to high value crops and/or less water intensive crops.

There will continue to be pressure for large surface water transportation systems in the Southwest. Controversies surrounding such systems will include the role of the federal and state governments in financing and management; the economic efficiency of transfers (as well as the inefficiency of artificial barriers to transfers with or without new delivery systems), and the environmental consequences of new water projects.

In many respects the battles over water in the future will resemble the battles of the past. The issues (allocation, cost, control) and the actors (state and federal politicians, water bureaucrats, and interest groups) will remain largely the same. The relative power, influence, and importance of both actors and issues, however, will change.

Budgetary constraints, fully appropriated water, and a growing economy in the region almost guarantee that water politics in the Southwest will be more confrontational.

This confrontation will be aided no doubt by a relatively new (or newly relevant) issue: pollution. And there will be relatively new participants: environmentalists, whose influence has been growing.

Whatever the future of the Southwest, there can be no doubt that knowingly or not it is being created today. Almost every contributor to this book has ended with a prescription or list of suggestions and alternatives to ensure a more desirable future than that which will most likely eventuate by continuing current practices or following accepted assumptions. In the future the quality of life in the Southwest may depend on whether the public and policymakers have heeded the advice of these authors and the others of similar good will who study that most crucial of resources—water.

NOTES

1. Allan V. Kneese and F. Lee Brown, *The Southwest under Stress* (Baltimore: Johns Hopkins University Press, 1981), p. 89.

2. *Idem*, p. 74.

3. Eugene W. Jones *et al.*, *Practicing Texas Politics*, 5th ed. (Boston, Houghton Mifflin, 1983), p. 170.

4. Zachary A. Smith, "Federal Intervention in the Management of Groundwater Resources: Past Efforts and Future Prospect," *Publius* 15, No. 1 (1985), p. 145.

5. *Ibid.*

6. Zachary A. Smith, *Interest Group Interaction and Groundwater Policy Formation in the Southwest* (Maryland: University Press of America, 1985), p. 133. [Hereinafter cited as *Interest Group Interaction.*]

7. Zachary A. Smith, "Stability amid Changes in Federal–State Water Relations," *Capital University Law Review* 15, No. 3 (Spring 1986), p. 479.

8. Zachary A. Smith, "Competition for Water Resources: Issues in Federalism," *Journal of Land Use and Environmental Law* 2 (Fall 1986), p. 177.

9. Helen M. Ingram, Nancy K. Laney, and John R. McCain, *A Policy Approach to Political Representation* (Baltimore: Johns Hopkins University Press, 1980), p. 5. See also: Ross R. Rice, "Amazing Arizona: Politics in Transition," in Frank H. Jonas (ed.), *Western Politics* (Salt Lake City: University of Utah Press, 1961), p. 58.

10. Smith, *Interest Group Interaction*, p. 142.

Contributors

ZACHARY SMITH received his Ph.D. in political science from the University of California, Santa Barbara in 1984. He has taught courses in public administration, public policy, environmental and natural resources policy and administration, and American politics at the University of California-Santa Barbara, Ohio University and the University of Hawaii-Hilo. He is the author of *Groundwater Policy in the Southwest, Interest Group Interaction and Groundwater Policy Formation in the Southwest,* and *Groundwater in the West.* He is an associate professor and director of the Master of Public Administration program of Northern Arizona University in Flagstaff.

RYAN J. BARILLEAUX is assistant professor of political science at Miami University, Ohio. A former aide to Senator J. Bennet Johnston, he was on the faculty of the University of Texas at El Paso. He received his doctorate in government from the University of Texas at Austin in 1983. He is the author of *The Politics of Southwestern Water* and other works on American government and public policy.

C. RICHARD BATH is professor of political science at the University of Texas at El Paso. He received his doctorate in political science from Tulane University in 1970 and is an authority on U.S.–Mexican relations and transborder resource issues.

LLOYD BURTON has had experience in natural resources policy dating back to service in the Washington (D.C.) offices of Congressman Morris Udall of Arizona, where he monitored the fate of legislation submitted to the House Interior and Insular Affairs Committee. He received the Ph.D. in jurisprudence and social policy from the School of Law (Boalt Hall), University of

California, Berkeley. He is currently assistant professor in the graduate school of public affairs, University of Colorado at Denver.

A. DIDRICK CASTBERG received his Ph.D. from Northwestern University in 1968. He has taught courses in public law and public policy at California State University, Los Angeles, and at the University of Hawaii at Hilo, where he is currently professor of political science.

R. MCGREGGOR CAWLEY is currently associate professor of political science at the University of Wyoming. Prior to this assignment, he was a member of the political science faculty at the University of Montana. He holds a Ph.D. in political science from Colorado State University, and his dissertation, "The Spanish Rebellion," was awarded an Honorable Mention by the Western Political Science Association.

CHARLES E. DAVIS received his Ph.D. in political science from the University of Houston in 1977. He has taught courses in public administration and environmental politics at the University of Arizona, Ohio State University, Suffolk University, and the University of Wyoming, where he also served as director of the MPA program. Dr. Davis is currently associate professor of political science at Colorado State University. He is coeditor of *Dimensions of Hazardous Waste Policy*.

TIM DE YOUNG is associate professor of public administration at the University of New Mexico, where he directs a certificate program in natural resources administration. He received his Ph.D. in government from the Claremont Graduate School. Before coming to UNM in 1979, he was assistant professor in political science at the Pennsylvania State University, Behrend College.

LAUREN HOLLAND is associate professor at the University of Utah, where she teaches courses in American government, state and local politics, public policy, and women's studies. She earned her Ph.D. in political science from the University of California at Santa Barbara. She has also taught at California State University, Fresno, and Dartmouth College.

HANK JENKINS-SMITH has taught and also done research in the areas of public policy and politics. Formerly a policy analyst for the U.S. Department of Energy, he earned his Ph.D. in political science from the University of Rochester. He has taught at Southern Methodist University, and now teaches political science and public policy at the University of New Mexico. He is currently deputy director of the University of New Mexico's Institute for Public Policy.

DANIEL MCCOOL received his Ph.D. from the University of Arizona. He has published two books: *Staking Out the Terrain: Power Differentials among Natural Resource Management Agencies*, with Jeanne Nienaber Clarke, and

Command of the Waters: Iron Triangles, Indians, and Federal Water Development. He is presently assistant professor of political science at the University of Utah and director of the Masters of Public Administration (MPA) program.

JOHN MERRIFIELD was born in West Germany in 1955 and became a U.S. citizen in 1966. He earned his Ph.D. in economics at the University of Wyoming and has served as the editor of the *Wyoming Quarterly Update.* He is currently assistant professor of economics at the University of Texas at San Antonio.

TIM R. MILLER is associate professor of management at Sangamon University. He received a Ph.D. from the University of Utah in 1984. He has taught at the Universities of Utah and Wyoming, as well as Northwest Community College (Powell, Wyoming). He received the Samuel C. May Research Award for his work on rapid population growth in western energy "boom Towns."

KENT OLSON is a professional economist who has combined teaching and research in several fields: forestry economics, water economics, public finance, and economic security. He has taught at Occidental College, Arizona State University, Indiana University-Purdue University at Indianapolis, U.S. International University, and Oklahoma State University. He holds a Ph.D. in economics from the University of Oregon.

OTIS W. TEMPLER is professor and chairman of the department of geography at Texas Tech University, where he has been a faculty member since 1968. He has been a member of the State Bar of Texas since 1959. After engaging in private law practice for several years, he earned a Ph.D. in geography from the University of California, Los Angeles. He recently served on the Board of Directors of the Water Resources Specialty Group of the Association of American Geographers. At present, he is a delegate from Texas Tech University to the Universities Council on Water Resources and is serving a second term as president of the Association for Arid Land Studies, an interdisciplinary group of scholars interested in the problems of the earth's arid and semi-arid lands.

ALBER E. UTTON is professor of law at the University of New Mexico School of Law. He is editor-in-chief of the *Natural Resources Journal* and director of the International Transboundary Resources Center. He is a member of the International Council of Environmental Law; member of the U.S.–Mexico Working Group on Transboundary Needs and Resources, and chairman of the Interstate Stream Commission. Dr. Utton is the coauthor and editor of *International Groundwater Law, The U.S.–Mexico Border Region: Anticipating Resource Needs and Issues to the Year 2000, International Environmental Law,* and *Pueblo Indian Water Rights.*